SMALL-BLOCK CHEVROLET
Stock and High-Performance Rebuilds

Larry Atherton & Larry Schreib

CarTech®

CarTech®

CarTech®, Inc.
39966 Grand Avenue
North Branch, MN 55056 USA
Phone: 651-277-1200 or 800-551-4754
Fax: 651-277-1203
www.cartechbooks.com

© 2015 Revised Edition

All rights reserved. No part of this publication may be reproduced or utilized in any form or by any means, electronic or mechanical, including photocopying, recording, or by any information storage and retrieval system, without prior permission from the Publisher. All text, photographs, and artwork are the property of the Author unless otherwise noted or credited.

The information in this work is true and complete to the best of our knowledge. However, all information is presented without any guarantee on the part of the Author or Publisher, who also disclaim any liability incurred in connection with the use of the information and any implied warranties of merchantability or fitness for a particular purpose. Readers are responsible for taking suitable and appropriate safety measures when performing any of the operations or activities described in this work.

All trademarks, trade names, model names and numbers, and other product designations referred to herein are the property of their respective owners and are used solely for identification purposes. This work is a publication of CarTech, Inc., and has not been licensed, approved, sponsored, or endorsed by any other person or entity. The publisher is not associated with any product, service, or vendor mentioned in this book, and does not endorse the products or services of any vendor mentioned in this book.

ISBN 978-1-61325-196-6
Item No. SA26

Library of Congress Cataloging-in-Publication Data

Atherton, Larry
  Small-block Chevrolet stock and high-performance rebuilds / by CarTech, Inc., [Larry Atherton, Larry Schreib].
      pages cm
  ISBN 978-1-61325-196-6
  1. Chevrolet automobile–Motors–Maintenance and repair. I. Schreib, Larry, author. II. Title.

TL215.C5A84 2015
629.25'040288–dc23

2014017491

Written, edited, and designed in the U.S.A.
Printed in China
10 9 8 7 6 5 4 3 2 1

Back Cover Photos:

Top Left:
Checking piston-to-cylinder wall (also called "skirt") clearance can be done with micrometers, or you can use feeler gauges with very little, if any, loss in accuracy.

Top Right:
Lubricate the threads on all the studs with assembly lube. Repeat this lubrication/installation procedure for the remaining 15 rocker arm nuts.

Middle Left:
Carefully position and lower the intake manifold onto the engine; don't slide it around or you may dislodge the gaskets.

Middle Right:
The carburetor should be in new, like-new, or just-rebuilt condition. Install a fresh base gasket on the intake manifold. The best gaskets are made from thick, heat-insulating material, with hard inserts at each bolt hole.

Bottom Left:
Begin installing the cam, twisting it slightly, and keeping it centered in the bores as you go. Apply assembly lube to the next cam journal and break-in lube to the next four lobes. Try to prevent the cam from "banging" against the bearings as you slide it in; this will keep as much cam break-in lube on the lobes as possible.

Bottom Right:
A variety of brackets are available for mounting the alternator or other accessories. In some applications, the alternator may require mounting on the opposite side to incorporate air conditioning or power steering.

OVERSEAS DISTRIBUTION BY:

PGUK
63 Hatton Garden
London EC1N 8LE, England
Phone: 020 7061 1980 • Fax: 020 7242 3725
www.pguk.co.uk

Renniks Publications Ltd.
3/37-39 Green Street
Banksmeadow, NSW 2109, Australia
Phone: 2 9695 7055 • Fax: 2 9695 7355
www.renniks.com

TABLE OF CONTENTS

Acknowledgments 4

What Is a Workbench® Book? 5

Chapter 1: Before You Begin 6
   The Small-Block Family 6
   Engine Building Tools 9
   The Workspace 11
   Cleaning Area 12
   Engine Handling 12
   Air Compressors 13
   Do You Need to Rebuild? 13
   System Diagnostics 13
   Removing the Engine 17

Chapter 2: Engine Disassembly 20
   Keep an Organized Workspace 20
   Tools and Supplies 21
   Safety First, Always! 22
   Step-by-Step Engine Disassembly 23

Chapter 3: Initial Parts Inspection 48
   Before the Machine Shop 48
   What To Do When Your Parts
      Don't Pass Inspection 48
   Initial Parts Inspection 51

Chapter 4: Selecting Parts 56
   Bearings 57
   Camshaft Drives 57
   Cam Bumpers and Drive Covers 58
   Camshaft Kits 58
   Carburetors 59
   Crankshaft and Connecting Rods 61
   Cylinder Heads 62
   Distributors and Ignitions 63
   Exhaust Manifolds 63
   Gaskets 63
   Intake Manifolds 64
   Oil System 64
   Pistons and Rings 66
   Rocker Arms and Studs 67

Chapter 5: The Machine Shop 69
   Finding and Dealing with a Machine Shop 69
   Who's Responsible? 70
   Before You Drop Off Parts 70
   Cleaning and Crack Detection 70
   Block Machine Work 71
   Head Machine Work 73
   Piston Machine Work 76
   Piston Rings 76
   Rod Machine Work 77
   Crankshaft Machine Work 78
   Engine Balancing 78
   Manifold Machine Work 80
   Other Machine Shop Services 80
   Picking Up Your Parts 81
   Things To Do After You Pick Up Your Parts 82
   Post-Machine-Shop Procedures 82

Chapter 6: Component Cleaning 85
   Tools and Supplies 85
   Important Considerations 86
   Precautions 87
   Component Cleaning Procedures 88

Chapter 7: Pre-Assembly Fitting 96
   Preparations and Supplies 96
   Precision Tools 98
   Special Considerations 98
   Final Tips 99
   Step-by-Step Pre-Assembly Fitting 99

Chapter 8: Final Assembly 116
   Tools and Supplies 116
   Final Assembly Tips 118
   Step-by-Step Final Assembly 118

Chapter 9: Installation, Break-In and Testing 146
   Installing the Engine 146
   Starting Your New Engine 147
   Step-by-Step Engine Installation 147

Appendix 154
   Cylinder Numbers and Firing Order 154
   Torque Sequences 154
   Torque Specifications 155
   Piston Ring Gap Alignment 156
   Timing Belt/Chain Alignment Marks 156
   General Specifications 156
   Work-A-Long Sheet 157

Source Guide 160

ACKNOWLEDGMENTS

This book would not have been possible without the generous assistance from manufacturers and the dedication of many individuals who ensured this S-A Design book would be up-to-date, complete, and accurate. The publisher, editors, and writers would like to extend their special appreciation to thank all of those who helped us with this publication:

Snap-on Tools	Sealed Power	Crower Equipment
The Eastwood Company	ARP Fasteners	Air Flow Research
Edelbrock Equipment Company	Fel-Pro	Pit Pal Products
MSD Ignition	Moroso	SCE Gaskets
General Motors Performance Parts	Goodson Tools & Supplies	AA Machine Shop
Holley	Comp Cams	Billy Graham's Hot Rod Shop

While a book like this requires an immense effort, some of the work was pure enjoyment. The many interviews I had with Jay Steel at Taylor Engine fall into this category. His boundless enthusiasm is matched only by his endless supply of terrific stories about engine building and racing. Thanks Jay!

—Larry Atherton

I wish to dedicate this effort to my friend Wally Cartwright. For over 40 years, Wally has been a professional engine builder, and I feel fortunate to have spent many pleasant hours watching Wally "stretch bolts." Over the years, his methodical philosophy has shown me the meaning of "precision engine building."

—Larry Schreib

I need to thank Mike Sharp for all of his help and for the 4-bolt block and steel crank. Also to Billy Graham for letting me borrow an engine as well as Mike O'Donnell at High Desert Machine and his expertise. Thanks Elizabeth for all of your patience along the way. Many others helped out along the way and opened their garages, toolbox, and engines to my camera.

—Todd Ryden

WHAT IS A WORKBENCH® BOOK?

This Workbench® Series book is the only book of its kind on the market. No other book offers the same combination of detailed hands-on information and revealing color photographs to illustrate engine rebuilding. Rest assured, you have purchased an indispensable companion that will expertly guide you, one step at a time, through each important stage of the rebuilding process. This book is packed with real world techniques and practical tips for expertly performing rebuild procedures, not vague instructions or unnecessary processes. At-home mechanics or enthusiast builders strive for professional results, and the instruction in our Workbench® Series books help you realize pro-caliber results. Hundreds of photos guide you through the entire process from start to finish, with informative captions containing comprehensive instructions for every step of the process.

Appendixes located in the back of the book provide essential specification and rebuild information. These include diagrams and charts for cylinder firing order, torque sequences and specifications, piston ring gap alignment, and timing belt/chain alignment. In addition, general engine specifications, including compression ratio, bore and stroke, oil pressure, and many other specifications, are included.

The step-by-step photo procedures also contain many additional photos that show how to install high-performance components, modify stock components for special applications, or even call attention to assembly steps that are critical to proper operation or safety. These are labeled with unique icons. These symbols represent an idea, and photos marked with the icons contain important, specialized information.

Here are some of the icons found in Workbench® books:

Important!
Calls special attention to a step or procedure, so that the procedure is correctly performed. This prevents damage to a vehicle, system, or component.

Save Money
Illustrates a method or alternate method of performing a rebuild step that will save money but still give acceptable results.

Torque Fasteners
Illustrates a fastener that must be properly tightened with a torque wrench at this point in the rebuild. The torque specs are usually provided in the step.

Special Tool
Illustrates the use of a special tool that may be required or can make the job easier (caption with photo explains further).

Performance Tip
Indicates a procedure or modification that can improve performance. Step most often applies to high-performance or racing engines.

Critical Inspection
Indicates that a component must be inspected to ensure proper operation of the engine.

Precision Measurement
Illustrates a precision measurement or adjustment that is required at this point in the rebuild.

Professional Mechanic Tip
Illustrates a step in the rebuild that non-professionals may not know. It may illustrate a shortcut, or a trick to improve reliability, prevent component damage, etc.

Documentation Required
Illustrates a point in the rebuild where the reader should write down a particular measurement, size, part number, etc. for later reference or photograph a part, area or system of the vehicle for future reference.

Tech Tip
Tech Tips provide brief coverage of important subject matter that doesn't naturally fall into the text or step-by-step procedures of a chapter. Tech Tips contain valuable hints, important info, or outstanding products that professionals have discovered after years of work. These will add to your understanding of the process, and help you get the most power, economy, and reliability from your engine.

CHAPTER 1

BEFORE YOU BEGIN

Whether you're rebuilding a street engine or building a high-performance racing engine, consider this your starting point. The information presented here will help you become familiar with the small-block engine family, give you some advice on the tools and workspace you'll need to work on it, and finally, you'll find out if your old small-block really needs to be rebuilt.

Let's begin with a quick look at one of the true "classics" of American engineering: the small-block Chevrolet engine.

The Small-Block Family

The small-block Chevrolet V-8 family is a rare phenomenon. Production engines have been offered in 10 different displacements—ranging from 262 ci to 400 ci—yet many of the major components and accessories are widely interchangeable. There have been, however, evolutionary revisions that you must keep in mind when buying replacement parts or interchanging components.

The displacement chart on this page lists the key specifications of all currently existing factory configurations. This reference will help you analyze production engine assemblies, but occasionally you may also need to recognize the origins and interchangeability of bare components. While we do not have space to discuss the components of every production engine in this book, we will highlight major design variations. For a great deal of additional information on the small-block, see S-A Design's *Chevrolet Small-Block Parts Interchange Manual*, by Ed Staffel.

The Original Design (1955 To 1962)

The original small-block introduced in 1955 had a 265-ci displacement and featured a 3.75-inch cylinder bore diameter and a 3.00-inch-stroke crankshaft. The cylinder block of first-year production engines has many unique features. The 1955 case (all GM parts books list bare cylinder blocks under the heading "cylinder case") doesn't have provisions for an integral oil filter; it does not have cast-in bosses on the sides of the block for engine mounts (the mounting bosses are on the front of the block); the lifter galleries receive oil through a metering slot ground into the rear camshaft bearing journal.

Small-Block Chevrolet Basic Engine Displacements and Related Specs
(Dimensions in inches unless otherwise noted)

Engine	Year	Bore	Stroke	Main Journal Diameter	Rod Journal Diameter	Main Bearings	Cylinder Volume	Rod Length	Compression Height
262 ci	1975-76	3.671	3.100	2.450	2.100	2 Bolt	32.811	5.703	1.750
265 ci	1955-56	3.750	3.000	2.300	2.000	2 Bolt	33.134	5.703	1.800
267 ci	1979-81	3.500	3.484	2.450	2.100	2 Bolt	33.520	5.703	1.560
283 ci	1957-67	3.875	3.000	2.300	2.000	2 Bolt	35.398	5.703	1.800
302 ci	1967	4.000	3.000	2.300	2.000	2 Bolt	37.718	5.703	1.800
302 ci	1968-69	4.000	3.000	2.450	2.100	4 Bolt	37.718	5.703	1.800
305 ci	1976-94	3.735	3.484	2.450	2.100	2 Bolt	38.479	5.703	1.560
307 ci	1968-73	3.875	3.250	2.450	2.100	2 Bolt	38.347	5.703	1.675
327 ci	1962-67	4.000	3.250	2.300	2.000	2 Bolt	40.861	5.703	1.675
327 ci	1968-69	4.000	3.250	2.450	2.100	2 Bolt	40.861	5.703	1.675
350 ci	1967-94	4.000	3.484	2.450	2.100	2 & 4 Bolt	43.803	5.703	1.560
400 ci	1970-72	4.125	3.750	2.650	2.100	4 Bolt	50.139	5.565	1.560
400 ci	1973-80	4.125	3.750	2.650	2.100	2 Bolt	50.139	5.565	1.560

All 265 crankshafts—along with the 283 and the "early" 327/302 cranks—have a 2.30-inch main bearing diameter and a 2.00-inch rod journal diameter. All blocks produced prior to 1968 accept this "small journal" crank design.

All small-block connecting rods are 5.703 inches long (measured from the center of the bearing bore to the center of the piston pin bore), with the single exception of the 400-ci rods (see the chart on page 6). Pre-1968 rod bearing bores are sized to accept bearings for 2.00-inch-diameter rod journals.

The 1956 block was modified to accept an integral, replaceable oil filter. The following year, 1957, the first displacement increase was made with the 283-ci small-block. This was done by enlarging the cylinder bores by .125 inch to 3.876 inches.

All 1957-and-later blocks featured a revised oiling system that solved recurring difficulties with the lifters and rocker arms. The oil slot in the camshaft journal was eliminated in favor of an annular groove formed in the structure surrounding the rear camshaft bearing. This groove joins the main oil gallery—above the camshaft housing—to the two lifter galleries, and provides continuous oil pressure to the lifters, pushrods, and rocker arms.

In 1958, the cylinder wall thickness was increased; this was a prelude to future bore diameter increases. In addition, in 1959, the troublesome "rope-type" rear crankshaft seal was replaced by a rubber lip seal, requiring an alteration to the seal groove in the block and rear main cap.

The Revolution (1962 To 1968)

The first major revolution in small-block design began in 1962 when the 327-ci engine joined the many 283 options (the 265 was discontinued in 1958). Throughout the next decade, the powerful 327 and the subsequent 350-ci

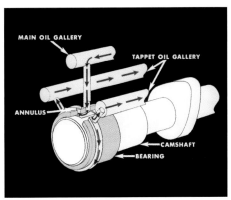

1955 and 1956 engines used a unique method of feeding oil to the lifter galleries. Lubricated in "squirts," once per cam revolution, by a milled flat on the rear cam journal, the system was found to be inadequate to ensure valvetrain reliability. In 1957, the oiling system was revised to provide a full-time pressure oiling to the galleries (the main gallery was modified to directly intersect the annulus passage that feeds the connecting lifter galleries).

configuration would build a legendary reputation for the GM small-block.

The 327 featured a .125-inch bore increase, resulting in a nominal 4.00-inch bore. The crank stroke was also increased .250 inch, resulting in a total stroke of 3.250 inches. This change required a minor revision to the cylinder block, and from 1962 onward, the bottom portion of each cylinder was relieved to clear the rotating journals/rods and larger counterweights of the increased-stroke cranks.

The main and rod journal diameters of the early 327 crank remained identical to the 265/283 cranks. The basic connecting rod design also remained unchanged, maintaining the 5.70-inch center-to-center length of the original 265 rod. However, some rods had reinforced beams and bearing housings to accommodate higher potential engine speeds (a practice that has continued through current options). To accommodate the longer stroke, the piston pin bore was moved closer to the deck (reducing the pin height specification).

As bore diameters and stroke lengths changed, the piston design had to change, too. During this period, and during future development, the compression ratios were modified through changes in the piston dome. As a result, piston design was very specific for each option, reducing interchangeability. This trend would continue throughout the 1960s and 1970s.

Before 1962, the small-block cylinder head had not significantly changed. Minor variations were made to the combustion chamber and piston to increase the combustion ratio, and the port volume had been increased slightly in castings fitted to some of the optional (increased output) 265/283 engines. Nevertheless, 1962 ushered in a new era of cylinder head development. For the first time since 1955, the intake valve diameter was increased (from 1.72 inches to 1.94 inches) in some 283 and 327 high-output options to improve intake efficiency at higher engine speeds. The exhaust valve diameter remained 1.50 inches.

From 1962 to 1968 progressive refinements continued to nudge power output upward, and a second important advancement was made in 1964 when some high-output 327-ci options were fitted with revised "big-valve" cylinder heads. These heads boosted high-RPM performance and incorporated several important features: the intake and exhaust port volumes were significantly increased, the intake valve diameter was boosted to 2.02 inches, and the exhaust diameter was enlarged to 1.60 inches (the first exhaust-valve size increase since the original 265 design).

The Late Development (1968 To 1996)

In 1968, the diameters of the main and rod journals of all small-block crankshafts were enlarged: the mains to 2.45

CHAPTER 1

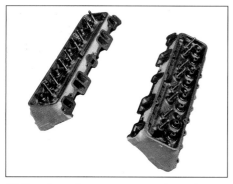

While minor changes were made to the combustion chamber and port volume, small-block cylinder heads remained virtually unchanged from 1955 to 1962. In 1962, the intake valve diameter was increased from 1.72 inches to 1.94 inches in some high-output 283s and 327s. Most differences remained within the valves, combustion chamber design, and other internal features. Externally the heads look much the same, other than the lack of accessory mounting holes.

inches and the rod journals to 2.10 inches. This required a corresponding change in the crank-bearing bore of the cylinder block. This alteration has carried through to the present day, so 1968 is the clear demarcation between early "small-journal" cranks/rods/blocks and late "large-journal" cranks/rods/blocks through the Generation II small-block.

The strengthened "4-bolt" block also appeared in 1968, and it has been used, along with various heavy-duty "forged steel" crankshafts, in several high-output production options. Nonetheless, other than the displacement variations created with different stroke and bore combinations, most of the major technical advancement in late small-block development has occurred in the induction and auxiliary systems.

A major exception to this generalization is the unique 400-ci combination introduced in 1970. Important alterations were made to the earlier cylinder block, crankshaft, pistons, and the connecting rods to expand the displacement to 400 ci. The cylinder bore diameter was increased to 4.125 inches, causing the internal surfaces of the water jacket core between the cylinders to touch. As a result, this unusual case is often called the "Siamesed-bore" block.

The stroke of the 400-ci engine was increased to 3.75 inches, the longest ever squeezed into a production small-block. To strengthen the long-stroke crank, the main-bearing journal diameter (and the corresponding bearing bore in the block) was increased to 2.65 inches. The rod journal diameter remained at 2.10 inches. However, for the first and only time, the connecting rod center-to-center length was altered. The designers could no longer move the pin higher in the piston (as had been done with every previous stroke increase) simply because there was not enough space between the pin bore and the deck of the piston to accommodate a conventional ring package with the longer stroke. The only alternative was to shorten the rod to 5.565 inches.

The 400-ci Small-Block

In the following years General Motors offered three other small-displacement configurations—the 262-ci (3.67-inch bore), the 267-ci (3.50-inch bore), and the 305-ci (3.75-inch bore)—that are very similar in external appearance, and any of them can easily be mistaken for a 350-ci (4.00-inch bore) engine. These lesser-known small-blocks are not commonly built into performance engines, so if you're obtaining a complete core for a rebuild, it's wise to insist on a warranty that will allow you to return the engine if the measured bore diameter isn't what you required or expected.

It's also important to note that a redesign of the rear crankshaft seal in 1986 caused minor changes in some later components. To decrease oil seepage past

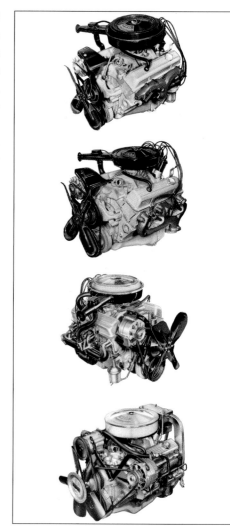

"Performance fever" drove General Motors to produce a wide variety of small-blocks to meet the needs of the average car buyer and the performance enthusiast. Here are some of the configurations produced in 1970: (from top down) 307-ci 2-barrel produced 200 hp; 350-ci 2-barrel developed 250 hp; 350-ci 4-barrel rated at 300 hp; and with the addition of large-valve heads, a high-rise manifold, and free-flowing exhaust system, a high-output 350-ci produced 370 hp, despite the addition of a "smog" pump.

the rear seal, the original two-piece seal was replaced by a one-piece design. In addition to the new seal and mounting appliance, this update caused subsequent changes in the design of the block, crank,

REBUILDING THE SMALL-BLOCK CHEVROLET

The 400-ci small-block was introduced in 1970. The bore was increased to 4.125 inches and the stroke was increased to 3.75 inches, the longest ever squeezed into a production small-block. The connecting rod length (rather than piston-pin height) was changed to 5.565 inches to accommodate the longer stroke.

oil pan, and pan gasket, as well as altering the flywheel bolt pattern.

Performance enthusiasts should also be aware of the wide array of performance components offered by GMPP (General Motors Performance Parts). They offer a variety of performance heads, intakes, rods, pistons, and even complete crate motors that are sold through local GM dealers. Many of these special parts are not used in regular production engines. If you're going to use any of these unique components during a rebuild or while building a racing or special-application engine "from scratch," you should study the GM Performance Parts Catalog (available from GM dealers) to ascertain compatibility and interchangeability details.

Engine Building Tools

Building a precision engine assembly requires a lot of tools. While most work is done with ordinary hand tools, a few specialized tools are also required. If you want to perform advanced building techniques, such as cylinder head assembly and valve face/seat preparation, even more special tools will be required. However, this section will focus on the basics. If more specialized tools are needed to complete a particular phase of the engine-building process, they will be mentioned at the beginning of upcoming chapters or included in step-by-step instructions. For example, the precision tools needed to complete initial parts inspection and pre-assembly fitting are discussed and illustrated in Chapter 3 and Chapter 7.

Hand wrenches are the most fundamental of all mechanical tools. These simple tools are available in at least a dozen variations, but every mechanic should own at least one set of combination (open-end and box-end combined) hand wrenches ranging in size from 1/4- to 3/4-inch (Snap-on set OEX707A).

Socket sets consisting of a ratchet handle, sockets, and extensions are the most versatile and efficient tools for engine work. Common drive-stub sizes are 1/4-, 3/8-, and 1/2-inch; 3/4- and 1-inch drives are also used in heavy-duty (usually commercial and truck) applications. The most common sizes used in engine building are 1/4-, 3/8-, and 1/2-inch drive. The 1/4-inch drive set (Snap-on 134MPB) is the most compact, but it's only suitable for small jobs (usually hand-tightened fasteners, such as valve cover bolts). The 3/8-inch-drive socket set (Snap-on 248FB, 6/12-point) will handle most of the common fasteners found in engine assemblies, and the 1/2-inch-drive set (Snap-on 344AMB, 6/12-point) is best suited for heavy-duty fasteners such as main cap and head bolts.

Sockets to fit typical engine fasteners are often sold in sets, commonly ranging from 3/8- to 7/8-inch, and are available in 6- and 12-point configurations. In most situations, 6-point sockets are the best choice, since they have considerably greater turning power with conventional hex-head bolts. Many specialty fasteners, such as those from ARP (see page 127), have 12-point heads that require 12-point sockets. If you're planning to use any of these specialty fasteners, make sure you add a set of 12-point sockets to your toolbox.

Sockets also vary in height, commonly referred to as "depth." You should have at least one ordinary "standard height" socket set. These short sockets are quite strong and will fit almost all fasteners. A set of "deep" sockets is essential if you'll be installing head or main studs (or any other studs) in your engine. Sockets can also be found with universal joints, sometimes referred to as wobble sockets, which allow you to get at bolts off-angle. These are a little more expensive, but well worth the extra bucks when it comes to getting at a hidden nut or bolt.

Torque wrenches are required for every engine buildup. There is a specific torque requirement published for every engine fastener. While some engine builders won't bother torquing small and accessory fasteners (we recommend torquing all fasteners), any critical fasteners must be torqued to establish proper bearing clearances, gasket sealing, and engine reliability. Some of these

Hand wrenches are the most fundamental of all mechanical tools. Every mechanic should own at least one set of combination (open-end and box-end combined) hand wrenches ranging in size from 1/4 to 3/4 inch. Quality sets are available from Craftsman and other companies.

CHAPTER 1

Snap-on Tools

Millions of people all over the world design, build, repair, or maintain automobiles. Within this number is a smaller, select group that instills an uncommon pride of craftsmanship into everything they do. For them, it's not how fast the job can be done or how much money they'll make, it's the quality of the end result that has become their personal "yardstick" of success. Some of these individuals are employed in new car dealerships, others in professional race shops and machine shops, and some work only on their own vehicles in their home garages. As varied as these individuals may seem, almost all of them have one thing in common: they own Snap-on tools. Some own entire Snap-on rollaway chests filled with tools, others own only a few tools, but all of them know from personal experience that Snap-on means top quality.

For example, consider the simplest socket. The gripping surfaces are like little ridges and valleys. However, when the twisting force exceeds the torque capacity of the bolt or nut, the tips of the hex "round off" and the wrench slips. It would seem that little can be done about this phenomenon, but Snap-on re-engineered the common socket with its unique Flank Drive wrenching system. The visual appearance is only slightly different from other sockets—the ridges are separated by broader, smoother valleys—but the result is that 15 to 20 percent more torque can be applied to the same fastener. This advantage may seem small, but it can make a real difference when you're wrestling with a stubborn fastener. When this technology was applied to Snap-on's open-end wrenches, the turning power increased by 40 percent! This is a notable improvement in any tool, but it's truly remarkable in a tool that has been the mainstay of mechanics for over 100 years.

All Snap-on sockets, wrenches, and many other tools are made from a steel alloy developed and patented by Snap-on. This allows Snap-on wrenches to have the thinnest sections without compromising strength and balance. And of course, their finish is legendary.

As popular as these sockets and wrenches are, the Snap-on story cannot be told by just describing a few tools. You can only begin to appreciate what Snap-on Tool Corporation offers when you look through its catalog. Hundreds of pages illustrate thousands of tools. Some are hand tools, some are air or electric powered, some are specialized and expensive, and others are simple and at a reasonable price. It's the sum total of all their tools that illustrates the awesome capability that Snap-on can put into your hands.

From a single ratcheting screwdriver to a complete "engine builder tool kit," Snap-on is the choice of professional mechanics. You will be amazed at the sheer number of tools on board a Snap-on Dealer's rig.

BEFORE YOU BEGIN

Snap-on offers a variety of useful shop tools as well. This compression-gauge kit is supplied with different high-pressure connections to fit a variety of applications. You'll notice that their wrenches have an unequaled feel and balance in your hands. Having a set of standard (open and boxed) wrenches along with a double-ended flare wrench (for fuel lines and other fittings) is a good idea. They also offer a wide range of micrometers and other precision instruments from dial indicator sets to a complete set of micrometers.

"critical fasteners" are the main- and rod-cap bolts, intake and exhaust manifold bolts, flywheel and clutch bolts, timing chain sprocket bolts.

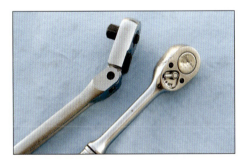

Socket sets—consisting of a ratchet handle, sockets, and extensions—are the most versatile and efficient tools for engine work. The most common drive sizes used in engine building are 3/8- and 1/2-inch drives. A 3/8-inch-drive socket will handle most of the common fasteners found in engine assemblies, while the 1/2-inch drive is best suited for heavy-duty fasteners.

You'll need at least one torque wrench with a range to about 100 ft-lbs. To obtain the highest precision, you should have a 3/8-inch-drive torque wrench with a range from about 5 to 75 ft-lbs (Snap-on part QJFR275E) and a larger 1/2-inch-drive torque wrench with a range extending above 200 ft-lbs (Snap-

You are going to need at least one torque wrench to properly tighten all of your new fasteners. Snap-on offers a variety of different styles from 1/4- to 1/2-inch drives. There are also dial wrenches and "click-types" available.

on part QJR3250A). This will cost some money (quality torque wrenches are not cheap), but if you expect to obtain long engine life and top performance, accurate torquing of fasteners is essential.

Additional hand tools will be required to complete your engine-building project. They're commonly found in most mechanics' toolboxes, and include screwdrivers, pliers, diagonal cutters, wire strippers, hammers, chisels, straight and taper punches, and other "simple" hand tools. Although a complete list of these tools would be quite long, most are not expensive, and they're often needed for other repair projects (all of these tools are available from Snap-on; see sidebar "Snap-on Tools" on page 10).

The Workspace

The essential first step to any successful engine project is to establish a clean, organized, well-lit workspace. Almost any small room with about 150 to 200 square feet of available space can be converted to a small engine assembly shop. The most likely and common location, of course, is a portion of your garage or a similar utility room with easy access and a sturdy floor. Accessibility is important; you need to be able to safely get a finished, assembled engine out of the assembly area, either on an engine cart or with a hoist.

Most home workshops are small, so it's important to measure the available floor space, give some thought to the organization of the main work areas, and carefully "lay out" the shop to your needs. The workspace should contain six fundamental areas:

- workbench
- tool storage
- component storage
- cleaning area
- space to position an assembly stand
- air compressor

Pit Pal Products (pitpal.com) offers some great, heavy-duty shelving, storage, and solid fold-up tables.

As you develop your workspace, don't underestimate the importance of light. When you're using a micrometer, inspecting the surfaces of a main-bearing insert, or probing the innards of a rusty cylinder block, you need every bit of light you can get.

Cleaning Area

Precision engine building requires a good deal of "cleaning" work (see Chapter 6, "Component Cleaning"). Industrial solvent (commonly available as paint thinner) is used to wash many engine components before pre-assembly or final assembly, so a solvent tank is an essential item. A commercial tank can be rented

Cleaning an engine before pulling it out of the car, or while you're disassembling it, can be a messy job. A pressure washer will help. During assembly, using a pressure sprayer that combines compressed air with a lubricant-based cleaner is your best bet. To handle this job, you will need a compressor rated at a minimum of 9 scfm at 90 psi.

from a company that will clean the tank and replace the solvent on a periodic basis, but this can be expensive (although it's environmentally respectable). The common solution for any small home workshop is one of the many bench-top tanks (we use a compact Snap-on solvent tank that includes a pump and filter, part PBD26). You can also purchase 10-gallon buckets of cleaners or even smaller pint-sized cans that are great for cleaning grimy bolts and hardware.

The workspace, especially around the cleaning tank, should be well ventilated, and you want to keep the window(s) or door(s) open to clear away fumes while cleaning. If the room isn't naturally ventilated, you should add a small exhaust fan. As an additional safety measure, keep a dry-chemical fire extinguisher close at hand.

Engine Handling

An engine stand is the centerpiece of every engine-building workshop. You'll be working with heavy, partial or complete engine assemblies, and a heavy-duty stand will make the difference between smooth sailing and a real headache. You'll never be able to build a quality engine if you have to roll it around on your shop floor. Don't start your engine project without a sturdy engine stand in your shop. Get one with four casters. A built-in drip pan is also a good idea; it'll help keep your work area drip-free and slip-free.

Engine stands appear to be relatively low-tech devices, and it's tempting to simply buy the cheapest one. This, however, isn't a good idea (see sidebar "Shop Safety" on page 28). Most complete V-8 engine assemblies weigh more than 500 pounds. This puts a big strain on cheap engine stands, particularly those with only three casters. If one of the wheels runs into a small dip in your floor, the stand can easily tip over. Furthermore, we've seen a cheapie stand actually fall apart and drop a completed engine! Don't take chances with your engine

Be sure that your new engine stand is up to the task of not only holding your engine firmly, but allowing you to be able to rotate it. Once you have a crank and heads on a block, it gets very heavy and you don't want to be stuck with a stand that doesn't allow smooth rotation.

BEFORE YOU BEGIN

This engine hoist, or cherry picker, can be easily knocked down for storage. You may just want to rent one from your local tool or parts store, or get a friend to split the cost with you and share one.

project or your safety; invest a few extra bucks in a heavy-duty stand.

Of course, you also need a way to lift and lower the engine assembly from your engine stand (and into and out of your vehicle). The usual method is to use

Don't skimp on an engine stand! Definitely get one with four heavy-duty casters; you may also want to consider one with a drip pan because an old engine will drip oil and grime for an eternity. The bracket assembly should be adjustable and welded to the center tube for a strong hold.

a hydraulic-arm hoist, often called a "cherry picker." Since the hoist will only be used occasionally, most amateur builders prefer to rent one. These are available from most tool rental sources and the cost is generally reasonable. If you do decide to buy one for yourself (and for most of your friends to borrow) look for one that disassembles or folds up for easier storage. (If a friend borrows it, tell him he has to store it until the next person uses it!)

Air Compressors

There are few automotive maintenance or rebuilding jobs that cannot be done more easily with compressed air. This especially applies to engine building, where compressed air is absolutely essential for block and component cleaning.

In addition to blowing solvent off parts, most home repair shops use compressed air for inflating tires, running small air wrenches, and perhaps some spray-painting chores. Each of these jobs makes very different demands on the airflow capacity of the compressor. Nevertheless, you can never go wrong with buying an air compressor big enough to handle the most demanding job, which will almost certainly be cleaning your engine block. Compressors just capable of this job will be rated at about 5 scfm at

Don't buy a compressor smaller than this for your engine project. This one is rated at about 5 scfm at 90 psi and uses a 20-gallon storage tank.

90 psi and use a 20-gallon storage tank. Air compressors of this size are usually portable, run on standard 110-volt, AC, single-phase power, and cost under $400. If you would like to get more "bang" for your buck, consider a vertical, 60-gallon, 220-volt AC single-phase compressor rated at about 9 scfm at 90 psi. Compressors of this capacity are big, heavy, non-portable, and they don't plug into a standard power outlet. However, they generally cost only a little more than their smaller siblings, and if you have the space (and a 220-volt outlet) the cost is well worth it.

Do You Need To Rebuild?

If you've decided to rebuild your engine, or if you're building an engine from parts for racing or other purposes, you can skip the remainder of this chapter (unless you'd like to learn more about troubleshooting). On the other hand, if you've bought this book to help you rebuild the engine in the car you're currently driving, the following information might save you a lot of money.

At first, it may seem like a relatively easy task to tell when an engine needs rebuilding, especially if it's running poorly, leaking water and oil, and refuses to start on most mornings. However, lack of maintenance and various problems in the ignition system, carburetor, and one or more of several other systems can produce many of the same symptoms. If you want to be certain that the mechanical condition of your engine warrants rebuilding before you open your wallet, use the following diagnostic information to build a case for either rebuilding or just repair.

System Diagnostics

During the rebuild it is generally a good idea to check the engine for problem areas.

CHAPTER 1

The usual suspects include the starting system, the ingnition system, engine mechanics, and the carburetor.

Starting System

Most engine cranking difficulties can be traced to the battery cables or the battery. Remove, inspect, clean, or replace both battery cables. If servicing the cables doesn't correct the problem, the battery should be removed, fully charged, load tested, and replaced if necessary (most auto parts stores will perform a battery test for free). If the starter fails to spin and no audible "clunk" is heard (indicating that the starter itself is attempting to operate), check the ignition switch and (if your vehicle has them) the neutral safety switch and the main fusible link. If there is still no noise from the starter, the solenoid, starter relay, or the starter may be defective.

The Ignition System

Many driveability troubles can be traced to the ignition system. Fouled spark plugs, a bad plug wire, or corroded terminals inside the distributor cap will all produce a misfire. Most ignition problems are related to the distributor. Breaker points, if used, should be checked for wear, alignment, pitting, burning, and correct adjustment. If the points or reluctor mounting plate is loose or worn, it will be impossible to keep the points (reluctor) in proper adjustment. Worn distributor shaft bushings will also produce this effect. Electronically triggered distributors can have a weak module and can also be affected by worn bushings. Also, check that the mechanical advance isn't corroded.

Check coil output by holding the distributor end of the coil wire (with a suitably insulated tool) about 1/2 inch from a grounded metal object and crank the engine. An intense blue-orange spark should jump from the wire. At most parts stores you can also find a clip-on load-test plug for testing the coil's output.

Make sure battery power is being applied to the coil during and after cranking. In breakerless systems, the magnetic pickup has one or more wires connected to it. These wires can break (internally), causing erratic ignition operation or a no-start condition. The electronic control module (ECM) may also be at fault. "Igniter" modules (that actually turn power to the coil on and off) are generally mounted in the engine compartment, and some are even mounted on the engine or distributor and are subjected to a lot of heat. Heat reduces the life of electronic components, so put them at the top of your checklist.

Examine the high-voltage spark plug and coil wires for missing or torn boots, cuts, abrasions, or burned spots. These conditions cause arcing and engine misfire. These wires can be tested with an ohm meter for proper resistance. Wire resistance should measure approximately 1,000 to 10,000 ohms per foot on stock-type wires, and lower on aftermarket sets. As long as all of the wires are close to each other's measurement, they're probably performing okay.

Frozen, worn, or binding advance mechanisms can cause hard starting and engine kickback, lack of power, poor fuel economy, engine stalling, and/or surging during light throttle operation. The mechanical advance can be checked with a timing light. As the engine RPM increases, the timing should change, then come back to normal as RPM drops to an idle. Use a vacuum pump, such as the Mityvac, to test vacuum advance mechanisms.

Also, remove and inspect the spark plugs for correct heat range, proper gap, worn electrodes, excessive contamination, and cracked insulators.

Ignition timing is an important part of the overall performance of your engine so you definitely need a quality timing light. There are many models available, but you should get a model with a metal inductive pickup. Plastic versions are prone to melt easily. Also, a starter bump-over switch is very helpful when you are adjusting the valvetrain on your new engine.

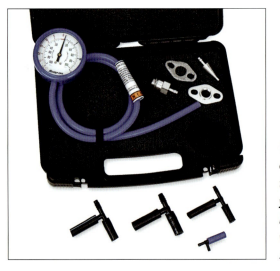

This Snap-on vacuum-gauge set is one of the most valuable diagnostic tools that you can own. It can help you evaluate engine condition and locate problems. This set includes a variety of fittings for general and specific applications.

Buying a Used Engine

Rather than pull the engine out of your daily driver and render the car out of service, you may want to obtain a replacement engine. When this second engine is fully reconditioned, all that remains is installation and swapping over some accessories, often taking little more than a weekend. There are many other reasons for buying a rebuildable "core," including putting together a race engine, replacing an engine that is damaged beyond repair, etc. However, once you've decided to buy, you have several options.

Perhaps the first thought that comes to mind is to scope out eBay, Craigslist, your local newspaper, or "car trader" paper. You'll probably find no shortage of ads placed by people trying to sell engines and parts. While you may find exactly what you're looking for, watch out for the pitfalls. Some people who place ads don't remove the engine until they get a "hot" buyer. Although this may play to your advantage if you can see the engine run before you buy, some individuals don't have the proper equipment to remove the engine or they just "can't find the time." While waiting for a few of these mini-entrepreneurs, you may waste several weeks or even months. If you do buy an engine from a private party, be sure you can get your money back if you discover it's not what they claimed.

Another option is to buy from a local wrecking yard. The first thing to ask is whether the engine you're buying is in "just removed" condition or whether it was assembled from miscellaneous parts. You'd be surprised what some junkyards manage to scrounge together. Find out if they offer a money-back or exchange warranty if the engine turns out to be the wrong displacement or is damaged. Do they guarantee that what you're buying is a "rebuildable core"? If you find something wrong, don't delay; return it to the junkyard as soon as possible.

Another option is to ask your machine shop to obtain the engine for you. While they might charge more, some shops will guarantee that all components are in rebuildable condition, and they'll pay for the testing and core charges to replace junk parts.

When you are looking at used engines, write down the casting number (on the rear top pad of the engine) and investigate what the block actually is. There may be other numbers stamped in the block on a small pad in front of the passenger side cylinder bank. S-A Design's *Chevrolet Small-Block Parts Interchange Manual*, by Ed Staffel, lists casting numbers and codes for blocks, heads, and intakes, so you'll know exactly what you are buying.

Remember, when you get ready to buy the foundation for your dream engine, don't get excited and forget about the very real possibility that you may be buying something that's little more than a dirty paperweight. Buy from a reputable person or company (call the Better Business Bureau and/or check on them any way you can), make sure you get a written warranty, and just to make sure everything turns out okay, always keep your fingers crossed when you hand them the check!

Buying a used engine can be a real adventure! Browsing ads in newspapers can often waste weeks or months of your time. Some wrecking yards manage to find the worst parts on the planet, assemble them, and have the gall to call it an engine; you'll call it junk.

CHAPTER 1

Engine Mechanical Condition

Power and economy both depend on the basic mechanical condition of the engine. A vacuum test will help you evaluate the engine and locate problems that may cause rough running, lack of power, or hard starting.

Use a quality undamped vacuum gauge for these tests. Begin by connecting the gauge to a direct manifold vacuum source (on the intake manifold). The following are some typical gauge readings and what each indication means:

- A steady reading between 16 and 22 inches (Hg) at idle. This is normal. Radically cammed engines have lower, less steady readings.
- Normal range at idle with sporadic drops below normal. This indicates a sticking valve.
- Normal range at idle with needle vibration of about 2 inches (Hg). This indicates an ignition problem. Check plug gap, dwell, coil, distributor cap, and plug wires.
- A steady reading slightly higher than normal. This can be caused by a dirty air filter or overly advanced ignition timing.
- A steady reading of 3 to 12 inches (Hg) lower than normal. This indicates one or more of the following conditions. Intake or carburetor vacuum leak, retarded ignition timing, worn piston rings.
- Gauge needle drifts slowly over a range of 4 to 5 inches (Hg) at idle. This indicates an idle mixture that is too rich or too lean.
- Gauge needle fluctuates rapidly between 10 and 21 inches (Hg) at idle. This occurs when one or more valvesprings are weak or broken.
- Gauge reads normal at idle but drops slowly as engine speed is increased to 2,500 rpm. This indicates a restricted exhaust system.
- Gauge reads below normal and fluctuates rapidly over a range of about 3 inches (Hg) at idle, then the needle becomes steady as engine speed is increased. Worn intake guides usually cause this reading.

Perform a compression test. It will indicate how well the piston rings, valves, and head gaskets are sealing, and it's one of the most important tests in helping you determine if your engine needs rebuilding. The cylinder-to-cylinder balance is the most relevant information. The lowest cylinder reading should be at least 75 percent of the highest reading. Before checking engine compression, make sure the valves are properly adjusted (mechanical camshafts) and all the spark plugs are removed. The engine should be at normal operating temperature. Disable the ignition system and make sure the throttle and choke plates are fully opened. The compression reading for a mechanically sound engine can vary from as low as 80 psi to more than 180 psi, depending on the mechanical compression ratio and camshaft profile; it should, however, be consistent among all of the cylinders.

You can also perform a leak-down test. This procedure eliminates the variables of cam timing and provides a better measure of piston, ring, valve, and gasket condition. Most engines have 5 to 10 percent leakage. If you measure 20 percent or more on any cylinder, the rings, valves, or head gasket are leaking, or there may even be a cracked bore or cylinder head.

Uniformly worn piston rings give consistently low compression readings, or consistently high leakage readings. To check for ring wear in a cylinder, remove the gauge and squirt some motor oil through the spark plug hole. Crank over the engine to distribute the oil and recheck the compression. The new reading should not increase more than 10 or 15 psi (or more than 5 percent leakdown flow). A larger increase indicates excessively worn piston rings.

If the engine overheats, check for combustion gas in the cooling system. Checking kits are available in parts stores, or have a professional perform the test for you. A positive result often indicates a leaking head gasket, but it could also mean a crack has developed in the block or cylinder heads.

Finally, look for signs of water in the oil. If the oil has turned a foamy yellow or there are water droplets on the dipstick, the block or heads may be cracked.

Carburetion

Flooding is one of the most common carburetor problems. First, check the float level, and then look for fuel contamination. The fuel pressure should also be checked, along with the condition of the fuel filter. Flooding is likely to occur if pressure exceeds 7.5 psi at the carburetor. Also check the following items: worn needle-and-seat assemblies, gas-soaked floats, and correct float arm and pivot alignment.

Also, check idle speed and idle mixture, vacuum leaks, and look for a stuck-open or leaking exhaust gas recirculation (EGR) valve. Check for a dirty air filter element, clogged air bleeds, or clogged-bowl vent tubes.

A defective accelerator pump system is most often the cause of stumbling or hesitation on initial acceleration. A quick movement of the throttle should produce a steady stream of fuel from the nozzles. Also check the float level, the power valve (or power circuit), and make sure the secondaries are not opening too soon.

Incomplete throttle opening caused by improperly adjusted linkage is often the reason for lack of power. With the engine shut off, have a helper operate

BEFORE YOU BEGIN

the accelerator and check for full throttle opening and closing. Also check for the following:

- clogged main jets
- plugged power valve channel
- restrictions (Holley carbs) or a power-enrichment circuit that isn't functioning
- low float level or a float that isn't dropping far enough
- fuel filters and the fuel delivery system
- make sure the air filter is clean and of adequate size

Finally, the carburetor can affect fuel economy but so can many other systems. Make sure the engine is "tuned up." Also check: 1) tires for proper inflation, 2) front-end alignment, 3) brakes for dragging, and 4) bad axle bearings.

Anything that overly richens the fuel mixture will decrease fuel economy. Improper choke operation, floats set too high, leaking needle-and-seat assemblies, power-circuit malfunction, or too much fuel pressure are common causes.

Removing the Engine

If you are rebuilding a used engine, it's time to remove the engine from your car to get it ready for your new power plant. In our project car we were replacing a worn-out 6-cylinder with a fresh 350 V-8. The following steps for engine removal carry over to any application.

Flooding is one of the most common carburetor problems. Check float level, and then look for fuel contamination. The fuel pressure should also be checked. Flooding is likely to occur if pressure exceeds 7.5 psi at the carburetor.

1 Prepare For Removal

Pulling the old engine out of your car won't take long, but be sure to use care, caution, and patience. You'll need a heavy-duty jack along with jack stands, a drain pan for coolant and one for oils (think about power steering lines, trans fluid, and more), and having a friend to help when the engine comes out is a good idea. We're pulling a 6-cylinder engine for an eagerly anticipated V-8 swap, but the procedure is the same if your vehicle already has a V-8 from the factory.

CHAPTER 1

2 | Disconnect Battery

Most major repairs performed on your car start by disconnecting the battery. Disconnect the negative terminal first and install it last.

3 | Remove Hood

The hood needs to be removed. Mark the location of the hood hinge mount so you'll have a better idea of the exact location to save time when aligning it for installation.

4 | Drain Coolant; Remove Hoses

As the coolant drains, work your way from the top down, starting by removing the upper radiator hose followed by temperature sensors. Next remove the heater hoses and lower radiator hose. Even if the radiator stops draining, more coolant will pour from the engine when the lower hose is removed so be prepared with your drain pan.

5 | Lift Rear of Car

With the coolant and oils drained, lift the rear end of the car. If you're pulling the transmission with the engine, you'll need the extra room, and even if the transmission is staying in, this will give you more work room to get to the converter and bellhousing bolts as well as help with the exhaust, transmission linkage, and more. The outer axle flange of the rear end is a solid location for the jack stands.

6 | Remove Radiator

Once the coolant has drained out, remove the radiator. Make sure the transmission lines are disconnected if you have an automatic transmission. Use care not to damage the fins.

7 | Disconnect Wiring from Starter/Alternator

Label and disconnect the wiring from the starter and alternator. The starter will have the main positive battery feed and another smaller wire on the large terminal with one or two wires going to separate terminals on the solenoid. The alternator will also have one large wire terminal and generally a connector to disconnect on the housing.

8 Remove Flywheel Bolts

Back under the car, there are three bolts that secure the flexplate or flywheel of the engine to the torque converter of the transmission. The transmission needs to be in neutral to get to all of the bolts. This is where a flywheel tool comes in handy to hold the wheel as you loosen the bolts and to spin it around to get to the next bolt.

9 Remove Bellhousing Bolts

There are six bellhousing bolts that need to be removed. Some of these may be accessible from the top, while others are best to get from under the car. Go ahead and remove them all; the dowel pins will keep the engine and transmission mated.

10 Remove Engine Mounts

Don't forget the engine mounts! There are two long bolts that slide through the chassis mount and the engine mount. Generally they require a 5/8-inch socket.

11 Secure Chain

With a heavy-duty chain, mount one link on the driver's side rear of the engine. Generally, on the back of the cylinder head, but in the case of this inline six we used the exhaust manifold bolt hole. The other end of the chain should be mounted to the passenger-side front of the engine.

12 Connect Chain to Hoist

Connect the chain to your engine hoist and lift up just until there is a little tension on the chain. Make sure that the chain and lift point are nearly centered, or just a little bit to the front of center to dip the rear of the engine down a little. Also, make certain that the transmission has a jack under it or has been secured so it doesn't move too far forward once the engine comes out. Go ahead and lift the motor a little bit more to get it to come loose of the mounts. Once there, use a pry bar to separate the engine from the transmission.

13 Slowly Pull Engine

Once the engine is away from the mounts and transmission, raise it slowly and constantly check to make sure it is not pulling on wires, brackets, or cables and it is not making contact with the air conditioning or heater housing. Continue lifting until it clears the radiator support and roll the cherry picker back. As soon as it is clear of the engine bay, lower the engine down where it can be moved easier and more controlled.

CHAPTER 2

ENGINE DISASSEMBLY

A well-known expert was asked what he could learn about the "past life" of an engine during disassembly. He responded, "Everything!" Removing each bolt was his equivalent of turning a page in a book titled "A Detailed History of this Engine."

While you may not have the experience to "read" this much detail, the disassembly steps in this chapter (and the inspection steps in Chapter 3) will act as your "expert" guide. They'll provide insights and tips that an expert might tell you if he was guiding you through the entire process. To get the most out of this book, take your time, read each of the upcoming steps thoroughly, and think through the procedure before you begin. If this is your first engine rebuild, it's essential to take the extra time to become familiar with the components you're removing. If you already have a good deal of experience with tools and engines, you can move along more quickly. However, regardless of your experience, don't lose your patience and begin skipping steps; you won't gain full benefit from the "resident expert" you're holding in your hands.

Engine disassembly can tell you a great deal about the "past life" of your engine. Be sure to keep your parts organized during disassembly so you can inspect them further.

Keep an Organized Workspace

One of the best ways to ensure that your rebuilt engine will provide both top performance and long-term reliability is to establish a comfortable workspace and keep it organized. Don't even attempt this project if you plan on rebuilding your engine while you roll it around on your driveway. You need a well-lit, clean, and relatively dust-free environment. You need a place where you won't be distracted by telephones, blasting radios, TVs, or a pack of your best friends. You need a clean workbench, a quality engine stand, the proper tools, and most important, you need patience and the unbending will to "do it right." Rebuilding an engine involves working with hundreds of components. Each part must be properly removed, reconditioned or replaced, and reinstalled. You can make the job considerably easier and stay more organized by obtaining several plastic storage bins from your local hardware store (warehouse stores such as Menards, The Home Depot, and Lowe's, etc. are excellent sources). Use small bins for small-part storage; use large bins to keep

ENGINE DISASSEMBLY

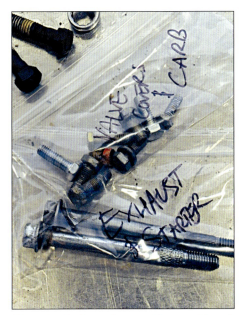

Use plastic zipper bags to keep bolts and other components sorted and identified. Use small bins for small part storage and large bins to keep pans, cylinder heads, and other large components off your shop floor.

exhaust manifolds, oil pans, cylinder heads, and other large components off your shop floor. Plastic bins can easily be cleaned to store reconditioned parts, and they can be stacked to take up less space.

Use plastic zipper bags to keep bolts and other small components sorted and identified (the freezer bags even have a printed panel where you can label the parts with a felt-tip marker). Many bolts look very much alike but are not interchangeable. If you're not intimately familiar with your engine's hardware, organizing fasteners can save you a lot of time and frustration during reassembly.

Make sure to use the Work-A-Long Sheet on pages 157–159 (also available for free download at cartechbooks.com) when instructed in the upcoming steps. It will not only help you keep track of your engine's "particulars," it will become a valuable permanent record of your engine rebuild. Having it neatly and accurately filled out can even add value to your engine in the eyes of a potential buyer.

Finally, many engine accessory brackets, hoses, and wires can become a confusing jumble later on. To avoid this problem, an upcoming step instructs you to take detailed notes and take a couple of photos before and during the disassembly. Don't limit your picture taking to these specific steps! Take shots at any point during the rebuild that will help maintain an accurate record. A digital camera is perfect, since there are no processing costs and you can take as many as you need, then file them away on your computer along with any accompanying notes about the photos.

Remember, in engine building neatness and organization count, big time!

Tools and Supplies

Aside from an organized workspace, plastic bins and bags, and basic hand tools (see Chapter 1, "Before You Begin," for more information on basic tools), you need a few specialized tools and supplies to properly disassemble an engine.

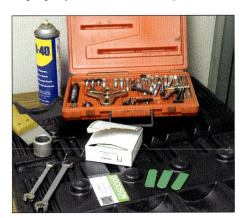

In addition to the standard array of hand tools, engine disassembly requires several specialized tools. Line wrenches (used to remove air-injector and other metal lines), a 3-bolt puller (required to remove the vibration damper), and rod bolt protectors (to prevent the crankshaft from being damaged) are just a few.

Rust Penetrant. To loosen rusted-on exhaust manifold bolts and other stuck fasteners, penetrating lubricants such as WD-40, CRC 5-56, PB Blaster, and others are a big help. These lubricants often make the difference between a broken or rounded-off fastener and successful disassembly.

Heavy-Duty Line Wrench. Line wrenches (box end with a slot that allows it to pass over tubing) are required to remove the air-injector lines on exhaust manifolds and the fuel lines from the carb and pump. We recommend Snap-on part RXS18 for the 9/16-inch wrench, or part RXS608 for a complete set. (See sidebar "Snap-on Tools" on page 10 for more info.)

Some heavy-duty equipment is also needed to rebuild your engine. The most important is a quality engine stand as well as an engine hoist, to lift the engine onto and off of your engine stand.

REBUILDING THE SMALL-BLOCK CHEVROLET

CHAPTER 2

Valvetrain Organizer. If you're reusing the rocker arms, valves, springs, and other valvetrain components, you must keep them in order. We recommend a plastic organizer tray, like one from Goodson or Eastwood. You can also quickly make one from a cardboard box (punch 16 holes, label it for front and back, then use the valvestems to "skewer" the springs, rockers, etc.).

Vibration Damper Puller. If you try to remove the vibration damper without the right tools, you'll ruin it. For removal, you need a simple centerbolt puller with three attaching bolts (see Step 32 on page 35).

Rod Bolt Protectors. Exposed rod bolts can damage the crank journals during disassembly and reassembly. Short lengths of 3/8-inch rubber hose or plastic protector boots slipped over the bolts are absolutely essential to protect the crankshaft. Goodson and others offer inexpensive protectors.

Rod Removal Tool (optional). A tool that attaches to a rod bolt and guides the rod down the bore when removing the pistons is very helpful. B&B Performance offers an inexpensive Pro model or you can make one yourself (see Step 48 on page 38).

Engine Stand and Cherry Picker Hoist. These items are a bit expensive but absolutely essential—avoid "cheap" models that don't roll well or barely hold the engine. Seeing your newly assembled engine lying on the floor is no fun! You can rent a cherry picker, but when you consider how long you'll need an engine stand, it makes sense to buy one of your own (or borrow one from a patient friend).

Generous Supply of Clean Rags. Rags can be purchased from home and business supply warehouses. You'll need about 25 pounds of "lint-free" cotton rags to complete your engine project.

Safety First, Always!

Like most jobs, engine disassembly isn't difficult. All you need are the right tools, patience, and a willingness to learn and think ahead. If you start rushing the job, you'll make mistakes that will cost you time and money, and you'll be sorry. If you ignore this particular facet of engine building, you'll be more than sorry; you could be seriously injured. There isn't a professional engine builder that can't tell you at least one story about an inexperienced "over-enthusiast" losing a finger, toe, or eye, or winding up with other mutilations. An engine weighs several hundred pounds; you can't catch it when it falls! A crankshaft propped up in your garage can tip over easily and cut off a toe. Without proper safety glasses or a face shield, metal shavings, solvent, or other debris can wind up in your eye. Without gloves, you can expose yourself to cancer-causing chemicals. The list is endless.

Read the sidebar "Shop Safety" on page 28 before you begin. Think about safety during your entire project. If you know you don't have the personality to rebuild an engine using the right tools and in a thoughtful and safe manner, you should not start the job. Instead, take your engine to a qualified engine-building shop; you'll get the job finished faster, maybe even cheaper, and certainly safer.

Taking photos of your engine (in addition to marking components) before removing it from your car and during the rebuilding process is a great idea. It will help you maintain an accurate record of your project, plus it can be a big help when you are trying to distinguish one mounting bracket from another.

ENGINE DISASSEMBLY

Step-by-Step Engine Disassembly

1 Ready to Begin

Before we pulled the engine for rebuilding, we noted the different brackets and accessories. Note that this AC bracket goes over the valve cover. If we swap to taller valve covers, chances are that this bracket won't fit anymore. Also, the two intake bolts are a little longer to secure this bracket.

2 Record Engine Observations
Documentation Required

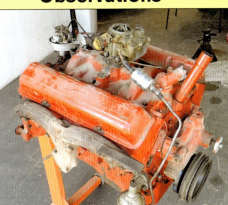

This is a 283 out of a 1966 Chevy II. There are many subtle variations in small-block Chevy engines and their accessories. However, there are more similarities than differences and most of the disassembly steps that follow are applicable to all small-blocks. Regardless of whether your engine has all the accessories attached or is partially stripped, your first step should be to use the Work-A-Long Sheet. Record your knowledge of the engine, including previous operational notes. Also, check off the attached accessories and note any damaged or missing components. This basic information will begin the permanent record of your rebuilding project.

3 Record Engine Observations
Documentation Required

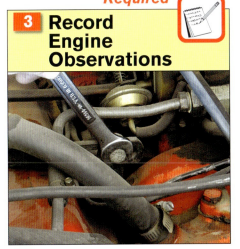

Note the way the alternator bracket mounts to the intake manifold (where the wrench is). If you use an aftermarket intake, be sure there is a mounting hold in the same location. This is why it is a good idea to take photos and notes before disassembly.

4 Before Mounting on Stand
Safety Step

Several components must be removed (or are easier to remove) before you mount the engine on an engine stand. To prevent the engine from falling over while you perform the next few steps, and to prepare to lift the engine onto an engine stand, use a "cherry picker" hoist. Attach a lifting chain to the engine. Raise the hoist just enough to take the slack out of the chain. Chain tension will keep the engine upright.

CHAPTER 2

Removing Stubborn Fasteners

Removing very tight or frozen fasteners requires special techniques to avoid damaging the bolts or component parts. Carelessly applying brute force usually results in stripped or broken fasteners.

Here are some tips that will help you successfully remove all but the most stubborn fasteners. The most important tip is: be patient! When you encounter a stuck screw or bolt, STOP! Don't apply excessive force. Use the following to increase your odds of easy removal.

Chemical Wrenches

Applying a liberal amount of a chemical penetrant such as WD-40 often makes the difference between success and failure. Allow the penetrant to soak in for at least 5 to 10 minutes. When possible, strike the center of the bolt or stud with a light hammer and drift several times. This tends to break down the corrosion between the threads and helps the penetrant to work its way in. However, don't deform or damage the head of the fastener. Applying some penetrant to troubled-looking retainers before you begin disassembly is always a good idea.

Special Tools

Use only a high-quality tool that is not worn and fits the fastener tightly. This is essential! Removing stuck fasteners with cheap tools is almost always doomed to failure. If possible, use a 6-point socket or wrench, since 12-point sockets don't allow as much torque before "rounding off" the fastener. Never use an open-end wrench on a frozen bolt or nut, unless a socket, box-end, or line wrench simply cannot be used. Long-stem, 6-point, box-end wrenches are usually effective for breaking loose stuck bolts when a socket can't be used. Top-quality line wrenches are a must for stubborn flared fittings.

Techniques and Tricks

Make sure that the tool is fully engaged on the fastener before you apply force. Always use deep sockets on studs with nuts to ensure full engagement on the hex surfaces of the nut. If a fastener starts to unscrew but then locks up, screw it in slightly and apply penetrant to the threads. Continue screwing the fastener in and out and adding penetrant until it can be removed.

A little patience and the right tools will make removing stubborn fasteners much easier. Leave the hammers, chisels, and hacksaws to the less-patient "mechanics."

A liberal application of penetrating lubricant should be your first step when you encounter a stubborn fastener. Allow the penetrant to soak in for at least 5 or 10 minutes.

If your best efforts fail and the fastener breaks off, these extractors Tools will drill and back out the broken fastener in one step. We tried them; they really work!

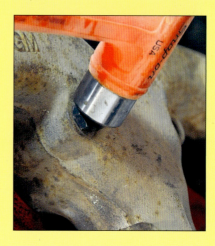

Lightly striking the fastener or fitting several times with a hammer and drift can help break down corrosion and allow penetrating lubricants to enter the threads.

24   REBUILDING THE SMALL-BLOCK CHEVROLET

ENGINE DISASSEMBLY

Documentation Required

5 Remove Crank Centerbolt

Locate the large centerbolt holding the damper and front pulley onto the crankshaft. Some engines do not use a centerbolt; indicate its presence or absence on the Work-A-Long Sheet. If your engine does not have a centerbolt, skip to Step 6. Loosen and remove this bolt with a 1/2-inch-drive breaker bar (or impact wrench). The crankshaft will probably rotate as you attempt to loosen the bolt. Lock the crankshaft by inserting a pry bar or large screwdriver through one of the flexplate holes or in between the ring gear and starter housing (see Step 4). If there is no flywheel or flexplate on your engine (and you don't have an impact wrench), leave the centerbolt in place, you'll remove it later.

6 Remove Flywheel or Flexplate

Make sure the engine is not resting on the ring gear. Loosen and remove the six bolts that retain the flywheel or flexplate. These bolts are also very tight; use a 1/2-inch-drive socket and a long breaker bar. Be careful as you remove the flywheel; don't let it fall on your fingers! Note that the flywheel bolts use star-type lockwashers and have fine threads. Keep them together in your parts bins or bags. If your engine is equipped with a flywheel and clutch assembly, the pressure plate and clutch disk must be removed first. The six bolts holding the clutch disk in place should be loosened evenly before being removed. Use care not to drop the pressure plate or clutch disk as you remove it.

7 Remove Rear Oil Gallery and Water Jacket Plugs

In this step you remove three oil gallery (pipe) plugs and two water jacket core plugs installed in the rear of the block (the large cam plug will be removed later). If you can't remove any of these core plugs, ask your machine shop to remove them before they clean your block. The gallery plugs are extremely tight and often must be drilled and removed with an extractor. However, they can sometimes be loosened with a special 1/4-inch square-drive pipe-plug socket (Snap-on set 211PPPMY). Never use a 1/4-inch drive ratchet or extension; it will break off and remain jammed in the plug! Remove the two core plugs by first driving them in the water jacket with a large 1/2-inch-drive socket ($1\frac{1}{16}$ inches usually works). Then work the plugs to one side, grab them with a Vise-Grip or adjustable pliers, and lever them out.

CHAPTER 2

8 Mount Engine on Stand

You cannot build a quality engine if you have to roll it around on your garage floor! A heavy-duty engine stand is an essential part of your engine-building project. Use a "cherry picker" to lift the engine into position, then attach the engine to the stand using at least grade-5 bolts that thread into the block no less than 1/2 inch. Be sure to get the engine secured and put the lock pin in to hold it steady or tighten the lock bolt/setscrew on the stand.

Safety Step

9 Drain Oil

Make sure the engine is securely mounted on the engine stand. Remove the lift point and/or attaching chains. Before you proceed, consider placing a drip pan on or under your engine stand. If you don't, engine oil, antifreeze, grease, dirt, rust, and other unpleasant gunk will wind up underfoot as you tear your engine apart. Now, drain engine oil from the pan and remove the oil filter. Remember, used engine oil is a toxic waste; keep it off your hands (latex gloves available at most paint stores work nicely) and dispose of it in an environmentally appropriate manner.

10 Remove Accessories and Mounting Brackets

If your engine is so equipped, begin accessory removal by unbolting the air-conditioning compressor and its mounting bracket. Next, remove the fan, smog pump, power steering pump, and alternator. Unbolt all remaining mounting brackets located on the front of the engine.

Documentation Required

11 Remove Distributor/Spark Plugs

Distributors are positioned to optimize engine-compartment clearance. Record its general position on your Work-A-Long Sheet before you loosen it. Start by removing all spark plug wires. Then unbolt and remove the distributor hold-down clamp. Remove the distributor by twisting and lifting it by the bottom of the housing. Note that, as you lift up, the rotor turns. This is due to the helical gear. Don't apply excessive force to the rotor, cap, or vacuum-advance housing. Finally, remove the spark plugs. Since the appearance of the insulators can help diagnose some engine malfunctions, you may want to number the spark plugs (masking tape works well) for future reference. While you're working on top of the engine, strip the intake manifold of the EGR valve, carb, and thermostat housing.

ENGINE DISASSEMBLY

Professional Mechanic Tip

12 Apply Penetrant

13 Remove Exhaust Manifolds and Air-Injection Lines

PRO TIP *Before you attempt to remove any exhaust system bolts and fittings, apply a liberal amount of rust penetrant to each fastener and allow it to soak in for at least 10 minutes. (See sidebar "Removing Stubborn Fasteners" on page 24.) If any of the bolts don't break loose, don't apply excessive force. STOP! Apply more penetrant, and try again.*

Before you remove the exhaust manifolds, mark them with an "L" or "1" (left bank) or an "R" or "2" (right bank). Some stock manifolds are already marked (as ours was). Now bend back any locking tabs on the exhaust manifold bolts, and remove the bolts and manifolds. If your engine has them, remove the spark plug heat shields that are attached to the top edge of the block. If you have AIR tubes to remove from the manifold (if using the same manifolds, leave them in place), soak them in penetrant. Then, use a quality 9/16-inch line wrench, such as this thickheaded Snap-on model (part RXS18), to remove the lines. If an injector tube starts to twist with the nut, STOP! Apply more penetrant and work the nut back and forth until it turns freely.

14 Remove Motor Mounts and Starter

Some motor mounts/brackets may be left/right interchangeable, while others are not. If you feel there may be any confusion during reassembly, mark each bracket with a tag or stamp. Remove the front motor mounts and/or mounting brackets from each side of the cylinder block. Next, remove the starter support bracket (if your engine has one). Then remove the two starter attaching bolts. The starter is heavy, so be careful as you remove the final bolt.

15 Remove Fuel Pump and Pump Support Plate

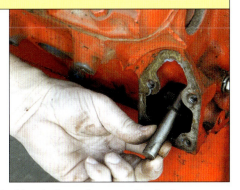

Remove any fuel lines still attached to the fuel pump. Unscrew the two 3/8-inch pump attaching bolts and remove the fuel pump. Next, remove the two 1/4-inch bolts holding the pump mounting plate to the block. Use a gasket scraper or screwdriver to pry the mounting plate loose. Finally, slide the fuel-pump pushrod out of the block. Set these components aside in your parts bins.

CHAPTER 2

Shop Safety

Engine building can be a fascinating and rewarding experience. If you often feel rushed, are easily excited, and you rarely think about safety, you could be "building" more than an engine. You could have a disaster in the making.

There are a thousand ways you can injure yourself working on automotive parts and components. Fortunately, most injuries are minor and more irritating than anything else. However, keep this in mind: if you regularly bang your fingers, cut yourself, or have other "minor" accidents, you're getting a warning message. The hand of fate may be ready to deal you a real catastrophe. Many "over-enthusiasts" have lost fingers, toes, eyes, and much worse.

Be sure to use safety glasses, even when you're cleaning parts, as debris or cleaners can easily fling into your eyes. Earplugs are a good idea when you're power washing or using air tools. Respirators or masks are great when you're working with cleaners or painting your nearly complete engine. Common sense is one of your most important safety tools. Use it!

Engine Stands

Don't use cheap engine stands. More than one has broken, dropping the engine to the floor. Stay away from models that use three, instead of four, casters. A slight depression in your garage floor or one wheel locking up can cause three-wheel stands to tip over. Finally, keep the lockscrew (that prevents engine rotation) tight; if the engine rotates quickly, it can flip the stand off its wheels.

Chain Hoists

If you are using a chain hoist attached to a ceiling beam make absolutely sure that the supporting beam will safely support at least 700 pounds. If you're not sure of the load carrying ability of your ceiling, don't take any chances—rent a quality cherry picker.

Take Regular Breaks

More accidents, and poor quality work, happen after long hours on the job than any other time. Take a break at least once each hour, even if you are eager to continue. Stretch your legs or sit down and relax. Think about how your project is coming and how you can improve the quality of your work. Review a chapter of your book, or parts catalogs, to make sure you have everything to complete the steps you're involved in. When you feel composed and relaxed, resume your project.

Stay Patient

If you feel yourself starting to rush, STOP. Take a minute or two to take a deep breath and slow down. If you lose your patience, you'll stop having fun, the quality of your work will suffer, and you're almost certainly one step away from an accident.

Don't Drink

Building an engine is not the time to call up your buddies and break out the beer. Engine building is a complex job that requires your full attention. Don't work when you're tired, when you feel distracted, or when you've had a drink. Your safety and the quality of your work depend on it.

There are a thousand ways you can injure yourself working on automotive parts. Having the correct tools for the job is important—and using them smartly and as they are intended is just as important. When you're working under your car during the engine installation, having a good set of jack stands in position is imperative. The same is true with a good floor jack. Even having a cleaning bin where parts can soak, and cleaner is stored, is good for keeping things neat and for keeping cleaners out of harm's way. Always wear safety glasses when working with cleaners and power tools. A good set of earplugs and a mask are also good to use when grinding. Be prepared and work safe!

ENGINE DISASSEMBLY

16 Remove All Topside Accessories

Remove all remaining accessories from the intake manifold, including the carburetor and choke bi-metal housing. Also, remove the oil pressure sender from the rear of the block. Snap-on and other manufacturers offer special sockets for "idiot light" and gauge-type units. However, a deep socket, open-end wrench, or adjustable pliers will remove most types. Don't apply force to the plastic on small senders, or to the "can" on larger sending units.

17 Remove Water Pump

 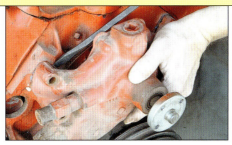

Remove the water pump by removing the four bolts that secure it to the engine block. When the bolts are removed, you may need a small pry bar or large screwdriver to break the pump loose from the block, but don't pry against the timing chain cover—you could easily damage it.

Chevrolet used two different length water pumps through the 1960s and early 1970s: a short pump (right) and a long pump (left). The short pumps were used on engines in Corvettes, Novas, and other engines that were short on space between the pump and the radiator. Be sure to use the same style that you had before, or your brackets and pulleys will be all wrong.

18 Remove Valve Covers

Remove all remaining components that may still be attached to the valve covers. Then remove the cover bolts and covers. If you have to pry the covers loose, take your time because excessive force can easily bend them.

In about 1986, Chevy changed the retaining arrangement of their valve covers. No longer were the four bolts on the outer edge of the cover and head. The bolts were actually moved to the center of the valve cover (such as the grungy model shown). These were much less prone to oil leaks over time.

REBUILDING THE SMALL-BLOCK CHEVROLET

19 Remove Intake Manifold

Remove all remaining bolts attaching the intake manifold to the cylinder heads. Most manifolds will come loose after prying with a screwdriver inserted between the manifold and the end-rails of the block. If your manifold seems to be "really stuck," STOP! Make sure all the manifold bolts have been removed. When the manifold has been removed, note the heat-riser passage configuration (providing it hasn't been burned out) of the intake gaskets on your Work-A-Long Sheet for future reference.

20 Remove Rocker Arms and Pushrods

Remove each of the rocker arms by unscrewing the self-locking nuts. It is recommended that you replace these lock nuts, but try to keep the old ones for your visual inspection. Goodson offers a helpful tray just for valvetrain disassembly. Lift the rocker arm off the stud and pull out the pushrod. Roll each pushrod on a clean, flat surface to make sure none are bent. Mark or label them and note any damage on your Work-Along Sheet for future reference.

21 Remove Head Bolts

First, make sure the lock-bolt on the engine stand that prevents block rotation is tight. Use a long, 1/2-inch breaker bar and a 5/8-inch 6-point socket. Break all the head bolts loose, then go back with a short-handled ratchet and remove all but two bolts in each head. Leave one bolt near each end of each cylinder head (four total). Unscrew these four remaining bolts only two or three turns.

22 Remove Cylinder Heads

In most cases, the cylinder head will be stuck to the block with sealing compound and corrosion. To coax it loose, insert a breaker bar or pry bar into one of the intake ports and smoothly apply pressure until the head pops up against the two remaining head bolts. If the head resists prying loose, STOP! Make sure all but two bolts have been removed and the two remaining bolts are loose. After the head is loose, mark it with an "L" or "1" (left bank) or an "R" or "2" (right bank). Now remove the two remaining bolts and lift the head onto your workbench. Use the same technique to remove the other cylinder head.

ENGINE DISASSEMBLY

Block Performance Tips

The most notable feature of performance on heavy-duty cylinder blocks is the addition of four-bolt main caps on the three intermediate bulkheads. Some production four-bolt iron blocks have slightly thicker bulkheads and cylinder bores, and should be selected for performance use, since this improves overall strength and ring seal. Used four-bolt blocks are becoming harder to find but are still out there. New performance blocks can be purchased from GMPP (see page 60) or other aftermarket sources. Aluminum and special iron-alloy blocks are also available.

Once a block is selected, you must notify your machine shop that the core will be used in a performance or racing buildup. General performance prep includes boring/honing the crank bore to the "tight side" of tolerance to maximize bearing crush. Cylinders are bored and/or honed with deck plates installed. Some shops prefer to bore new blocks to center the individual bores before honing to final size. Much care must be given to the surface finish of the bores to ensure proper ring seal.

Additional modifications may be desired for some applications. When a long-stroke crank or racing rods are used, the block may have to be modified to gain clearance for the rotating pieces. Many of the aftermarket blocks have extra material to allow for increased clearancing. If the engine is fitted with roller-bearing rocker arms, flow restrictors are often installed in the lifter galleries to reduce oil supply to the valvetrain. In some instances, the cooling passages in the block decks are closed off or restricted to alter coolant flow. Most of these mods are straightforward and well documented, but it is important to discuss these decisions with your machine shop when you deliver the block.

The most common feature of performance heavy-duty cylinder blocks is the addition of four-bolt caps (hence, the four bolts per cap). The main cap on the top is a four-bolt design, and the lower model is the two-bolt version. Performance Bow Tie castings are available from GMPP and other aftermarket sources.

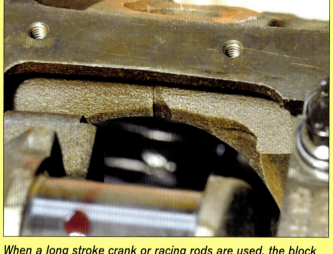

When a long stroke crank or racing rods are used, the block may have to be modified to gain clearance for the rotating pieces. Some high-performance GMPP Bow Tie blocks are much less likely to break into water jackets when clearance grinding.

For performance use, cylinders must be bored and honed with deck plates installed. Surface finish must be optimum to ensure best ring break-in and seal.

REBUILDING THE SMALL-BLOCK CHEVROLET

23 Remove and Tag Head Gaskets/Remove Dowel Pins

Remove the cylinder head gaskets—they usually remain stuck on the cylinder block.

Tag each gasket "LEFT" or "RIGHT" and note its type on your Work-A-Long Sheet. The cylinder heads and gaskets are located on the block by two dowel pins on each deck surface. Most machine shops remove and replace these pins as a matter of course when machine work is performed. If you have the proper tools, you can remove them now. But don't drive them into the water jackets. They can become stuck below the deck surface or you may even crack the block and render it useless. The best way to remove them is to first tap them with a hammer and brass drift, and then use a 5/16-inch collet-type puller, such as this tool from Goodson.

25 Remove Oil Pan and Dipstick

Before you rotate the engine on your engine stand, remove the fourteen 1/4-inch and four 5/16-inch pan bolts (the larger bolts are located at each end of the pan). If the pan is stuck to the block (most are), insert a gasket scraper or screwdriver between the block and pan rails, but try not to bend the pan. Gently pry on both sides until the pan comes loose. Also, remove the dipstick and dipstick tube by twisting it back and forth by hand. If it doesn't come out, insert a 5/16 x 1-inch bolt into the tube and use a pair of adjustable pliers to twist it out.

Documentation Required

26 Remove Crank Pulley

Remove the 3/8-inch bolts that hold the crank pulley to the vibration damper. Before you toss the bolts into a bin, carefully inspect them, and indicate on your Work-A-Long Sheet whether they have fine or coarse threads. Fine threads are used more often, but there is no way to predict what you'll find.

24 Remove Lifters

If you're considering reusing the camshaft and lifters, each lifter must be reinstalled in the same lifter bore, or you will doom the cam to destruction. Label each part upon removal or use a disassembly tray like those from Goodson or Crane Cams. Remove each lifter by using a hooked probe to pull it up, then grasp and remove the lifter body with your fingers and/or needle-nose pliers. Some lifters may also be so worn (mushroomed) that they do not slide out of their bores. If you find any, just pull the lifter up as much as possible, and leave it in the bore. You'll remove it later. Note the location of any suspect lifters on your Work-A-Long Sheet.

ENGINE DISASSEMBLY

27 Install Damper Puller

Documentation Required

You must use a 3-bolt puller to remove the vibration damper. This puller is used in a variety of applications so adding one to your toolbox is a good idea. We got ours from Snap-on. Before you begin, check three important things. First, make sure you're using the correct puller. Don't use a puller that grabs the outer ring; you'll pull the ring right off the damper! Second, make sure the puller draw bolt does not damage threads in the nose of the crankshaft. If you have any doubts, reinstall the crank bolt (without the washer) and allow the draw bolt to push against the head of the crank bolt. Third, make sure the threads on the three attaching bolts match the threads in the damper and that the bolts have been screwed into the damper at least 3/8 inch.

28 Remove Vibration Damper

29 Remove Timing Chain Cover

Now, remove the 10-1/4-inch timing chain cover bolts—they often use separate star-type lockwashers. Place the bolts and lockwashers in your parts bin. If the top dead center (TDC) timing indicator plate is held on with two cover bolts, indicate the attaching bolt locations on your Work-A-Long Sheet. Pry the cover loose by inserting a gasket scraper or screwdriver between the cover and the block; gently pry until the cover comes free.

30 Remove Crank Key

When you're sure the puller is properly installed, tighten the draw bolt. To prevent the crank from turning, insert a wood handle between the crank and the block. The damper usually breaks loose with a "pop." If the draw bolt gets very tight and the damper won't budge, STOP! Make sure the draw bolt is properly contacting the crank and that the three attaching bolts are not pulling out of the damper (you should have screwed them in at least 3/8 inch). If everything looks okay, continue tightening until the damper comes loose.

Remove the vibration-damper locating key in the crank snout by using a 5/16-inch (maximum) non-tapering drift punch. Drive the key toward the front main. As the key moves back in its slot, it will climb out of the crank. When two-thirds of the key is visible, use pliers to pull it free. If the crank slot is enlarged or the key is loose, the crank may be unusable (more on this in Chapter 3).

REBUILDING THE SMALL-BLOCK CHEVROLET

Head Performance Tips

Excellent production cylinder-head designs were achieved in the late 1960s (with the "186" and "492" castings) when the valve diameters in factory hi-po options were increased to 2.02 inches (intake) and 1.60 inches (exhaust). Port volumes were also enlarged in some versions of these "big-valve heads." Combustion chamber volumes have varied, depending on production compression requirements. Later heads use "angled" spark plugs that may improve combustion.

Specific cylinder head design and modification will depend on compression and RPM requirements. In many stock applications, the "small-valve" performance head (1.94-inch intake and 1.50-inch exhaust) is a desirable choice since smaller port volumes often increase mid-range throttle response and fuel economy. Big-valve heads (2.02/1.60) are best suited to high-RPM operation (above 4,500 rpm) in 302- to 350-ci engines. Small-chamber heads (64 to 65 cc) increase compression ratios with flat-top or low-volume piston domes.

Late-model performance cores are relatively plentiful on the second-hand market. However, certain early hi-po heads are becoming quite scarce. If you are using a set of older heads, be sure to update to hardened valveseats. Leaded fuel actually acted as a lubricant to the valves and valveseats to prevent wear. Since leaded fuel is no longer available from gas pumps, the valveseats will need to be upgraded to hardened seats.

In many cases, the best bet may be to obtain new cores from GMPP (see page 60), Air Flow Research (see page 129), Edelbrock, Crower, Holley, or other aftermarket source. The design features of these specialty heads vary widely. Some are for extreme-RPM racing, others may be suited for street, some are even "smog legal." Always review the suitability and the preparation details recommended by the manufacturer before you buy. Give their tech line a call or look at their website to find out which head will best meet your goal.

Performance modifications should also be discussed with your machine or porting shop. The list of modifications is nearly endless, but typical work includes porting the intake and exhaust ports and gasket matching. Combustion chambers are often reshaped to improve airflow and equalize volumes. Lightweight, small-stem valves are used in many racing classes. Non-stock valveguide inserts can be used, some will offset valvestems to permit installation of even larger valves. The spring seats are often enlarged to accept large-diameter valvesprings; however, the thin-wall castings on production heads often limit this procedure.

While late-1960s performance heads work well, GMPP aluminum Bow Tie heads have a lot to offer. They have extra material where it's needed, efficient chambers and ports, and can accept offset pushrods and other valvetrain tricks. There are a lot of aluminum racing heads available in the aftermarket today.

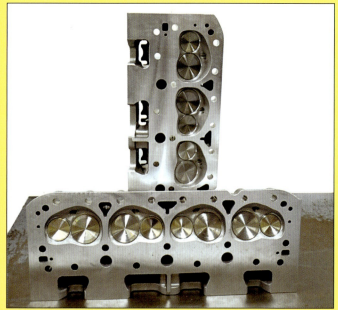

There are several sources for ready-to-run replacement cylinder heads for performance, street, and even "smog-legal" applications. GMPP, Edelbrock, Holley, and other companies offer cylinder head upgrades that are ready to bolt on your small-block.

ENGINE DISASSEMBLY

31 Remove Timing Chain and Sprockets

Loosen and remove the three bolts that hold the upper sprocket to the camshaft. The sprocket will usually come off with a slight "tug." If it's stuck, gently pry each side of the gear with a screwdriver wedged between the sprocket and the block face. The timing chain will come off with the upper sprocket. Sometimes the lower sprocket will slide off of the crankshaft with little effort; however, it is often firmly attached. If yours is tight, a gear puller will be needed to remove it. If you don't have the proper tool, don't worry about it; your machine shop will remove the lower sprocket for you (usually at no charge) when they inspect or regrind your crank.

Professional Mechanic Tip
32 Remove Camshaft

Removing the camshaft is easier if you install a "handle" like the ones offered by Goodson. You can also use a long, 3/8-inch NC bolt, or temporarily reinstall the cam sprocket as a handhold. Twist the cam back and forth, as you remove it. Keep the cam centered and prevent it from "falling" against the bearings as it slides out of the block.

Professional Mechanic Tip
33 Rotate Engine in Stand

Most engine short-blocks contain residual coolant, dirt, rust, and other debris that will fall to your garage floor when you rotate the block upside down. If you don't have a drip pan under your engine stand, spread rags on the floor to catch as much of the spillage as possible. Turning the engine slowly will also help keep the mess contained. Note: If the pump driveshaft falls out, just set it aside for now.

34 Remove Oil Pump

If you are planning to install a new or special oil pump (see Sidebar "Oil Pumps" on page 44), now is a good time to remove the pickup from the pump body. If you will be reusing the old pump, do not remove the pickup. First, make sure that the pickup tube has not been welded or brazed to the pump cover. If it has, remove the weld with a small die grinder before you proceed. Insert a pry bar into the pickup pipe loop as shown. Twist once or twice while pushing the pickup away from the pump cover. The tube should quickly loosen up enough to be removed by hand.

Remove the single bolt holding the oil pump to the rear main. Wiggle the pump while you're pulling upward to free the pump from the two dowel pins in the cap. When loose, continue lifting straight up. In most cases, a plastic attaching sleeve will keep the short pump driveshaft attached to the oil pump. If the shaft separates from the pump, it may fall through the distributor hole and to the floor; this may have happened already when you rotated the engine upside down. Set the pump and driveshaft aside.

CHAPTER 2

Documentation Required

35 Remove Oil Filter Adapter

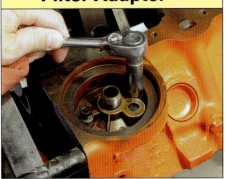

Remove the two 1/4- or 5/16-inch bolts that hold the oil filter adapter to the block. Your filter adapter may look different from the one pictured here. When the bolts have been removed, lift the adapter free, note the adapter type on your Work-A-Long Sheet, and set it aside in your parts bin.

Professional Mechanic Tip

36 Turn Crankshaft

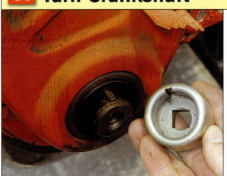

In the following steps, you need to rotate the crankshaft to continue disassembly. You can use a handy crank socket, such as this Snap-on example, which allows you to turn the crank in either direction. In a pinch, you can reinstall the crank centerbolt with a spacer (right photo), then use a standard 5/8-inch socket and breaker bar.

Important!

37 Number Rod and Main Caps

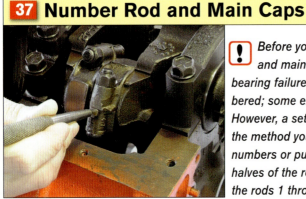

Before you begin bottom-end disassembly, it is essential that you number the rod and main caps. They are not interchangeable, and mixing the caps is a sure road to bearing failure. Don't skip this step even if you notice that the caps are already numbered; some engines come with duplicate numbers! You can use center-punch marks. However, a set of 1/8- or 3/16-inch steel number stamps does a nice job. Regardless of the method you choose, don't stamp the caps across the parting lines. Position your numbers or punch marks only on the flat areas adjacent to the parting lines. Stamp both halves of the rods, and to ease assembly, stamp the main caps and the block. Number the rods 1 through 8 and the mains 1 through 5.

Important!

38 Reduce Excessive Cylinder Ridge

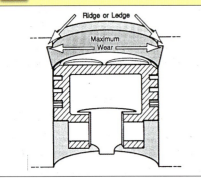

If your block has a ridge in the bores deeper than about .008 inch, it will catch the rings during assembly. You can use a ridge reamer to remove the ledge and save the pistons, but this may be false economy (especially when you consider that more good blocks are scrapped by the incorrect use of a ridge reamer than any other single mishap). When a deep ridge has been worn into the bores, the pistons are usually worn out too. So the best solution is simply to drive the pistons out. Although the rings or ring grooves may break, the block will not be damaged. To save the pistons, use a top-quality reamer, such as Snap-on's (part WR30A), or have your machine shop cut the ridge.

36 REBUILDING THE SMALL-BLOCK CHEVROLET

ENGINE DISASSEMBLY

39 Begin Rod/Piston Removal

Begin the rod/piston removal by rotating the crankshaft so that the piston being removed is at BDC; piston is at the bottom of the stroke.

40 Loosen Rod Cap

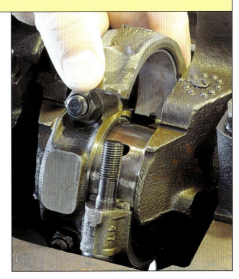

Use a long-handled ratchet or breaker bar to loosen the two connecting rod nuts and unscrew them only a few turns. Don't remove them yet.

Important!

41 Protect Journal

It is not essential to use a special tool to remove the rods and pistons. However, it is essential to use some method of protecting the crank journal as the rod bolts slide by. Rebuilders often install short rubber hoses over the bolts. Companies such as Goodson sell a set of rod bolt covers that are very durable and handy. (If you use the removal tool described in Step 43, you should install one sleeve and wrap the tool with tape to protect the crank.)

Critical Inspection

42 Don't Crack the Bore!

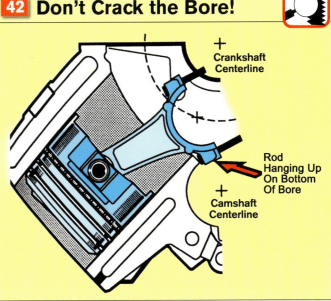

Regardless of the method you select to remove the rods and pistons in the upcoming steps, it is absolutely essential that you keep the big end of the rod centered as it moves down the bore. If it drifts up or down, it can catch on the edge of the cylinder bore. Unfortunately, some engine builders don't realize the cause of the "hang-up" and deliver several potent hammer blows. This sometimes breaks chunks off the bottom of the cylinder bore, which can convert a perfectly fine block into scrap metal. Don't let this happen to you! Keep the rod centered as it moves down the bore, and if it gets stuck, make sure you know why before you apply additional force.

REBUILDING THE SMALL-BLOCK CHEVROLET

43 Remove Rods/Pistons

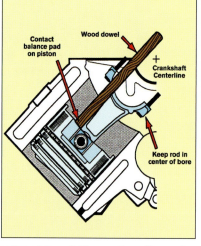

If you do not have a special rod removal tool, use a wooden dowel (an old broom handle works well) that is about 24 inches long. Once the rod is loose from the rod cap, position the dowel on the piston balance pad (see drawing) and drive the piston out. Remember to keep the rod centered. Be ready to catch the piston before it drops to the floor. You can also make a special tool by welding a nut that goes over the rod bolt to a steel rod. Be sure to wrap the rod with tape to prevent scuffing the crank journal. B&B Performance and other companies sell a professional version.

44 Replace Rod Caps and Nuts

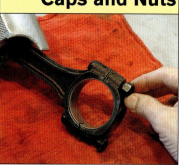

Once the rod/piston is removed, replace both bearing shells, put the cap and nuts back on, and set the assembly aside. Keeping the bearings with the rod can help you "read" possible problems (such a rod misalignment, insufficient oiling, bolt stretch, etc.) when we inspect these components in Chapter 3, "Initial Parts Inspection."

45 Remove Remaining Rods/Pistons

Now, jump back to Step 39 and repeat the disassembly procedure for the remaining seven rods and pistons.

46 Remove Main Bearing Caps

Make sure the main caps have been numbered before you remove them from the block (see Step 37). Using a breaker bar and a 5/8-inch 6-point socket, loosen and remove all ten main-cap bolts. If your engine has 4-bolt main caps, also remove the six side bolts on the three center caps. The main caps are fitted to the block with a slight interference fit and may require a tap or two with a plastic hammer to free them. Keep the bearing shells with their respective caps.

47 Remove One-Piece Rear Main Seal

If your small-block was manufactured after 1986 and uses a one-piece rear main seal, perform this step; otherwise skip to Step 48. The crank seal appliance must be removed before the crankshaft can be lifted from the block. First, unscrew the two long and two short bolts that hold the seal support on the rear of the block. Then, pry the appliance loose and slide it straight off the end of the crank.

ENGINE DISASSEMBLY

Piston Performance Tips

As with other small-block components, the selection of pistons available through the aftermarket is nearly unlimited. GMPP, JE, TRW, and many other companies can provide pistons for nearly any compression, configuration, or special feature a builder can imagine.

Piston manufacturers use various aluminum alloys and methods of manufacturing, such as casting, forging, billet machining, or the Speed Pro hypereutectic process. The specific criteria will vary with the application, but you should discuss piston requirements with your machine shop or the piston manufacturer before making a selection. In many cases, pistons require widely varying skirt clearance that can make a substantial difference in the suitability of the piston for a specific application. In general, the smaller the permissible skirt clearance, the more stable the piston will remain in the bore, resulting in better oil control and ring seal. This is especially important for street applications, where cold and low-temperature operation is more commonly encountered.

The number and width of the ring grooves can be specified if a custom piston is ordered. Occasionally the rear wall of the ring grooves is modified to increase oil drainback or sealing. The location of the piston pin bore can also be varied–altering the pin height and, possibly, deck clearance. The configuration and volume of the dome and the size and location of the valve reliefs can also be prescribed in some custom designs.

Intricate piston modifications are very common in racing applications. In some cases, the dome is custom-made or hand-contoured. If very high compression is required, the dome must fit tightly inside the compression chamber, but the finalized shape must not block or hinder combustion distribution. Sharp edges are radiused and the dome is often glass-beaded. In some instances, the underside of the dome and pin bosses may be machined to reduce overall weight.

At only 340 grams, this FSR Tour Series GP piston by JE Pistons is a lightweight piston for a performance-built small-block Chevy. The Forged Side Relief (FSR) forgings are stronger and lighter than a typical "full round" piston designs. These pistons have a smaller skirt and stiffer structure, which is favorable in racing applications. In addition, FSR pistons use a shorter wrist pin to help reduce the total weight.

This is a high-compression JE Chevy piston for open-chamber heads. The tall dome helps achieve a compression ratio as high as 16.0:1. The small gas ports in the top ring groove help combustion pressure push the top ring outward and improve ring seal.

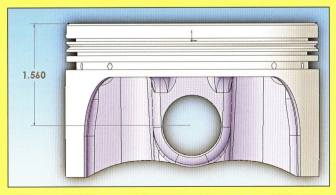

Today, products are designed on a screen before ever going into prototype stages. 3D design software such as SolidWorks are used to model a piston prior to manufacturing. Engineers can verify many design features such as deck thickness, dome/dish volume, piston weight and more. This image shows an SRP Professional piston for a small-block Chevy.

REBUILDING THE SMALL-BLOCK CHEVROLET

Rod Performance Tips

Heavy-duty production rods are often adequate to withstand up to 5,500 rpm. When additional strength is required, special performance rods can be purchased from GMPP (see page 60), Crower, Eagle, Arias, and others.

Many premium steel or titanium rods can be custom finished to any specification. The same is true of aluminum rods, although aluminum alloy rods are usually restricted to short-duration engines (e.g., drag racing applications). In most instances, you (or your machine shop) must contact the rod manufacturer to discuss finish details.

Typical performance preparation includes crack inspection (Magnaflux, Magnaglo, Zyglo, etc.); for all-out racing, steel rods may also be X-rayed to locate internal flaws. The big end of the rod should be reconditioned after new, premium-grade steel bolts and nuts—or capscrews and washers—are installed. Rods that have pressed-in bolts, such as stock engines, should not have the bolts removed after resizing. Installing new nuts (available from ARP or B&B Performance and other manufacturers) at each teardown is, however, recommended.

Rod bolts on racing engines should be tightened using the stretch method: a special micrometer measures bolt stretch as the fastener is tightened. The relaxed length of each new bolt also should be measured and recorded. Bolts should be checked against this length at each teardown; fasteners that have "grown" .001 inch or more should be discarded.

In many cases, heavy-duty rods will not clear the block or camshaft. Special machine work and careful hand grinding on both the rod and block may be required. In some cases, particularly with long-stroke cranks, deep reliefs are required and a thick-wall Bow Tie or aftermarket block must be used.

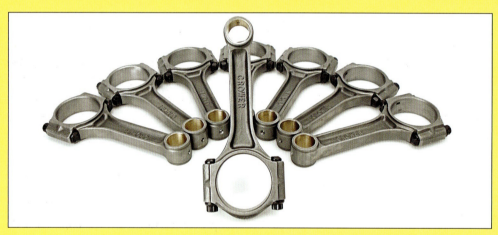

This set of Crower rods is designed for Sportsman racing and is an excellent choice for a high-performance street or bracket-racing engine. The machine work is top-notch.

While rod bolts should not be removed without resizing the rod, new nuts can be installed at each teardown to improve reliability in high-performance and racing engines. This kit from ARP is supplied with rod bolts and nuts for a complete rebuild.

ENGINE DISASSEMBLY

48 Remove Crankshaft

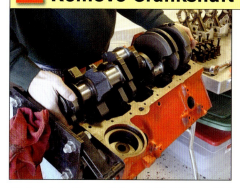 

Lift the crank straight up out of the block; you may have to wiggle it slightly (end to end) as you lift to clear the thrust faces on the rear main bearing. Some of the bearing shells may remain stuck to the crank journals as the crank is lifted free. Before they fall off and get mixed up, remove them—along with any bearing shells remaining in the block—and keep them with their respective main caps (Goodson offers parts tags that are great for use in such a situation).

49 Remove Two-Piece Rear Main Seal

If your engine is a late-model design with a one-piece rear main seal, jump to Step 50. Use a metal probe or a small screwdriver to pry out the rear main seal halves from both the block and rear main cap. Note the seal type on your Work-A-Long Sheet, and then discard the old seal. Also remove the dipstick tube by tapping it from the oil pan deck surface out.

50 Remove Water Jacket Plugs

Now, remove the remaining core plugs from the side and front of the block using the same technique described in Step 47. Finally, remove the two water-drain plugs from each side of the block with a 9/16-inch 6-point socket and a 1/2-inch breaker bar. Don't use a 12-point socket on these plugs; they are usually very tight.

51 Remove Remaining Plugs

Rotate the engine right-side up. Remove the 1/8-inch pipe plug in the oil pressure access at the front of the block. Next, remove the two 1/4-inch oil gallery plugs at the back of the block using the techniques described in Step 47. A final cup-type plug is located in the oil passage just under the rear main cap. Although most engines are rebuilt without removing this plug, you cannot thoroughly clean the passage with it in place. To remove the plug, insert a 1/4-inch-diameter, 24-inch-long steel rod (found at most hardware stores) into the oil-pressure access at the rear of the block. A few taps with the hammer will drive the plug out. Also, if you have any stuck lifters, that you could not remove earlier, now is the time to drive them down and into the block.

REBUILDING THE SMALL-BLOCK CHEVROLET

52 Cylinder Head Disassembly

Many of the steps involved in rebuilding cylinder heads are well outside the capabilities of most home shops. For an overview of these procedures, refer to Chapter 5, "At the Machine Shop." Because of these technical requirements, you may choose to take your cylinder heads to a qualified shop and leave the disassembly and reconditioning to them. On the other hand, if you have a valvespring compressor and you'd like to disassemble the heads yourself, proceed with Step 53.

53 Compressing the Valvespring

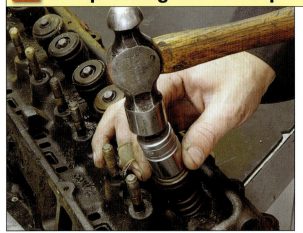 

The valve locks often become firmly stuck in the spring retainers. To free them, position the head with the chambers facing down on a soft wooden surface. Use a hammer and socket to strike each retainer several times (with moderate force) until you "feel" it break loose. Reposition the head with the intake ports facing down and try your valvespring compressor. If the retainer won't budge, give it a few more hammer raps.

54 Remove Locks and Springs

When the spring is compressed and the valve-locks are exposed (adjust your spring compressor to almost fully compress the valvespring), remove the locks with a probe or magnetic tool (this one is from Goodson). Now release the spring compressor. Sometimes the rubber O-ring on the valvestem becomes so hard that it will not let the retainer slide off. You may have to pry the retainer loose with a screwdriver.

ENGINE DISASSEMBLY

Crank Performance Tips

All factory small-block Chevy cranks are sturdy and durable. Cranks with either 3.000-, 3.250-, 3.500-, or 3.750-inch stroke have been offered by GMPP in either cast or forged versions (the GM 3.750-inch crank is cast only). Cast cranks are suitable for power levels to about 375 hp. Forged cranks are stronger and the common choice for high-performance and racing engines. Stock and racing crankshafts are available from GMPP (see page 60) and many aftermarket sources.

Details of crank preparation and modification should be discussed with your crank-prep shop. Basic crank preparations and modifications include crack inspection (Magnaflux). The oil passage openings are often lightly chamfered to remove burrs and increase oil dispersion across the journals. Small-block cranks used in racing applications are usually cross-drilled to provide 360-degree oiling to the rod journals. Every crank should be dynamic balanced, and the journals should be micro-polished. (Balancing non-stock rod/piston combinations may require adding heavy metal to the counterweights. This process is quite expensive—discuss the options with your machine shop.)

Special performance preparation may also include Tuftride heat-treating, hard-chrome plating, or other special coatings to increase surface hardness and wear resistance of the bearing journals. Increasing the fillet radius between the journals and the throw arms increases strength but can require special modifications to the bearings. The leading edges of the counterweights may also be hand-shaped—sometimes called "knife-edging"—to reduce oil windage losses. In short, a lot of time and work will go into a performance and racing crankshaft.

Cast cranks are suitable for power levels to about 375 hp. Forged cranks (right) are stronger and the common choice for high-performance and racing engines. Telling them apart is not difficult. A cast crank will have a thin parting line while a forged crank usually will have a wide mark on the first throw.

For applications where engine speed will regularly exceed 6,000 rpm, the crank should be cross-drilled through the main journals. This ensures the rods will receive high-pressure oiling during the full 360-degree crank rotation, keeping them thoroughly lubricated and cooled. Cross-drilling is the preferred method of providing 360-degree lubrication; grooved journals form a significant stress point from which cracks can develop, and fully grooved bearings don't offer the load carrying ability of non-grooved lower bearing shells.

55 Remove Keeper Burrs

Important!

In some cases, the valvelock grooves in the valvestem can develop a raised "burr" that will prevent the valve from sliding through the guide. Do not drive the valve out with a punch. Use a small, fine file (positioned flat against the valvestem) to remove the raised lip around the lock grooves. Rotate the valve head while you gently file the stem. When all of the raised edge is removed, the valve will easily slide out of the cylinder head.

CHAPTER 2

Oil Pumps: Blueprinting and Modifying

The internal pressurized oiling system of the small-block is considered by many engine builders to be just about bulletproof, and the oil pump is equally well designed.

The oil pump is mounted on the rear main cap and contains a pair of 1.200-inch-tall 7-tooth gears. They are driven by the connecting shaft from the bottom of the distributor, which in turn, is driven by the camshaft. The pump draws oil from the sump in the pan and directs pressurized oil to the main oil gallery by way of passages in the rear main cap and block.

Inspecting and replacing the oil pump is a wise investment in almost every engine rebuild. To determine the condition of the pump, disassemble and clean the components in solvent. When dry, visually inspect the spur gears. Look for pits or wear on the teeth. The inside of the pump housing should have virtually no detectable wear. Install the gears in the pump housing and measure the end clearance with a depth mic or feeler gauge. Normal clearance is between .002 and .006 inch. Inspect the pump cover for wear; there should be only light surface marks from gear contact. Remove the roll pin holding the pressure-relief spring in the pump cover. The relief valve should move freely.

If your oil pump passes this inspection, it is almost certainly reusable (it must have seen very limited use). Chances are that you'll replace the pump anyway, at lease just for peace of mind. If the only thing wrong is excessive (or insufficient) end clearance—and this should be checked on even brand-new oil pumps—have the housing or pump gears machined (some builders sand them on a flat surface with 400-grit wet/dry paper) until you have .003 inch, ±.0005 inch. Before you install a new oil pump, take it apart and perform the same inspections.

The pickup should be tack-brazed or welded to the pump cover to prevent it from moving during engine operation (see Step 40 on page 113 in Chapter 7, "Pre-Assembly Fitting," for instructions on positioning the pickup). However, brazing/welding should only be done when the cover is removed from the pump and the pressure-relief

56 Keep Parts Organized **Important!**

If you are planning to simply replace parts or perform other limited reconditioning work (to save money or if the heads are in very good condition), you should keep everything together. This plastic organizer from Goodson does the job in style.

57 Engine Disassembly Complete

This completes disassembly. In Chapter 3, we'll take a closer look at the piston assemblies (the rings, pistons, rods, and rod bearings), the cylinder heads, the block, crank, and other components before they are sent to the machine shop. It is in this and other upcoming chapters that you'll determine what parts can be reused and/or rebuilt. Upcoming chapters will also discuss component selection and cleaning, and will go through a pre-assembly fitting session to make sure all parts work together efficiently and reliably.

valve is removed from the cover. After welding, check the cover for flatness, clean any oxidation from the relief valve bore, and make sure the valve moves freely.

Before reassembly, deburr all edges with emery cloth. Then thoroughly wash all components with clean solvent and blow dry. Pre-lube the gears, gear shafts, and pressure-relief valve during assembly with assembly lube or engine oil. When you install the cover, apply a drop of Red Loctite to the threads of each bolt and torque to 10 ft-lbs.

Oil Pump Driveshafts

The oil pump is driven by a short shaft that connects the stubby shaft on the oil pump to the bottom of the distributor gear. A plastic sleeve keeps the driveshaft aligned with the pump, preventing it from slipping to one side, wobbling, and possibly breaking. The plastic sleeve also "locks" the driveshaft to the pump, preventing the shaft from falling out of the engine when the block is turned upside down (during assembly).

While the stock pump, driveshaft, and plastic collar are adequate, we strongly recommend replacing them with a high-performance part (available from B&B Performance and others) in all engine buildups, including street-stock engines. Replacement shafts are made of a stronger material and use a permanently attached metal sleeve instead of the plastic collar. This ensures that the shaft will stay aligned with the pump, reducing the chance of shaft failure and subsequent loss of oil pressure. Always use a high-performance driveshaft when you are using a high-volume or high-pressure pump.

If you decide to use the stock pump driveshaft, make sure to use a new plastic attaching sleeve to keep the driveshaft securely aligned and attached to the pump. This will generally be supplied in engine overhaul kits.

Oil Pump Modifications

Several modifications can be performed to the pump, pickup, and pressure-relief system for high-performance and racing applications. Some enthusiasts replace the pump with high-volume housings available from Moroso (see sidebar "Moroso" on page 138) and several other sources. Another common upgrade is the replacement of the stock pressure-relief spring with the Chevrolet "white stripe" spring for racing applications. For more information on performance applications, refer to the S-A Design books catalog.

The internal oiling system of the small-block Chevy is just about bulletproof. The pump is mounted to the rear main cap and contains a pair of 1.20-inch-tall, 7-tooth gears. They are driven by a connecting shaft, referred to as an intermediate shaft, from the bottom of the distributor.

Check the inside of the housing. It should have virtually no detectable wear. Install the gears in the pump housing and measure the end clearance. Normal clearance is between .002 and 0.006 inch, but many pros prefer no more than .0035 inch.

Oil Pumps: Blueprinting and Modifying CONTINUED

After it is adjusted to provide proper pan clearance, the pickup should be brazed or welded to prevent it from moving during engine operation. Welding should only be done when the pump is completely disassembled and by a seasoned welder (we did not put this example in our engine!).

The intermediate shaft connects to the oil pump shaft through a tongue-and-groove connection that is locked together by a plastic retainer in stock applications. Performance applications use a steel connector and if you're using a high-volume oil pump, the steel locking shaft should be used.

Removing and Installing Cam Bearings

There are two things every engine builder needs to know about cam bearings: 1) they should be replaced in virtually every rebuild, and 2) this operation should be performed by a professional engine builder or machine shop. This may sound a bit inflexible, but here's why it makes sense.

Cleaning and Cam Bearings Don't Mix

Any engine that needs rebuilding almost always needs chemical cleaning (hot tanking, spray cleaning, etc.). Unfortunately, cam bearings have a soft surface material that is easily damaged by strong chemicals or high-pressure sprays. If the cam bearings are in good shape before the block is cleaned, they will almost certainly have a badly oxidized and/or pitted surface afterward.

If you are working on a very clean engine block that does not require steam or chemical cleaning, you may not need to replace the cam bearings. Nevertheless, even in this case there is another important factor you should consider. In all but the earliest small-blocks, the cylinder block has grooves machined in the cam bearing bores that feed oil to the main bearings. These annular grooves (hidden behind the cam bearings) can trap dirt or metal particles, especially if the engine has suffered from a component failure, such as a flat cam lobe or spun rod bearing. In other words, considering the oiling system design of the small-block Chevy and the relatively small cost of chemical cleaning, replacing cam bearings makes good sense.

Unfortunately, replacing cam bearings is not an elementary procedure. However, if you're determined to attempt it yourself, or would like to learn more about cam bearing installation, here's a quick look at the process and a few tips that may save you some time and frustration.

Cam Bearing Removal/Installation

The key to removing and installing cam bearings is using a properly designed tool, such as one offered by Goodson. The tool adjusts for any size bearing. Rubber sleeves protect the bearing surfaces, while a tapered cone keeps the tool—and the cam bearings—in line during installation.

Installing new bearings requires a good deal more care than removal. Here are some important tips:

- Locating the proper fore-aft position for the new bearings (especially the inner ones) is a bit easier if

ENGINE DISASSEMBLY

Removing and Installing Cam Bearings CONTINUED

you scribe alignment lines in the block bore sizes before you remove the old bearings.
- Before installing new bearings, chamfer both edges with a scraper. This will prevent the force of the arbor from deforming the bearing surface, the most common cause of tight spots in cam rotation.
- The diameter of all small-block camshaft journals is the same, but the bearing bores in the block are three different diameters: bore number-1 (front) is 2.020 inches; bore number-2 and bore number-5 are 2.010 inches; bore number-3 and bore number-4 are 2.000 inches. Check all bearing bores with a dial-bore gauge. Some blocks have undersize bores that should be honed to size before the bearings are installed (small bores can result in insufficient cam bearing clearance). Occasionally, a block may have an oversize bore or bores. In this case, you may need to obtain a bearing from another cam bearing set, or even special oversize bearings.
- 1955 and 1956 265-ci engines used a special, wide rear bearing (number-5) with two oil holes. The oil holes on these early engines must line up with the feed passages in the block, and the rear journal on the camshaft must have a "flat" machined in it.
- All cam bearing oil holes in 1957-and-later engines can be installed in any radial position; however, many installers line up the oil holes with the feed passages to the main bearing bores.
- After you've installed a couple of bearings, wipe them clean, apply a little lubricant, then install and rotate the cam to ensure that it does not bind. If the cam gets progressively tighter as each bearing is installed, make sure the cam is not bent (if you don't have a dial indicator and V-blocks, take it to a machine shop and have it checked).
- The front edge of the front cam bearing should line up with the inner edge of the chamfer in the front of the block.
- The rear edge of the rear cam bearing (number-5) should not protrude into the core-plug counterbore at the rear of the block.

The diameter of all small-block camshaft journals is the same, but the bearing bores in the block are three different diameters: bore number-1 (front) is 2.020 inches; bore number-2 and bore number-5 are 2.010 inches; bore number-3 and bore number-4 are 2.000 inches.

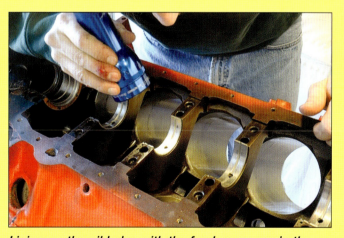

A properly designed arbor tool is essential for working with cam bearings. This tool, available from Goodson, adjusts to a wide variety of bearing sizes and works equally well for removal and installation. Don't forget to wear eye protection when using a hammer.

Lining up the oil holes with the feed passages in the front four main bearing bores is not required. However, some installers believe that this practice offers advantages. Here a high-intensity light is being used to check hole alignment.

CHAPTER 3

INITIAL PARTS INSPECTION

You may think that taking time to inspect engine components right after disassembly isn't necessary. After all, you pay your machine shop to inspect and recondition your engine with the latest, high-tech equipment. They'll find anything wrong before money is spent on machine work, won't they?

Before the Machine Shop

In the best of all possible worlds, machine shops never make mistakes. However, in this world, machine shops do, and there can be some question about who is ultimately responsible. If you don't know that it's right, presume that it isn't. When you're knowledgeable about all aspects of your rebuilding project, it will likely succeed with flying colors.

This chapter will help you inspect the main components of your engine before you take them to the machine shop and before any money is spent on reconditioning. The following inspection steps are not meant as a substitute for comprehensive testing with precision equipment. Rather, this summary inspection (requiring some precision tools) will give you sufficient familiarity with your components to speak knowledgeably with your machinist. At best, you'll find nothing outside of the ordinary; at worst, you'll come across one or more pieces that are damaged beyond repair. A real advantage of the small-block Chevy is that you can easily obtain replacement parts, and most are reasonably priced. Even major components such as engine blocks and crankshafts probably won't break your budget. Information about replacement "cores" and their approximate costs follow at the end of this chapter.

This chapter will help you inspect the main components of your engine before you take them to the machine shop. You may discover nothing wrong, or you may find some components damaged beyond repair. The worn thrust surface on this crankshaft is more costly to repair than buying a replacement core.

A very in-depth component inspection will be done in Chapter 7, "Pre-Assembly Fitting," after all the parts have been reconditioned by your machine shop. Remember, the more critical your eye, the less money you'll spend on your engine building project.

What To Do When Your Parts Don't Pass Inspection

The old saying "anything can be fixed" is nearly true. However, it should read, "anything can be fixed for a price." Unless you have a defective part that is very rare and cannot be replaced, it's much cheaper to have your machine shop obtain a replacement core or a new part from the aftermarket and continue with the work.

If you purchase a core from your machine shop, you'll pay slightly more than from a typical wrecking yard. Despite this, it's generally preferable to purchase cores from the shop doing most of your machine work. Why? When you take into consideration that a machine shop may buy a large number of used blocks, heads, or cranks, clean them, inspect them, test them, and then find out a certain number are

48   REBUILDING THE SMALL-BLOCK CHEVROLET

INITIAL PARTS INSPECTION

Using Precision Tools

Part of the enjoyment of engine building is working with a variety of basic and specialized tools. Perhaps the most interesting tools are precision measuring instruments. While basic engine building requires only a few micrometers, a dial indicator, and a dial caliper, it is easy to get the "bug" for precision tools and continue adding to your collection. And that's great! Because the more measuring capability you have at your fingertips, the more capable and confident you will become.

There is, however, a difference between owning a drawer full of micrometers and being able to perform reliably precise measurements. As with most skills, using precision tools is only learned by applying patience, practice, and the desire to do it right. When you use a micrometer, the tool alone does not measure the thickness of a spring shim or the diameter of a main bearing journal. You, literally, perform the measurement with the tool. The firmness of your grip, the keenness of your eye, and the precise feel in your fingertips are just as important as the precision calibration of the tool.

The best, and perhaps the only, way to develop a "feel" for precision tools is to practice using them. The best things to practice with are the calibration standards supplied with every micrometer. At room temperature, these "gauges" are accurate to within a .0001 inch. When you become comfortable holding and operating micrometers, you should be able to get reliable "zero" readings using the standards with your eyes closed (some micrometers must be adjusted to obtain precise zero readings with their standards. Refer to the instructions that came with your micrometer for details).

After you pick up your mic and get repeatable results with your standards, measure a component (a lifter, for example) then attempt to get the same reading with your dial calipers. Next, measure a rod pin bore with your calipers. Measure the same rod with a snap gauge, then mic the snap gauge with your outside micrometer. Compare the readings from each method of measurement. When your precision tools regularly produce readings within ±.0005 inch of one another (it won't happen overnight), you have developed the skill to begin depending on your precision tools. (For additional info on selecting and using precision tools, refer to the S-A Design book *Engine Blueprinting*, by Rick Voegelin.)

We use many precision tools, but there are a few that stand out as our favorites. The 0-to-6-inch micrometer set from Snap-on (part PMF115) is an important part of our measurement center and would be the "prized possession" of any engine builder. You can also find a micrometer that is supplied with spacers so one mic can be used in a variety of applications. A dial-bore gauge (part MMCB-06 from Goodson) is graduated in .0001-inch increments and measures from 2.0000 to 6.0000 inches. It is very precise, and a joy to use. Other very helpful Goodson tools include their valve- and spring-height gauges (parts SWIFTY and MVS-130). The universal deck-clearance gauge from B&B Performance (part 4010) is inexpensive and easy to use. Finally, the cam-timing fixture for the small-block Chevy from Iskenderian Cams (parts 200-PCK and 200-DI) works so well that we fight over who can use it next!

A dial indicator, along with a deck-height stand and a magnetic stand, will make your life much easier and your measuring more precise. The magnetic base and adjustability of the arm will help in hundreds of measurements.

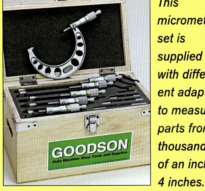

This micrometer set is supplied with different adapters to measure parts from thousandths of an inch to 4 inches.

Another of our favorite tools is a dial-bore gauge.

REBUILDING THE SMALL-BLOCK CHEVROLET

junk, you soon realize that there's more to buying used parts than meets the eye. On the other hand, if you purchase a core from a wrecking yard, there's usually some question whether it's even returnable, and even if you can return it (haggling at the front counter not withstanding), you'll have spent a considerable sum of (nonrefundable) money on cleaning, inspection, and testing. So spending a bit more for a "guaranteed core" from your machine shop makes a lot of sense. However, if you decide to buy parts from a wrecking yard, make sure you establish that defective merchandise can be returned before you write the check.

Unless you're knowledgeable about component interchangeability, discuss cores and replacement parts with your machine shop before you buy. Remember, the quality of your engine is truly the sum of its parts!

A typical engine overhaul may require one or more of the following replacement cores.

Blocks

Cores will run anywhere from $100 to $250. If you're looking for a special, hard-to-find casting, expect to pay much more for a dirty, unmachined piece.

Heads

Cores run about $50 to $100 per head. Remember, it's almost always cheaper to replace a cracked head than attempting a repair, especially with today's aftermarket. Common "882" castings are not the best head but are acceptable. "624s" are a very thin-wall design and should always be avoided, even for street-stock applications. "186" or "041" castings, at about $100 to $200 per pair, are probably the best replacement castings per dollar spent. These heads were made in late 1969 and 1970, came on 300-hp 350s, used 1.94/1.50 valves, have small chambers, straight plugs, and good flowing ports. Despite the fact that they were made for only two years, we have it on reputable word that there are "a million of 'em" still around.

Also consider the late-model, four-bolt (valve cover) heads. They're about 3 pounds heavier than earlier factory designs, making them less prone to cracking, plus they're plentiful and cheap.

There are now a variety of bare and complete heads available from the aftermarket that may offer increased metal in vital areas, and often have better flowing ports. In some cases, these may cost a little more, but in the long run, after machining costs, and new components, you may end up with a better head at the same cost. In all cases, make sure the chamber volume is compatible with your pistons; some 305, small-chamber heads (available everywhere) have under 60 cc and can easily develop 11:1 with flat-top pistons.

Cranks

When choosing a cast-iron replacement crank make sure it has the correct counterweight pattern (305 and 350 have the same stroke and journal size, but the factory balance is greatly different). Steel cranks are just about impossible to find at wrecking yards and machine shops. You might as well buy a new steel crank from GMPP or other aftermarket company for about $200 to $700.

Rods

Rods are a few bucks each. Many machine shops supply cores at no charge to their good customers.

Valves

Used valves are also inexpensive, but don't even consider them. Clearances (angles and tight tolerances) and different applications produce too many variables. Go with a new set.

Vibration Damper

Replacement cores run about $35. New ones can range from $100 and

Inspecting components can "tell a story" about what is right and what is wrong with the engine. When you inspect the piston/rod assemblies look for a skewed wear pattern on the sides of each piston. This would indicate that a rod is slightly bent. While not too serious of a problem, it is certainly something that should be corrected before reassembly.

Small-block Chevy heads are notorious for cracking, especially late-model castings. Make sure you have your heads crack-checked, and if you purchased them used, also have them pressure-tested. Fortunately, there is no shortage of replacement cores, and several aftermarket sources produce excellent performance castings in aluminum or iron.

INITIAL PARTS INSPECTION

higher. If you need a damper for performance or racing, consider a Fluidampr a high-performance unit from B&B Performance.

Flywheel and Flexplates

Flywheel cores run about $50 and will need to be resurfaced. Depending on the condition, a new one may be worth the cost, especially if you're planning on a performance engine. If you're replacing the flexplate, make sure to get one with the correct number of gear teeth! Same goes for the flywheel.

Other Cores

EGR (exhaust gas recirculation) intake manifolds are very hard to find (just about all factory manifolds are cracked). Legal replacement manifolds are available from many aftermarket companies, including Edelbrock, Holley, Weiand, etc. These intakes are considerably lighter than the stock cast iron ones and often will flow better for improved performance. Prices generally start just over $140 for new ones, or hit a swap meet to find a used one.

Initial Parts Inspection

1 Inspect Cylinder Block

Every engine has its own "personality." Here are a few common problem areas on the small-block (a high-intensity light, such as the one used here from Remington, is very helpful). First, inspect the valley area for water jacket cracks. They sometimes run horizontally, just above the lifter bores. Cracks also occur on the outside of the block, just below the deck surfaces. Check the decks for cracks or combustion-gas gouges from blown head gaskets. Check all threaded holes for stripped threads or cracking, including the oil-pump mounting hole on the rear-main cap. If the engine was purchased from a junkyard, look over the exterior of the block for damage, like broken off chunks (especially around starter mount), etc., and have the block Magnafluxed and pressure-tested.

2 Inspect Cylinder Block CONTINUED

Check that the main caps fit snugly in their recesses on the block. The parting edges between the cap and the block bores should line up and be smooth to the touch (if they aren't, the caps may have been switched). Inspect the camshaft upper-sprocket thrust face for gouges. If you have access to precision measuring tools, mic the cylinder bores, check the main bores for proper size and out-of-roundness (many blocks may need align boring), and mic the lifter bores to make sure none are worn or oversize. Finally, look for any cracks in the bottom end, particularly at the bottom of the cylinder bores (from previous improper disassembly techniques), around the main bolt-holes (from excessive over tightening of the bolts), and in the main webs (often due to excess stress from detonation).

3 Inspect Cylinder Head

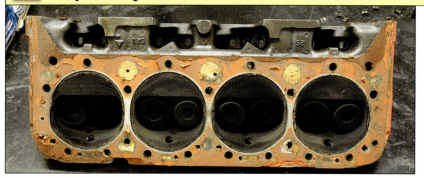

Cylinder heads, particularly late-model castings, are weak points. It is not uncommon to find cracks in the valveseats, bolt holes, exterior surfaces, and elsewhere. Some factory castings are so prone to cracking they should be avoided. Probably the worst of all is the 624 head ("624" refers to the last three casting numbers—462624—located over or under two of the intake ports). If your engine has these heads, consider scrapping them and finding replacements. Possible replacements are the 882, 487, 493, 993, 545, and others. Ask your machine shop for help in selecting replacements (make sure they have the accessory mounting holes needed for your application).

Continue looking for cracks in the valve seats, across the lower row of bolt holes, and in the exterior parting line across the centerline of the exhaust ports. You may find evidence of previous weld repair work, since about 25 percent of all small-block heads have small repair spots from the factory. GM does a nice job on these "touch ups," and repaired heads should not necessarily be tossed aside. Look for eroded valveseats and head surfaces between chambers. Inspect the valves for stem, lock groove, tip, and face wear. Also, look for hairline cracks across the face and head. Check for excessive guide wear by wiggling the valves in the guides. Examine the rocker studs for looseness, damaged threads, or side wear from rocker arm contact. Look over the spring splash shields for wear.

4 Inspect Crankshaft

Remarkably, about 50 percent of all small-block cranks are reusable directly after cleaning and polishing. Unfortunately, some cranks may look fine at first glance but turn out to be unusable. Here are the common things that can turn your crank into scrap metal. Check the crank thrust surface by running your finger over the thrust flange. It should be smooth and perfectly flat. Check the keyways on the nose; they should not be enlarged and the keys should fit snugly. Mic the journal diameters; they should not be more than .030 inch undersize or look badly discolored. Inspect the rear seal surface; it should be smooth and have no annular grooves. If your crank doesn't pass these initial tests, consider obtaining a replacement from your machine shop.

INITIAL PARTS INSPECTION

Thread Repair

Threaded holes in engine components must be in top shape to allow bolts to be tightened to full torque. Damaged threads can lead to gasket failure and oil, water, or fuel leaks. Fortunately, many threads can be easily restored.

If the threads are merely corroded or slightly damaged, repair can often be accomplished by carefully retapping the threaded hole with a cutting and/or bottoming tap of the proper size and thread pitch.

For threads that are stripped or require more than minor repair, there are two repair methods commonly available to the do-it-yourselfer. The first technique involves drilling out the remaining threads, retapping with a special tap, and installing a stainless-steel threaded insert that returns the hole to its original thread size. Helicoil manufactures a well-known brand of threaded inserts. This repair method is suitable for nearly every threaded hole in the engine and many external accessories. Helicoil inserts are extremely strong. In fact, when carefully installed, they are often stronger than the original threads.

A second method of repair uses a very strong epoxy to replace the stripped threads. This "chemical" repair is suitable for small fasteners used in non-critical applications, such as an accessory mounting hole on the intake manifold, some small carburetor screws, etc. Loctite Corporation produces a two-part chemical epoxy mix that is first inserted in the damaged bolt hole. While the epoxy is still a liquid, the fastener is coated with a "releasing" compound and screwed into the damaged hole. Extra epoxy is forced out between the thread, and once it hardens and the bolt is unscrewed, the hardened epoxy becomes a rock-hard substitute for the missing threads.

Each of these repair methods has advantages and disadvantages. Both allow fasteners to be tightened to their full recommended torque, but for pure thread strength, Helicoil inserts are superior. Moreover, Helicoil repairs are ready to use immediately while epoxy requires a minimum of 30 minutes to harden. However, the epoxy method is less expensive since a special tap, installation tool, and stainless-steel thread inserts are not required. Furthermore, a drill motor, the correct bit, and some degree of skill is required for successful Helicoil repairs, while the Loctite epoxy technique requires no special tools and can be performed almost anywhere.

Whichever technique you choose, if the repaired threads will not allow the fastener to reach the full recommended torque, the damaged component will require replacement.

Helicoil manufactures the most popular brand of threaded inserts. Their kit includes a special tap, inserting tool, and several Helicoil inserts to repair a number of threads.

5 Inspect Crankshaft
CONTINUED

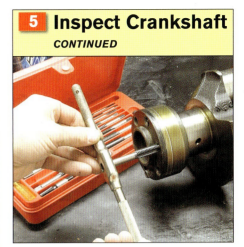

Continue inspecting the crank by looking for less serious problems. Inspect the flywheel flange and crank nose for damaged threads (this thread-chasing tool set from Snap-on, part RTD42, cleans threads without reducing thread strength). Look at the rod side-thrust faces on each rod journal; they should be smooth and have no discoloration. If you're going to be using a manual transmission, make sure the crank has a pilot bushing installed (or that it's machined to accept one). This Snap-on puller kit (part YA6100) removes old pilot bushings from just about any crankshaft. Finally, the crank should be Magnaflux-inspected by your machine shop. If your engine is out of a car with a manual transmission, make sure to remove the pilot bearing from the crankshaft (and be sure to install a new one). Snap-on and other companies offer a puller tool, or you may be able to remove them yourself with a screwdriver or grease gun.

CHAPTER 3

6 Inspect Main and Rod Bearings

Inspect the main and rod bearings for excessive wear. Signs of poor lubrication or dirty oil will show scores or light scratches. If there is other engine damage you may see metal particles embedded into the bearing material. Discoloration indicates inadequate oiling or excessive heat. These two rod bearings show signs of detonation. Also, look on the back of the bearing for signs of excessive loads or detonation. While you're looking, there may be numbers such as ".020" that indicates the bearing is .020 inch oversized meaning that the crank has been turned prior.

7 Inspect Rods and Pistons

Make sure the rods and pistons are all the same type. If the engine has been previously rebuilt, it's possible you may find an oddball rod/piston or two, and if the weight is different, the engine may have had an out-of-balance vibration. Inspect the piston skirts for uniform wear patterns; canted or twisted patterns indicate a bent rod. Check the big-end inside diameter for roughness or discoloration (probably due to a spun bearing; rod may not be rebuildable). If you have the necessary precision tools, check the big-end bore for correct size and out-of-roundness. Mic the width of the rods and compare them to the width of the crank throw; clearances should be between .005 and .012 inch for most applications.

If your cylinder bores have almost no detectable wear and you're planning on reusing the pistons, mic the outside diameter (usually at the bottom of the skirt) to verify that none of the pistons have "collapsed." Check the width of the ring lands (they should have no more than .003 inch clearance with a new ring; measure using a feeler gauge), and give the pistons a careful visual inspection. Have your machine shop clean and test them for proper pin fit, piston-to-cylinder wall clearance after honing, and piston/rod alignment. As with the crankshaft, cracks in the rods and pistons are almost impossible to find with the naked eye. You may want to ask your machine shop if it would be more expensive to have all the rods Magnafluxed compared to buying a new set. Your choice.

8 Inspect Camshaft and Lifters

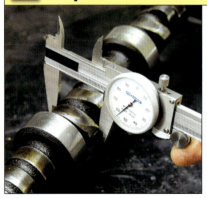 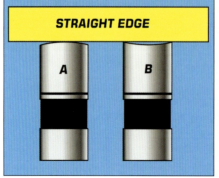

Chances are that you are going to replace the cam and lifters for an improved set. The only time the cam and lifters are reusable is: 1) when all the lifters have contact surfaces that are smooth and uniform in appearance, with a slight crown [A], not a concave shape [B], 2) the lifters have no detectable outside diameter wear, 3) all the cam lobes show no signs of galling or excessive wear (mic the lobe heights to verify lack of wear), 4) the distributor-drive gear teeth on the cam show no significant wear, 5) the lifters have been organized so that they will be reassembled in exactly their original position, and 6) the cam and lifters will be reassembled into the same engine block. If you have one of these rare small-block cam and lifter sets that pass all these tests, you can reuse the camshaft. Oil the cam and lifters and wrap them in wax paper to prevent rust during storage.

54   REBUILDING THE SMALL-BLOCK CHEVROLET

INITIAL PARTS INSPECTION

9 Inspect Oil Pump and Pickup

Most engine builders reuse the oil pickup but replace the pump. Refer to sidebar "Oil Pumps: Blueprinting and Modifying" on page 44, for inspection, rebuilding, and performance modifications. Check the pickup/screen carefully for damage. Look for cracks in the tubing seam, especially where it enters the pump cover. Make sure the wire screen is not loose or plugged with debris; the pickup should get a thorough soaking in carburetor cleaner before reuse. Finally, inspect the oil pump and rear main cap mating surfaces; no gasket is used between the oil pump and the main cap, any damage to these surfaces will result in high-pressure oil leaks.

10 Inspect Vibration Damper

The vibration damper can become worn or damaged in several areas. First, make sure that the keyway in the hub is not enlarged. Check the pulley-attaching threads (if damaged, they can be Helicoil repaired), and make sure the rubber is not working out from between the inner hub and the outer damper ring (if it's oozed out even slightly, consider replacing the damper). If possible, put the damper in a lathe and measure how much it wobbles; the maximum is about .020 inch. Finally, check the hub oil seal surface for a grooving that can lead to an oil leak. The contact lip on all replacement seals is moved inward, so if the hub groove is shallow, the new seal will ride on an undamaged surface. If the groove is deep, a slide-on metal sleeve is available; it can be used with factory or replacement front seals.

11 Inspect Intake Manifold

Many factory small-block manifolds have a heat shield riveted under the riser passage. Hard carbon deposits build up under this shield; it must be removed before the manifold is hot tanked or jet washed. A small chisel and light hammer taps will usually work the rivets out. Inspect the riser passage for heat cracks. If the manifold is equipped with EGR (exhaust gas recirculation), carefully inspect the plenum for cracks running down between the large throttle bore. EGR manifolds get very hot, and cracks in this area are quite common. Finally, inspect the manifold-to-cylinder head surfaces for cracks, erosion from rust, or other damage.

12 Mark Your Parts

This completes the initial inspection of major engine components. If any of your parts did not pass inspection, refer to page 48. Regardless of the outcome of your inspection, put your own individual mark or stamp on every part before you take it to the machine shop. Use a number stamp, center punch, or an engraving tool, and mark only on non-machined surfaces. Identifying your parts will prevent possible mix-ups and disagreements in the future.

REBUILDING THE SMALL-BLOCK CHEVROLET

CHAPTER 4

SELECTING PARTS

An important step performed in every engine rebuild is selecting replacements for worn or defective parts. Trying to pick the best parts is an awesome task, considering the seemingly endless variety of substitutes available for virtually every piece in a typical engine. Some of these replacements are claimed to be "identical" to the stock parts; others are advertised as more durable, or more efficient, or less expensive, and so on. Ultimately, selecting "the right pieces" requires a good deal of research and careful decision-making.

The task is even more crucial if your goal is to increase engine performance. The range of performance components is truly staggering. A simple decision to modify one component may require other alteration(s) to other components or systems.

No matter what your goal—durability, fuel efficiency, high performance, or simply low cost—it's important to consider the selection of each component using the best advice (often obtained from your machine shop), common sense, and a good dose of cold logic. For instance, it would be fruitless to put a mechanical-secondary performance carburetor on an engine that will be driven on the street, or to put a racing intake manifold with large runners on cylinder heads with small intake ports, etc. In each of these examples, improving one specific area (in this case a portion of the induction system) would be a waste of money and effort. If you want to gain more performance by improving induction efficiency, you must be prepared to improve complementary aspects of the engine, or the result may produce less power and use more fuel than if you used stock components.

This isn't to say that single modifications can't produce modest performance improvements—in fact, such mods are relatively common. For instance, adding a better ignition system, or a less-restrictive air cleaner, or a better-flowing exhaust manifolds/headers can realize gains. However, in these instances the modifications corrected a specific limitation in the engine. What is very difficult (virtually impossible) is for an amateur engine builder to select a group of components and predict that the final result will be an improvement in engine function. There are now companies such as Edelbrock and Holley that put together complete performance packages with a specific carburetor and intake matched to a camshaft and even cylinder heads. That's a good way to go, but there will always be other decisions you need to make when it comes to component selection.

When selecting parts for your engine build, it helps to have clearly defined goals. Although many choose quality stock components for their rebuild, this stage is the perfect opportunity to upgrade your components to extract more power and efficiency from your engine. Aftermarket performance companies, such as Comp Cams and Edelbrock, offer excellent, complete packages to help simplify parts selection.

The bottom line to selecting parts is to clearly identify your goals in advance and discuss these goals with knowledgeable engine builders who have firsthand experience with the equipment you're considering. Then make well-thought-out decisions to achieve the desired results. If you have a limited budget or limited time (who doesn't?), the success of your project depends heavily on using your resources as wisely as possible. Selecting the components that give you the most for your money is a major part of this plan. These decisions must be made well in advance so that all machine work and component preparation is performed after the component selection variables have been nailed down. Finally, all parts must be on hand well before final assembly, so that pre-assembly fitting and clearance checks can be performed to verify the compatibility of every component in the engine.

Bearings

Many engine components have improved dramatically over the past several years. Today, it isn't unusual for a rebuilt street engine, even a high-performance engine, to last well over 100,000 miles. In fact, many engines that are built "right" last 200,000 miles or more! This kind of extended engine life wasn't possible with the Babbitt bearings of just a few years ago. The rod and main bearings that sit on the shelves of parts stores today are the result of nearly 100 years of development.

Because most engine bearings are so well designed, selecting the "best" bearing is an easy task. When your crank returns from the grinder and the size of the journals is known (usually .010-inch undersize), a matching bearing set can be selected. While every engine builder has his own preferences, most major brand-name bearings provide excellent service.

Many professionals feel there is probably an "edge" to using a bearing with tri-metal construction, versus a bi-metal bearing. This refers to the number of underlayers of metal that are used to manufacture the bearing. Most believe that tri-metal bearings can withstand greater loads and are less likely to suffer from Babbitt separation. Tri-metal rod and main bearing sets are available from Speed Pro, TRW, Clevite, and others.

Cam bearings are usually a simple, soft Babbitt bearing. Because the cam

Modern rod and main bearings incorporate the knowledge of billions of miles of "experience." As amazing as it sounds, combined with modern lubricants, engine bearings will experience virtually no wear in more than 100,000 miles of driving.

Because the cam turns at one-half engine speed and is subjected to only a fraction of the loads of rod or main bearings, "standard" soft Babbitt cam bearings work well in all applications. As long as the bearings are properly installed in the block and the cam is not bent, cam bearings will last just about forever.

turns at one-half engine speed and is subjected to only a fraction of the load of rod or main bearings, virtually any cam bearing will work fine. As long as the bearings are properly installed in the block and the cam isn't bent, cam bearings should last just about forever.

Camshaft Drives

The stock "silent chain" used to drive the camshaft in production engines is adequate for low-demand applications. However, over the normal life span of an engine, the chain stretches enough to affect the cam timing. And in very "tired" engines, the chain may become so loose that it jumps a tooth, throwing cam timing and engine performance way off. During every rebuild, the stock chain should be replaced or upgraded. Never use upper sprockets with nylon-coated teeth. They're notorious for chipping and failing. If the stock upper and lower gears are in good shape (a rarity), they can be reused, but always replace the chain.

If you elect to upgrade the cam drive, the most common choice is a double-row chain, often called a double-roller chain. Specialty chain drives are available from several aftermarket sources, including Cloyes, Milodon, Iskenderian Cams, Comp Cams, Crower, and others. Most of these specialty drives come as a matched set and include one-piece steel upper and lower sprockets and a high-strength chain. The lower sprockets are often broached with multiple keyways, allowing the cam timing to be easily advanced or retarded (typically 4 degrees). The few extra dollars spent for one of these rugged drives can add significant reliability.

Many racing engines are fitted with gear drives. There are several unique designs available, and most of them provide extremely high engine speeds, where a chain drive tends to stretch and

CHAPTER 4

The single-row cam-drive chain used in production engines is adequate for many applications (but never use upper sprockets with nylon-coated teeth). Many performance versions use lower sprockets broached with multiple keyways (left), allowing easy timing changes (typically ±4 degrees). Offset bushings can also be used to vary cam timing. The most durable chain drive is the double-row set, often called a double-roller chain. These are available from several manufacturers. The Milodon chain drive (right) also has an upper sprocket machined for a Torrington thrust bearing. The block requires no additional machine work to accept the Milodon drive.

retard cam timing. The downside is their high cost and audible gear noise, although some gear drives are designed for non-racing applications and are nearly silent.

Cam Bumpers and Drive Covers

The stock stamped-steel chain cover does an adequate job in most stock or performance applications. Racing or custom engines are often fitted with specialty cast-aluminum chain covers. These super-sturdy covers do not distort as easily as production covers, providing a positive oil seal. Cast covers also work well with cam bumpers (sometimes called "anti-walk" devices) that counter forward camshaft movement and the associated ignition timing variations.

In stock engines, camshaft movement is controlled only by the timing chain, but when the valvetrain has been modified, excessive camshaft "walk" can occur. A cam bumper is simply a needle-roller assembly attached to the front of the upper cam sprocket. The bumper contacts the inside surface of the chain cover and prevents the cam from walking forward during high-speed operation. However, the thrust action may push the bumper forward with sufficient force to bend a stamped cover or, especially in an endurance engine, the thrust bumper may actually wear through or crack the cover. A stock cover can be reinforced to resist cam thrust, but a stout cast-aluminum cover (used with a cam bumper) eliminates the problem entirely.

Camshaft Kits

Selecting camshaft and valvetrain components is one of the most important decisions affecting overall engine performance and durability. Stock-profile cams are readily available from GMPP and replacement-part sources such as Speed Pro. High-performance street cams and racing profiles are as common as dust. Iskenderian, Comp, Crower, Crane, Speed Pro, GMPP, and similar suppliers offer virtually an unlimited selection.

Cam selection is one area where the builder can, in a sense, put his personal signature on the engine. Unfortunately, one of the most common mistakes is to put in "too much cam." The temptation to seek more power is a strong one, but if the airflow path through the engine isn't suited to higher capacities, increasing the valve lift and duration won't produce more torque or power. In fact, it's likely to reduce combustion efficiency, power output, and economy. Consequently, if there is one nearly universal truism in cam selection, it's to be conservative!

If you want to build a high-performance street engine, limit maximum valve lift to .500 inch and valve-open duration to around 290 degrees. Most of the major cam companies have excellent catalogs that contain helpful selection guides, or you can telephone the cam maker of your choice and discuss the selection with one of their experts. Don't forget to ask the experts at your machine shop for advice as well.

After you select a suitable profile, consider purchasing a complete cam kit, which usually includes lifters, valvesprings, retainers, and accessories. Unless you're an experienced engine builder, it's not a good idea to cross select these critical components. When you buy a kit, the manufacturer (usually)

Milodon Products offers a variety of timing chain and gear sets. These small thrust bumpers attach to the cam sprocket and contact the inside of the timing chain cover to reduce forward movement of the cam, which causes inherent timing variations. A stock timing chain cover would flex and eventually fail so a stout cast cover needs to be used, such as this one offered by Milodon, as well.

SELECTING PARTS

makes certain you have compatible pieces. You'll double-check everything in Chapter 7, "Pre-Assembly Fitting," so if they screw up (and it happens) you'll catch it before it's too late.

When choosing a cam, remember these basic guidelines. It's hard to beat hydraulic lifters in an engine that is driven daily. In the not-too-distant past, solid lifters were considered more reliable in performance engines, but they require periodic adjustment of the operating clearance (also called lash adjustment). However, modern high-bleed-rate hydraulic lifters operate well at relatively high RPM, and they do not require bothersome lash adjustments.

Most cam manufacturers now offer special cams designed for hydraulic roller lifters. These lifters combine the best of both worlds. The roller-bearing foot allows the lifter to operate with aggressive lobe shapes that often produce more horsepower and torque and reduces the chance of lobe or lifter failure that isn't uncommon when high spring pressures are used. The roller also eliminates the difficulties associated with inadequate camshaft lubrication during initial engine startup.

Carburetors

Carburetor selection is a science unto itself. If you wish to study carb selection and functioning in detail S-A Design offers some excellent books. The initial decision, however, boils down to staying with the stock-type carb, substituting an aftermarket replacement, or possibly, opting for a fuel-injection system.

If smog regulations limit your selection to stock equipment, you should purchase a suitable replacement or, at the very least, carefully rebuild the old carb to make certain the new engine has the benefit of optimum fuel-air mixtures.

The selection of aftermarket performance carburetors is dominated by three highly respected brand names: Holley, Edelbrock, and Demon (by Barry Grant).

The Edelbrock Performer 4-barrel is a so-called "spread bore" style of carb (the secondary venturis are larger than the primary venturis) with vacuum-actuated secondary air valves. It's essentially a Quadrajet replacement and, as such, is a tried-and-proven design and provides a responsive and flexible induction for any performance street engine (smog regulations permitting). Technical details and selection recommendations are included in the Edelbrock catalog and on their website.

The venerable Holley 4-barrel carburetors are performance legends. Available in a wide variety of configurations, including numerous square bore (all four venturis are equal in size) and spread bore arrangements, and in a wide selection of flow capacities, the Holley modular construction is an outstanding racing design, and it can also be used in street applications (Holley produces "emissions legal" replacement carburetors). The most common street selection is a vacuum-secondary model (either square bore or spread bore) with a flow rating of about 600 to 700 cfm. There are hundreds of fine-tuning and modification accessories available for this carburetor, both from Holley and from third-party suppliers.

Lifter design and camshaft profiles are designed to work as a set; they should never be switched. The hydraulic lifter (left) is the most common design while the hydraulic roller pair (middle) is used on many late model applications. Solid roller lifters (right) are used in high performance/racing applications only, as they are noisy and require adjustment.

This kit from Comp Cams contains a cam, lifters, valvesprings, retainers, seals, and a timing chain gear set. Having all of these components in one kit can save you a lot of time and you won't need to worry about compatibility.

Edelbrock offers an extensive line of carburetors in their Performer Series. These are all-new and calibrated at Edelbrock for optimum performance. The carbs are easy to adjust and are complemented with a variety accessories such as throttle brackets, fuel lines, and more.

GMPP

General Motors Performance Parts Division (GMPP) is the corporate division that researches, creates, and markets Chevrolet replacement components—including all high-performance parts. These special components are commonly referred to as Bow Tie parts and are listed in the General Motors Performance Parts Catalog. They can only be purchased through local GM dealerships. Dealers who do not stock performance components can special order them. Check with your local dealer to get a catalog.

Blocks

GMPP offers bare four-bolt cylinder blocks in iron and even aluminum. The iron version is molded from a high-tin alloy (to increase strength) and is available with either a standard 4-inch bore or a Siamesed-bore variation that finishes to 4.125 inches. Their aluminum blocks have replaceable 4-inch bore iron sleeves. All Bow Tie blocks are set up for a 2.45-inch main journal crank.

Cranks

Ready-to-run Bow Tie cranks are available with either 3.25- or 3.48-inch strokes. The 3.25 crank is forged with 2.30-inch mains and 2.00-inch rod journals. The 3.48 crank is finished to late 2.45/2.10-inch specs. Two "raw" steel forging blanks are also available, allowing the experienced builder to obtain a premium forged crank with either small or large journals and virtually any stroke length from 2.7 to 3.75 (plus) inches.

Heads

There are a variety of heads available from GMPP these days. Ranging from Bow Tie heads with 2.02/1.60 valves, 64-cc chambers, angled spark plugs, and hardened valveseats to newer Vortech-style heads. These Vortech models flow well and can be used on earlier blocks, but will require different-style intake manifolds and valve covers. Both cast-iron and aluminum versions are available, and both are suitable for street use or mid-level racing. However, specific design details change with some frequency; check with your local GM dealer for updates.

Rods

GMPP offers special rod designs for high-speed engines (up to 7,500 rpm). Premium versions of the production rod are available.

Pistons

A variety of performance pistons are available for 4-inch bores. High-compression designs—nominal 11:1—have been available for 3-, 3.25-, or 3.48-inch strokes. However, most of the currently available designs are for 3.48-inch-stroke engines. These include pressed-pin and floating-pin versions and racing types with 12:1 compression. Some have relocated piston pin bores for 6.00-inch-long connecting rods. Overbore pistons (4.030 and 4.060) are also offered.

Accessories

The catalog also lists a wide variety of performance accessories and specialty items. There is much to choose from: intake manifolds, aluminum valve covers, high-pressure oil pumps, special ignitions, electric fans, aluminum water pumps, etc. All have been tested and approved by factory engineers.

The Phase 6 aluminum Bow Tie head (non-production is available with 2.02/1.60 hardened inserts or in a "bare" version without seats. Pushrod holes are not machined to allow intake porting. Both have 55-cc chambers.

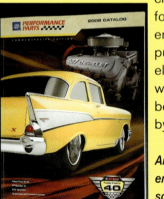

Any Chevrolet performance enthusiast is going to love scanning through the pages of the GMPP catalog.

Demon carbs are offered in a variety of styles and sizes as well. Their line of Road Demon Jr. carbs are perfect for street engines with vacuum-operated secondaries and even have electric chokes on them. Demon models are available in street and strip models and have unique features like billet fuel blocks and clear float windows that aid in setting float levels.

It's been quite a few years since a carburetor fueled a new car so it's only fitting that Holley, Edelbrock, ACCEL, and others now offer electronic fuel-injection systems for street engines that can be installed on original carbureted engines. These systems require additional modifications to the fuel delivery system and are more costly than a standard carburetor, but they deliver performance, economy, and emissions advantages that even a precisely tuned carburetor can't equal. In the not-too-distant past, traditionalists scorned electronics and microprocessors, but now only the most diehard relic can ignore the advantages of these ultra-precise fuel systems. Aftermarket EFI systems are becoming more and more popular. For more information, check out *Engine Management: Advanced Tuning* by Greg Banish.

Crankshaft and Connecting Rods

Crankshaft selection for the small-block Chevy is usually straightforward. Production cranks are divided into two broad categories: cast and forged. Factory cast cranks are very stout. Forged cranks are preferred for racing or extreme street performance. Cast cranks are inexpensive and forged cranks are expensive. Simply, you pay your money and take your choice. Add to that list that there are now complete CNC machined cranks, but get your checkbook out! These precise cranks are used for high-end racing. We'll stick with the basics in this book.

Small-block crank cores in most standard stroke lengths are plentiful. The most notable exceptions are 3.00-inch forged and 3.750-inch cast production cranks, both of which are somewhat rare. The 3.48-inch hi-po crank is the most commonly available production forging. As a result, combining the 3.48 stroke crank with the 4.00-inch-bore four-bolt block (producing 350 ci) is generally the most practical and economical forged-crank setup.

However, with enough money you can build virtually anything you desire. In addition to the cast and forged production cranks, GMPP offers "raw" (unmachined) premium steel forgings that can be finished to small-, large-, or 400- journal specs and any stroke length from 2.70 to 4.00 inches. In addition, if you believe the old axiom that more is better, it's relatively easy (although expensive) to assemble a long-stroke "small-block" that displaces in excess of 500 ci.

Specialty and racing rods abound. GMPP offers the tried-and-true large-journal "pink rod" for hi-po street and limited competition applications. Similar to the standard rod forgings used in performance engines of the 1970s, this rod is made from premium steel, uses 3/8-inch through-bolts and a pressed pin, and is inspected and fully prepped at the factory. GMPP also offers the "Bow Tie rod" in finished lengths of 5.700 and 6.000 inches (to fit racing combinations needing longer-than-stock rods). This very stout rod is suitable for most levels of competition and uses high-grade 7/16-inch cap bolts that thread directly into the rod body. It's factory-prepped for pressed pins and, because of its added weight, requires special balancing considerations.

The aftermarket selection of small-block rods is, for all practical purposes, unlimited. Numerous sources produce premium steel forgings or machined billets. For the most part, these rods are made-to-order and can be finished to almost any length, journal diameter, and pin configuration the builder desires. This type of work is expensive and is usually reserved for all-out racing efforts.

Some sources also offer a "sportsman rod," designed as a budget-oriented alternative for amateur or low- to mid-level racing engines. The example shown on page 62, offered by Crower Cams, is based on a custom-designed premium steel forging, and is delivered with a finish prep suitable for all-out racing. These rods are more expensive than standard production

Holley Replacement Parts produces a line of "emissions legal" carburetors that include all vacuum hookups and bowl venting to the charcoal canister.

Crower offers their Sportsman Rod, designed as a budget-oriented alternative for amateur or racing engines. A custom forging of 4340 chrome-moly steel, the machine work on these rods is first class. SPS bolts are used.

The Holley electronic fuel-injection systems for street engines delivers performance and economy that even a precisely tuned carburetor can't equal. Main jet size, choke, and accelerator pump are all adjusted by simply turning a knob. In the not-too-distant past, traditionalists scorned electronics and microprocessors, but now only the most diehard relic can ignore the advantages of these ultra-precise fuel systems.

Want to build a 500-ci small-block? Here's how. This GMPP "raw" (unmachined) steel forging can be finished to any stroke length from 2.70 to 4.00 inches.

rods, but they provide a tough and reliable alternative for racing buildups or high-buck street engines.

Cylinder Heads

Stock factory heads produce good power levels: 300 to 500 hp with emissions-legal equipment is a realistic goal. If you're determined to further increase power output, you must replace the stock heads with high-performance factory or specialty castings.

A wide array of factory performance and racing cylinder heads are currently available from GMPP. The list is too extensive to discuss in detail (see the latest edition of the GM Performance Parts Catalog). Briefly, the range of possibilities includes cast-iron 2.02/1.60 replacement heads with either 64- or 76-cc combustion chambers, and the Bow Tie cast-iron replacement head (non-production) with the 2.02/1.60 valve combo and 64-cc chambers. Several aluminum heads are also offered, including the production Corvette H.O. (High Output) head with 1.94/1.50 valves and 58-cc chambers. The "Phase 6" aluminum Bow

Edelbrock offers several cylinder heads for the small-block. All performance heads can accommodate 2.150-inch intakes and 1.650-inch exhaust valves with offset guides. Ductile iron seats "interlock" to prevent loosening.

Tie head (push rod holes are not machined) is available with 2.02/1.60 hardened inserts or in a "bare" version without seats. Both have 55-cc chambers. There is also a rare version of the "raised runner" aluminum Bow Tie and several variations of the latest Chevy racing

There are now many smog-legal aftermarket heads available, such as these from Air Flow Research. They offer many improvements over factory castings and use 2.02/1.60-inch valves, bronze guides, and hard seat inserts—not to mention weight savings. You may want to look into what the aftermarket has to offer in heads by checking with GMPP, Edelbrock, Holley, and many more.

setup, an aluminum design with large runner volumes, small 45-cc chambers, and unique 18-degree valve angles.

The range of aftermarket cylinder heads is equally impressive. Several custom shops offer trick heads for the small-block with virtually any feature you can imagine. The possibilities range from cast-iron or aluminum heads suitable for highly developed street engines to completely unique designs (requiring custom manifolds and special valvegear) for extreme RPM competition engines. Both Edelbrock and Holley offer good aluminum small-block heads.

The 190 aluminum heads available from Air Flow Research are a popular example of high-performance aftermarket street heads. These heads are "emissions legal" replacements. However, they offer so many improvements over factory castings that at first glance they look like custom race-only heads. The 190s are available with various chamber volumes, use the large 2.02/1.60 valve combination, incorporate bronze guides and hard seats, and gain additional valve-to-valve position (stock rockers can be used). Despite all these "trick" features, port volume is only slightly increased to ensure good throttle response and low-speed performance.

Distributors and Ignitions

The advent of solid-state electronics has totally changed the modern ignition systems. Old-fashioned breaker-point ignitions, which required frequent "tune-ups," are (or should be) keeping company with the dinosaurs. Every street, performance, or racing engine worth its salt is fitted with a breakerless electronic ignition.

The late GM factory HEI (High-output Electronic Ignition) distributors are satisfactory for street and modest-performance applications. There are several accessories and upgrade kits available that boost the output (voltage delivered to the spark plugs) and increase the timing reliability at high RPM. If you're approaching the performance limits of the stock HEI, one of these upgrade kits should be the answer.

All racing engines and some high-performance street engines are fitted with complete specialty ignition systems. The current selection and various options can leave you breathless. Most well-designed and proven systems provide better performance (than a standard ignition), but a few key points should be remembered. For any sort of street application, a vacuum-advance mechanism is required to meet emissions requirements and obtain good part-throttle fuel economy. Vacuum advance can be eliminated in racing applications. Many systems allow the builder to alter the advance curve either mechanically or electronically. Unless you have enough experience to know the exact curve needed for your application, have the fine-tuning done at a chassis dyno shop.

MSD Ignition is well known in the racing world for their powerful ignition offerings. Their impressive line of MSD (Multiple-Spark Discharge) ignitions offers something for nearly every application and many of these ignition controls are emissions-legal. They also offer ready-to-run distributors that are perfect for replacing breaker-point models or for applications where the large-cap HEI model won't fit. They also offer spark plug wires and coils that can top off any ignition system.

Exhaust Manifolds

Without question, the easiest and cheapest option is to stick with the stock exhaust manifolds, but in most cases, this limits the power output of the engine. Stock manifolds are designed to be compact, durable, and most of all, cheap. These are important goals—especially from a mass-production viewpoint—but if improved power is one of your goals, there are some excellent alternatives.

Several exhaust components from GMPP have been designed with performance in mind. The "ram's horn" cast-iron manifolds are available in the GM Performance Parts Catalog. These manifolds have the appearance of stock iron manifolds, but the collection chamber has a large 2.5-inch outlet. This setup isn't as efficient as tube headers but the manifolds are durable, quiet, and surprisingly efficient. However, they do not accommodate the late AIR (air injection reactor) emission systems if the system must be retained. If AIR tubes are required for your application, consider changing to a set that came in mid-1980s Camaros or Corvettes. They're compact and fit many applications.

The range of aftermarket tube headers for the small-block is staggering. Extra cost and effort is usually required when a non-standard exhaust system is used, but most Chevy small-blocks respond very well to low-restriction exhaust systems. There are now "shorty" headers available that position the flanges higher to help with ground clearance. If you think the number of headers available is high, start looking at the custom mufflers that are available! When you're interested in more performance, a free-flowing exhaust is one of the best buys for your money.

Gaskets

Selecting engine gaskets is probably one of the easiest decisions you'll make. Most gasket packages for the small-block are high quality and quite complete. Combined with the assembly techniques described in Chapter 8, "Final Assembly," your small-block should be water- and oil-leak free, and stay that way for many years.

CHAPTER 4

A performance engine puts additional demands on gaskets. Higher cylinder pressures, increased internal oil flow, and sealing non-stock components are just a few of the things a gasket has to deal with. In performance situations, many professionals want the most reliable gaskets money can buy, and one of the best names in performance gaskets is Fel-Pro. Their head gaskets incorporate the latest design technology and require no gasket-sealing compounds. In fact, they never need to be retorqued for the life of the engine. Fel-Pro offers complete gasket packages, individual gaskets, and many unique gaskets and seals for special and racing applications. Another company that offers great gaskets is SCE, with a variety of copper and traditional high-performance gaskets.

Intake Manifolds

Selecting an intake manifold can be a complex decision. The simplest and cheapest approach is to simply reinstall the original manifold, but there are numerous options that can readily improve efficiency and engine output.

As you might expect, GMPP offers several performance-oriented manifolds. They offer a high-rise cast-iron manifold that works well in racing classes restricted to a single 2-barrel carb. They also offer a cast-iron, dual-bore manifold for spread-bore or square-bore 4-barrels. There is also a new updated version of the venerable, aluminum high-rise 4-barrel (square flange) manifold used on the early Z/28 and LT-1 engine options. The race-only selections include aluminum Bow Tie manifolds to fit standard or relocated runner heads.

The range of aftermarket performance manifolds is virtually beyond description. The major suppliers include Holley, Edelbrock, Weiand, and numerous other specialty and racing manufacturers. Whatever kind of induction you can imagine (2-barrel, 4-barrel, multiple Webers, fuel injection, superchargers, or turbochargers for street or racing, for your car, truck, or boat), someone, somewhere, makes it for the small-block Chevy.

When selecting a manifold, keep these basics in mind. For a conventional stock- or street-performance engine, dual-plane designs generally offer better low- and mid-range torque. Single-plane manifolds are often suited to racing applications. For any street-driven engine, make absolutely certain the manifold is compatible with all emissions-related equipment (it should also have an E.O. number; see sidebar "Meeting Smog Requirements" on page 65).

Some manufacturers offer a complete package with their manifolds. For example, Edelbrock has developed several cams and cylinder heads specifically for their intake manifolds. Developed on the dyno and in the emissions lab, they comprise proven designs that would take the average engine builder thousands of dollars and hours of dyno time to duplicate (see sidebar "Dyno Testing" on page 152).

Oil System

The production Chevy small-block has an effective and reliable oiling system. For day-to-day driving, there is little reason to modify the system. If the oil passages are unobstructed, the oil pump is in good shape, and the filter is properly maintained, the stock oiling system will handle any reasonable demands. (See sidebar "Oil Pumps: Blueprinting and Modifying" on page 44 for more information on small-block oiling system preparation.)

If you're building a performance engine, you may wish to increase the bypass pressure or replace the standard pump with a high-volume model. GMPP offers a bypass-valvespring that raises delivery pressure to approximately 70 psi. The stock high-pressure pump used in the hi-po Z/28 and LT-1 engines is also available.

MSD Ignition offers a variety of distributors. Shown here are their standard Pro-Billet model and their ready-to-run version. Both use a maintenance-free magnetic pickup and have an adjustable mechanical advance. They also offer multiple sparking ignition controls, such as the 6AL shown, performance coils, spark plugs, and more.

Fel-Pro head gaskets incorporate the latest design technology and require no gasket-sealing compounds. In fact, they never need to be retorqued.

SELECTING PARTS

ARP is the leader in fastener technology. You may think, "a bolt is a bolt," but you won't feel that way once you work with ARP products. Their website and catalog are filled with great information and you'll be amazed at the technology behind fasteners.

High-pressure and high-volume replacement oil pumps are also available from aftermarket sources including Milodon, Speed Pro, and TRW. We chose a Milodon 18750 pump for one of the small-blocks built for this book. The pump was extremely well built, had rotors 3/8-inch taller than stock, and delivered a solid 65 psi during all of our dyno testing.

Meeting Smog Requirements

Every rebuilt engine that is operated on streets and highways must be assembled with an understanding of current emissions requirements. Regulations specified by national legislation, and enforced by the Environmental Protection Agency (EPA), have severely restricted the amount of pollution that a street-driven vehicle can legally emit. In some cases, state or local legislation may impose additional restrictions that are even more severe than national standards. Every builder of street engines should be familiar with these regulations.

Although this may seem like an imposing or nearly impossible task, your prospects of building a "smog legal" engine are not as dim as they first appear. Some forward-thinking manufacturers have invested time and effort to have their components "certified" as legal replacement parts. In other words, even though these parts were not installed on production engines at the factory, they are legal replacement parts (from an emissions standpoint).

An example is the Edelbrock Performer-Plus series of camshafts. These products are delivered with a copy of the Executive Order Number (usually called the E.O.) issued to Edelbrock by the California Air Resources Board (CARB). This affirms that the product has passed all emissions testing and is legal for use on the prescribed vehicles operated on California roads. Edelbrock also provides a sticker that should be attached to the inside fender to indicate the product is covered by a legal E.O. If there are any questions or difficulties during the biennial emissions check (required by local legislation), the E.O. statement should provide sufficient proof, or the purchaser can contact Edelbrock for assistance in verifying the legality of the components.

Some parts of the country are less restrictive than others (California is often the most restrictive), but if you are building a modified street engine, you would be well advised to consider using only emissions-certified components.

Both camshaft kits pictured here have an E.O. exemption number and are considered smog-legal in all 50 states. Crane and Comp offer a variety of grinds and accessories for street-legal performance. Most performance aftermarket companies offer parts that CARB approved for use on pollution-controlled vehicles. Check with the manufacturer.

CHAPTER 4

Stock small-block pans allow an adequate oil volume, usually a total of 5 quarts, but increasing the volume is a good idea because greater volume reduces oil temperature, assists engine cooling, and improves lubrication. Aftermarket suppliers, such as Moroso, offer many different styles of pans, pickups, and special pumps for the small-block. We selected a Moroso pan that has a hinged insert to help keep oil in the sump area during hard acceleration and deceleration. However, if you're thinking about increasing oil capacity, keep in mind that deeper pans often reduce ground clearance and can interfere with chassis members.

Pistons and Rings

Many years of factory and racing development have produced an extraordinary range of stock and specialty pistons for the small-block Chevy.

However, designs vary considerably depending on the bore requirements. The broadest selection is available for the 4.00-inch-bore blocks (302/327/350 ci) and the most common overbore, 4.030 inches. The selection for both early and late small-bore blocks is less plentiful, but generally adequate for low-compression rebuild projects. Recent interest in high-performance large-displacement small-blocks has produced several interesting designs for the 4.125-inch (400-ci) block. High-compression pistons (11:1 or higher) are readily available for the 4.00- and 4.125-inch bores, while similar designs for the small-bore blocks are not commonly available.

In some instances, you may have to consider the difference between a "cast" and a "forged" design. Without becoming too embroiled in detail, the considerations are: Cast pistons with thermal-expansion limiters used in most production small-blocks, do not expand very much when they become heated. As a result, they can be fitted with a tighter skirt clearance, which increases ring support and reduces wear. Forged pistons are stronger than cast (important in high-performance engines) but they expand more and must be fitted with greater skirt clearance, which reduces ring support, especially during cold startup. Bottom line: Cast pistons are best suited to low-RPM engines; forged pistons work well in high-RPM engines, but can reduce ring life.

The hypereutectic process has changed this traditional view. This process produces a strong, relatively heat-stable piston. It is, in effect, a kind of crossbreed that effectively retains the best features of both cast and forged pistons. This type of piston is installed in some late factory high-output engines, and would be an excellent choice in any performance engine buildup.

GMPP offers standard replacement pistons and overbore models for all production small-blocks. Their performance catalog also includes numerous specialty pistons with nominal compression ratios ranging from 9:1 to 12.5:1.

Manufacturers including TRW, Ross, Childs & Albert, Cosworth, and JE Pistons also provide forged or machined billet pistons for the small-block. These sources build to the customer's specifications. For all practical purposes, these pistons are for pure racing or special applications (such as a custom short-block combination with longer-than-stock connecting rods).

In most cases, piston ring selection depends on the piston design. The current "standard" ring package used by

Edelbrock developed this Performer package for a smog-legal small-block. It includes their 3701 intake manifold, a 2102 camshaft and lifters, and a 1902 QuadraJet-type carburetor. Developed on the dyno and in the emissions lab, they comprise a proven design that works "right out of the box" (see sidebar "Dyno Testing" on page 152).

This Moroso oil-pump pickup screen is nice because it has a bracket that attaches to the oil pump cover. This way you don't worry about welding the pickup tube to the pump.

most engine builders is a three-ring combination with a molybdenum-faced top ring, a conventional cast-iron second ring, and a three-piece oil ring. The "moly" top ring is favored because it achieves optimum seal after a brief break-in period. A segmented oil ring, with two narrow steel "rails" and a stainless "expander," is standard in most production and racing engines.

The final bore diameter, ring width, and whether the gap will be set by the engine builder or the factory are decisions that should be coordinated with your machine shop. All late-production small-blocks have 5/64-inch-wide compression rings and a 3/16-inch-wide oil ring. Many performance and racing pistons have narrower top and second rings (1/16 inch) to reduce ring weight, but for many street engines, conventional-width rings increase long-term reliability.

Rocker Arms and Studs

The small-block's production ball-mounted, stamped-steel rocker arms are simple and deceptively rugged. They provide 100,000+ miles of service in the average street performance engine—after all, GM used them in all of their high-output production engines during the muscle car boom. Specialty rocker arms are only required in racing engines and special applications (see Sidebar "Rocker Arms" on page 135), for example, when valvespring seat pressures exceed 120 pounds, and maximum engine speed exceeds about 6,500 rpm.

An excellent stock-type rocker is available from Speed Pro and some other specialty sources. It's a stamped arm, just like the production model, but the metal is thicker and it has other refinements. When combined with a sturdy mounting stud, this rocker arm is ideal for stock and high-performance engines. Crane and Comp also offer a variety of upgraded rocker arms for mild-performance engines.

In some cases, the rocker studs may also require attention. If seat pressures will exceed about 100 pounds and maximum engine speed will be above 5,500 rpm, premium-grade screw-in studs are required. Aftermarket sources such as ARP (see page 127) also offer 3/8- and 7/16-inch studs made from premium steel.

Most late-model factory heads with screw-in studs are also equipped with pushrod guideplates mounted between the base of the stud and the stud boss. Factory heads with pressed-in studs do not have guideplates. The pushrod openings in the heads are narrow slots that keep the pushrods aligned with the rocker arms. Heads with pushrod slots can be converted to screw-in studs, but guideplates must not be used with these heads (unless the stock guide slots are machined out). Some late-model heads use soft-steel guideplates and pushrods, but only hardened steel guideplates and pushrods provide reliable service.

The Milodon 18750 pump (right) for the small-block is extremely well built, uses 3/8-inch-taller rotors, and delivers a solid 65 psi. It is an excellent choice for a high-performance buildup.

K&N are known for their excellent line of FilterChargers, their air cleaners. Now they're taking much of the same technology into oil filters. These are three different filters designed for the small-block Chevy. The majority of applications use the two smaller versions.

Production engines were fit with 5/64-inch-wide compression rings and a 3/16-inch oil ring. When selecting a piston, keep in mind the ring dimensions and ask the manufacturer about your plans for the engine and application. Total Seal offers a variety of piston rings for small-block Chevys.

CHAPTER 4

Hypereutectic pistons have changed the traditional view of a forged piston. This piston is strong and heat stable. It is, in effect, a kind of crossbreed between cast and forged pistons. This type of piston would be an excellent choice in any performance buildup.

These roller-tip rocker arms are a nice update to any engine. There are also a variety of valvetrain components that you can upgrade with during your rebuild. Check offerings from Comp, Crane, Iskenderian, Crower, and others.

Edelbrock Engine Parts

From intakes to exhaust systems, Edelbrock manufactures a variety of components required to assemble a top-quality engine. The company markets a vast array of engine parts including aluminum heads, intakes, camshafts, and carburetors.

In addition to individual parts, Edelbrock offers engine and cylinder head Power Package Top End Kits that include intake, carb, and camshafts coordinated to produce more than 400 hp in a variety of different applications.

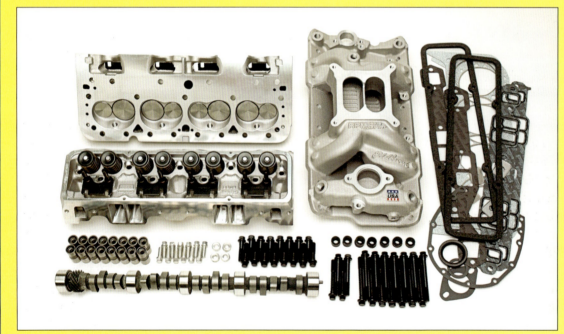

This is an Edelbrock Top End Power Package for a small-block Chevy. The kit includes a Performer RPM Air Gap intake manifold, aluminum heads ready to bolt-on, matched camshaft, timing gear and chain set, plus all the gaskets you'll need for the installation.

CHAPTER 5

THE MACHINE SHOP

Thorough engine rebuilding requires a number of specialized tools that few non-professionals can afford (or operate). But even if you won the lottery and packed your garage full of the latest high-tech machining equipment, you would need one more essential element to bring all those machines to life: experience. Combined with a passion to produce quality work, experience is the key to quality, precision machine work.

Finding and Dealing with a Machine Shop

Since most of us don't have the equipment or the time to learn how to use it, we must rely on a machine shop to prepare our blocks, cranks, heads, and other parts for assembly. But how do you find a top-notch shop? Start by looking for a company that has been in business for several years and has a good reputation. While this isn't a guarantee of quality, it's a good place to start. Next, discuss your engine project with machine shop personnel. Are they willing to listen? Do they take the time to explain what is required? Are they easy to get along with? If they don't pass these initial tests, consider another shop. People who are difficult to get along with before they take your money won't be very helpful if you run into problems after the job is finished. Finally, tell them (in a nice way) you'll be checking their work and you would like to know about their policy for customer satisfaction.

While no machine shop is perfect, quality shops regularly turn out quality work and should be prepared to absorb the cost of mistakes without giving you a bad time. The shop you select should say something like "We are dedicated to quality, and we'll do what's required to make sure you're completely satisfied with our work." If you hear these magic words, find people you like, and the shop is reasonably clean and organized, you probably have found a company that offers experience, dedication to perfection, and top-quality machine work.

Obtaining "customer satisfaction" from your machine shop depends on more than just the attitude of the personnel at the machine shop. It also depends on your attitude! We've talked to many shop owners and they all have the same lament. If something goes wrong—and they all readily admit to being human—their worst nightmare is

Locating a machine shop that is dedicated to quality isn't easy. If you find people you like, they seem dedicated to customer satisfaction, and the shop is reasonably clean and organized, you've probably found a shop that offers quality machine work.

REBUILDING THE SMALL-BLOCK CHEVROLET

CHAPTER 5

the customer who storms in and starts screaming at them about how they "screwed up" their engine. While it's understandable that you, as the customer, might feel a lack of control over the machine operations that you're paying for, having a chip on your shoulder doesn't help. Explaining the problem in a calm tone usually gets the desired results. If you would like your machine shop to do whatever is required to make sure you're completely satisfied with your purchase, treat them like the dedicated professionals they are.

Who's Responsible?

Since you're reading this book, you'll presumably be disassembling, making decisions about replacement parts, and finally, reassembling your "new" engine. By taking on this responsibility, it's generally accepted that you're also responsible for making sure everything is done correctly. No one else will accept this responsibility. If a faulty machine operation or defective part "slips through the cracks" and fails in service, you'll almost certainly be the one paying for (or performing) engine removal and reinstallation, disassembly,

It is generally accepted that you are responsible for making sure everything is done correctly if you will be disassembling, making decisions about replacement parts, and reassembling your "new" engine. No one else will accept this responsibility.

and reassembly, and the cost to replace damaged parts.

While reputable machine shops stand behind their work, many shops feel they're only responsible for the specific work they perform, not how the finished product is used or whether it's compatible with the hundreds of other components you may install in your engine.

To verify the quality of the work you're purchasing from your machine shop, Chapter 7, "Pre-Assembly Fitting," guides you through a careful inspection of critical machined surfaces and spells out how to verify the compatibility of replacement parts. If there's one thing we hope you'll gain from reading this book, it's this: Don't take anything for granted! If you don't know that it's right, presume it isn't.

Before You Drop Off Parts

Before you load up your vehicle with engine parts and head off to the machine shop, make sure you're fully prepared to discuss your project requirements with the machinists.

The upcoming sections in this chapter detail specific operations that are commonly performed by machine shops to prepare a variety of engines, from street stock to all-out racing power plants. Becoming familiar with these procedures will give you the background you need to intelligently discuss your project and determine if your machinist's recommendations are appropriate for the intended use of your engine.

Here are four additional tips:

- Make sure that you have identified your parts as explained in Chapter 3, Step 14, on page 55. Putting your own individual mark or stamp on every part prevents possible mix-ups and disagreements.

- Don't forget to take your Work-A-Long Sheet (or a copy) with you to the machine shop. Check off all new parts and engine components that you leave at the machine shop (make sure you also get a detailed receipt).

- Have the machine shop give you a written price quotation for the services they will perform.

- Remember to read this entire chapter (and preferably the entire book) before you have the machine work done. Especially review the step-by-step procedures at the end of this chapter. They will familiarize you with important procedures, some of which are not "automatically" done by machine shops.

Cleaning and Crack Detection

Many machine shops clean blocks, heads, and other components in pressure-washer blast cabinets, although heat-bake cleaning is becoming more common. Both cleaning methods work quite well. Although the now-less-common "hot tanks" do remove surface grunge, they don't do as good a job cleaning deep in recesses and oil passages.

Make sure that all of the plugs in the block and heads (including screw-in and press-in plugs in the oil galleries and core plugs in the water jackets) are removed before cleaning. If you were unable to get them out, ask your machine shop to remove them (many shops don't charge for this service). Don't forget, pressure washers, baking cabinets, and other cleaning methods won't do a thorough job unless all the plugs have been removed.

After cleaning, major components (including the block, cylinder heads, crank, pistons if not new, and rods) should be thoroughly inspected for cracks. Magnaflux magnetic inspection is

70   REBUILDING THE SMALL-BLOCK CHEVROLET

THE MACHINE SHOP

Make sure that all of the plugs in the block and heads are removed before cleaning. Many machine shops will remove plugs at no charge as part of the cleaning process.

The golden rule of engine building is: Never Take Anything For Granted. While components occasionally fail for "no reason," keep the odds on your side; make sure you personally know that everything is right. With this attitude, your engine project will likely succeed with flying colors and you'll never have to experience a piston that looks like this.

Make sure that you identify your parts with your own individual mark or stamp before you drop them off at the machine shop. This can prevent component mix-ups and disagreements in the future.

the common choice for ferrous metals, while Zyglo or other "stain" methods are used on aluminum parts. In addition, if you purchased a used block or heads that you've never seen in operation, have them pressure tested to ensure they're free of pinholes or undetected cracks.

While crack inspection and pressure testing may not always produce positive results, you'll be even more disappointed if you invest money in machine work on components that do little more than fill your oil pan with water. Don't take chances; crack inspection is the cheapest engine-building "insurance" you can buy. For information on obtaining replacement cores for parts that do not pass inspection, refer to "What To Do When Your Parts Don't Pass Inspection" on page 48.

Block Machine Work

A basic part of machine shop procedures almost always includes removing old cam bearings (before cleaning) and installing a new set (after crack inspection). In fact, unless you're an expert and own the required tools (see sidebar "Removing and Installing Cam Bearings," on page 46), this job should definitely be on your list of requested machine work. Occasionally, cam-bearing bores in the block are slightly oversize or undersize. Quality machine shops will detect these variations and can make the appropriate modifications to ensure your engine has the correct cam bearings.

Almost every engine buildup includes boring and honing the cylinders. Unfortunately, the small-block Chevy, along with many late-model engines, uses thin-wall block castings that easily distort from stress. A particularly troublesome area is the top of the cylinder bores. When the head bolts are fully torqued, thousands of pounds of load can distort the top of the cylinder bores by several thousandths of an inch, resulting in poor ring seal and lost power. Simulating these distortions with torque plates during the boring and honing procedure greatly reduces bore distortion when the cylinder heads are installed. Although having your machinist use torque plates will cost you more money, many consider it an excellent investment that increases engine performance, efficiency, and longevity.

After the cylinders are bored oversize, a final honing operation first removes the last five thousandths, then the final tenths of thousandths of an inch of material. This precision process, if done properly, will finish bore diameters so that piston-to-cylinder-wall clearance (a dimension specified by the piston manufacturer) is exactly correct. In order to maintain this recommended clearance, each bore may finish at a slightly different diameter, sized to match the corresponding piston.

Honing also leaves a unique surface finish on the bores called a "crosshatch" pattern. The smoothness or roughness of this finish must be precisely established by using the correct "grit" honing stones and the right honing pressure. If all goes well, the cylinders wind up with a finish that is just rough enough to allow the rings to break in quickly, but also smooth enough so that the ring wear is minimized. Optimum bore finish is usually prescribed by the piston ring manufacturer.

Another task that your machine shop may perform is align-boring the crankshaft bearing bores. Small-block cylinder blocks, again because of their thin-wall construction, "move" under stress and loads. After thousands of hot

CHAPTER 5

Many machine shops clean heads, blocks, and other components in a pressure-washer blast cabinet (right). They are effective and fast. Bead blasters (left) are also very popular for cleaning heads, manifold, or other parts. They blast millions of tiny steel beads at high speed, removing all traces of dirt and giving metal surfaces a like-new appearance. However, many of those beads can remain lodged deep in water jackets and other recesses that make final-assembly cleaning more difficult. Chapter 6 offers tips for cleaning and preparing bead-blasted parts.

and cold cycles, the main bores often drift out of alignment, sometimes enough to cause the crankshaft to bind up. Many professional machinists recommend that virtually all small-blocks be align-bored as part of "standard" machining practice. This procedure will correct the main bore alignment and reestablish a parallel crankshaft centerline, while align honing will correct main bore alignment but not necessarily produce a crank centerline parallel with other block dimensions, such as cam bore centerline and deck surfaces. In most engine buildups, this is a very minor point. However, in a racing engine (where absolute minimum clearances and other dimensions are strictly maintained) having a parallel crank centerline is an important requirement.

The deck surfaces of most small-blocks "warp" into the shape of waves. This distortion is typically a few thousandths of an inch (which might cause gasket failure) to as much as .010 inch or more (which absolutely will cause gasket failure). "Cutting the decks to clean" is a common procedure used in most engine buildups where the machinist removes only enough material to return the deck surfaces to flat and parallel with the crank centerline. However, if you're building a racing or high-performance engine, you may want to delay machining until after pre-assembly fitting. During mock-up assembly (described in Chapter 7), you can measure actual deck clearance and calculate true compression ratios. When these measurements are completed, you can return your block to the machine shop and instruct them to remove a specific amount from each deck to produce the desired result.

In addition to these more-or-less basic block-machining procedures, there are several other "special" modifications that can be done for racing or other heavy-duty applications. These include adding a roller thrust bearing between the block and the upper cam sprocket, enlarging the main-feed oil passages with core drills, tapping the main oil galleries for screw-in plugs, installing four-bolt main caps, grinding or machining the block to clear a long-stroke crank, and much more! If you're building a race engine, thoroughly discuss the project with your machine shop. Hopefully, they have experience in preparing similar engines for racing or specialized use.

Also, see sidebar "Block Performance Tips" on page 31, for more information on racing and high-performance selection and preparation.

Finally, we recommend that you tell your machine shop not to install new oil-gallery and water-jacket plugs. With oil-gallery plugs installed, it's almost impossible to thoroughly clean

If you've purchased a used block or heads that you've never seen in operation, have your machine shop pressure-test them to ensure they are free of pinholes or undetected cracks.

THE MACHINE SHOP

Every machine shop uses a Sunnen or similar power cylinder hone. Using torque plates during the honing process improves ring seal, producing better economy and performance.

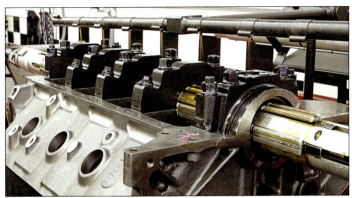

Align boring (as shown here) corrects main bore alignment and re-establish a parallel crankshaft centerline, while align honing only corrects main bore alignment. In most engine buildups this is a very minor point. In a racing engine, however, making sure the crank is parallel to other bores in the block (such as the cam centerline) is an important requirement.

Head and block surfaces can warp. If distortions are greater than .003 inch (or greater than .001 inch when using steel-shim head gaskets), have the block and heads "surfaced to clean." Make sure your machine shop uses a machine that uses multiple carbide cutters, not a stone wheel or sanding belts, since these alternative methods can result in poor gasket seal.

the block before assembly, as we'll discuss in Chapter 6. If the core plugs are in place, it's more difficult to remove soap and solvent residue from the water jackets. Install those plugs after you clean the block.

Head Machine Work

Cylinder heads should always be cleaned and crack-tested as described earlier. Finding cracked cylinder heads isn't uncommon, and as with cylinder blocks, it's much better to find a crack before any money is invested in reconditioning.

The surfaces of many small-block heads deform from use. If you or your machine shop detects distortions greater than .003 inch (or greater than .001 inch if you're going to use steel-shim head gaskets), ask the shop to have the heads "surfaced to clean." Your machinist will remove only enough material to return the head surface to dead flat. Ask if the machine they use for surfacing will grind or cut the heads. Grinding leaves a very smooth surface that may not have sufficient "grip" to hold the head gaskets securely in position. We suggest that all heads (and block deck surfaces) be surfaced with multiple carbide cutters, not ground with a stone wheel or sanding belts.

After cleaning, inspection, and surfacing, the valveguides and valveseats should be reconditioned. There are several options: valveguides can be sleeved or threaded to accept cast-iron or bronze inserts; the guides can be reamed and then fit with valves with oversize stems; the old guides can be machined out and new cast-iron or bronze guides pressed in place; or existing guides can be knurled to retain proper valve fit. All of these procedures produce acceptable results except knurling. This "quick-fix" method only lasts a few thousand miles, after which the valves rattle around as bad as if the guides were never knurled at all. Therefore, for all practical purposes, your choices boil down to using bronze or cast-iron sleeves or replacement valves and guides.

There is little consensus on what guide material works best; some machine shops prefer cast iron, others recommend bronze. However, many experts believe that guide life is directly linked to the type of valve seals used to control guide oiling (along with several other factors, including the type of lifters, pushrods, rocker arms, valvesprings, retainers, and even oil and frequency of oil changes). It's not so much a job of selecting a specific guide and a specific seal; it's using a combination of guides and seals that are known by your machine shop to provide good results. If they don't have any suggestions, consider these combinations:

For stock engines, use replacement, press-in, cast-iron guides with stock O-ring seals on the valvestems. In addition, use guide-mounted seals on the intake valves only (use black runner seals with thin, white stem scraper). If possible, also use the stock valvespring-mounted splash shields.

For high-performance engines, use cast-iron or bronze-wall guides with rubber guide-mounted seals on both the intake and exhaust valves. Eliminate valvespring-mounted splash shields but continue to use the stock O-ring seals on the valvestems, provided the valves are machined for them.

For racing engines, eliminate the O-ring seals on the valvestems, particularly when using needle-bearing rocker arms or restricted top-end oiling. Unless there is no other choice (such as using dual valvesprings), never use all-white Teflon/wire spring-type seals; they restrict guide oiling too much. When you must use Teflon seals, consider using bronze-wall guides, as they seem to survive better with less oil.

After the guides are reconditioned, your machinist can turn his attention to the valveseats. For any application requiring long life on unleaded gasoline, like virtually every street buildup, press-in hard inserts should replace the stock exhaust seats in the cylinder heads. While not inexpensive, they can add 50,000 miles or more of additional service. Some later-model or aftermarket cylinder heads have induction-hardened seats from the factory and may not require hard-seat inserts; discuss these options with your machinist.

Considering the affordable cost of new valves (about $80 per set), many engine builders opt for new instead of reconditioned valves. Speed Pro, TRW, Manley, and other manufacturers offer valves with hardened tips that can reduce wear with high spring pressures and mechanical (solid lifter) cams. However, if you're building a street engine and your valves are in good condition (showing little face, tip, or stem wear) regrinding the faces and stem tips is an acceptable option.

A quality, three-angle valve job should be performed using a 30-degree top cut, a 45-degree seat, and a 60-degree bottom cut. Seat widths should be about .065 inch (±.010 inch) for the intake and .075 inch (±.010 inch) for the exhaust. Seats should be held near the lower tolerance limit for performance use, and widened to near the upper tolerance

A quality three-angle valve job should be performed using a 30-degree top cut, 45-degree seat, and a 60-degree bottom cut. You can see the three different angles cut for the exhaust valve in the photo. Maintaining seat concentricity with the valveguide is also essential to good performance and long life.

There is little consensus on what guide seals work best. The blue rubber EOK press-on seals (right) are the recommended choice when it comes to valve-guide seals. Unless you have no choice, avoid all-white Teflon seals (left).

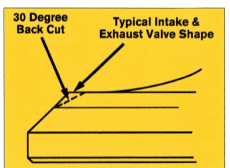

While it's considered questionable by some builders, grinding a 30-degree back cut on the intake and exhaust valves to just under the seat-contact position is often claimed to slightly improve port flow.

When seat pressures exceed about 110 pounds, screw-in rocker studs should be used in place of the press-in variety. Goodson offers a special tool to remove the factory pressed-in studs. Although these tools are not recommended for use in a hand drill, you can perform this operation yourself if you have a small mill or sturdy drill press and an angle plate. Tools include a stud puller, tap guide, and boss cutter.

THE MACHINE SHOP

Goodson Tools and Supplies

It is often difficult to locate the tools needed for precision engine work. Hardware and auto parts stores seldom stock what's needed, and even well-equipped tool shops may draw a blank when you ask for a spring-height gauge, a cylinder-bore mic, a plastic organizer, or even a box of parts tags. Goodson Tools and Supplies for Engine Builders can answer all of these engine building requirements and a lot more.

Some items in the Goodson catalog are designed for professional engine rebuilders, while others are suited to the needs of an amateur mechanic and auto enthusiast. Some are, simply, indispensable tools that even occasional engine builders will want to add to their toolbox.

The major portion of Goodson's business is direct sales to pro mechanics, but they do include a mail-order division.

Here are just some of the Goodson items used in our facility: dial-bore gauges, calipers, Plastigauge, component organizers, metal markers and tags, spray cleaners, paint. They have literally dozens of other useful gadgets. If it's something that can help with your engine-building project, Goodson probably stocks it on their shelves.

Many inexpensive items can be a big help during engine rebuilding. This valvetrain organizer is just one of several parts organizers that are "impossible" to find elsewhere.

---

limit for street longevity. To optimize performance, grind only the minimum amount necessary to clean the seats. The more the valves are "sunk" into the seats, the less efficiently the ports will flow. If the seats require a lot of grinding, consider installing hard-seat inserts in both the intake and exhaust sides, or look for replacement head castings.

The final steps in basic head preparation include installing the valvesprings so that they provide the cam manufacturer's recommended seat pressure. This involves measuring the compressed spring height at which the desired pressure is produced, then adding the appropriate valvespring shims so this pressure is applied to the valve. With the guide type, press-on stem seals are used and the top of the valveguides must be machined so that the OD (outside diameter) is concentric with the ID (inside diameter). If this isn't done, the seals won't contact the valvestem uniformly and excess oil may be drawn down from the guides, increasing oil consumption.

In addition to these basic head preparation procedures, there are several other "special" modifications that can be done for racing or other heavy-duty applications.

Porting and installing larger valves can increase mid- and high-RPM power. However, expect a reduction in low-speed throttle response and fuel economy. Unfortunately, stock factory thin-wall castings can't tolerate much grinding; if you're looking for a substantial power increase, consider GMPP Bow Tie castings or a set of performance heads from aftermarket manufacturers such as Air Flow Research, Dart, Edelbrock, Brodix, and others.

Screw-in rocker studs can replace the press-in variety; recommended when seat pressures exceed about 110 pounds.

Pushrod guideplates can be added to any head that uses integral pushrod guides by machining out the stock guide holes, cutting down the guide bosses, and drilling and tapping for screw-in studs (this is a good way to "salvage" a set of heads that have worn pushrod guides). When guideplates are used, hardened pushrods must also be used.

Finally, port flow and engine performance can sometimes be slightly enhanced by grinding a 30-degree back cut on the intake and exhaust valves to just under the seat contact position (see drawing on page 74). The margin of the valve (thickness from the top of the 45-degree portion to the top of the head) should be maintained as wide as possible. Also, see sidebar "Head Performance Tips" on page 34, for more information on racing and high-performance cylinder head selection and preparation.

To help you perform the pre-assembly fitting inspection in Chapter 7, ask your machine shop to deliver your heads to you in the following condition:

- unassembled (if you have a valvespring compressor)
- without the valvestem seals pressed on the guides (they're often damaged when removing the valves during inspection)
- no lubricant in the valveguides (makes final cleaning much easier)

If your machine shop has set up the springs for you, make sure the valves, springs, retainers, and any spring shims are numbered and kept together.

Piston Machine Work

The machine shop will disassemble your rods and pistons by pressing out the old pins with a hydraulic press (providing your rods use press-fit pins). After the rods are reconditioned, the pistons and rods can be reassembled.

Machine shops use two methods to install press-fit pins: 1) heating the pin bore of the connecting rod hot enough to allow the new pins to simply slide into the rod; or 2) pressing in the new pins with a hydraulic press. While heating the small end of the connecting rods in a furnace may sound as if it might damage the rod, in fact, if it's done properly, neither the rod nor piston are harmed. On the other hand, if a hydraulic press is used for assembly, the tremendous force required to push the pin through the connecting rod (about 8 tons) often scratches or galls the pin, and that scratches the pin bores in the piston. The result is a frozen or tight pin. But that's not all. The full load of the press is carried by one side of the piston, and that can distort the piston or further damage the pin bore.

The message is clear: Done with the right equipment by experienced personnel, installing press-fit pins by heating the rods is the better choice. If your machine shop uses the cold-press method, take your rods and pistons somewhere else.

If you'll be installing used pistons, have them cleaned (usually in an aluminum cleaning bath) and checked for cracks. If they pass professional crack detection and the inspections performed in Chapter 3, Step 7 on page 54, plus a thorough once-over by your machine shop, they should be serviceable.

Most pistons do not require additional machine work, except balancing. Exceptions to this rule can be found in high-performance or racing engines where deeper valve notches, dome contouring, special ring grooves, piston lightening, or other machine work is often performed. If you'll be using a high-lift camshaft (over .500-inch lift), high-compression ratios, a long-stroke crankshaft, or special connecting rods or cylinder heads, you should not have the assembly balanced until you complete all the pre-assembly checks in Chapter 7. If balancing is done before these checks are completed and your pistons or other rotating components need additional machine work, the assembly may have to be balanced again. For more information on racing and high-performance piston selection and preparation, see sidebar "Piston Performance Tips" on page 39.

Piston Rings

Piston rings are one of the most critical components of your engine. When they seal properly, they will provide good performance, reliability, and economy. If they fail to seal, your engine will have excess blow-by, poor performance, use too much gas, and generate excessive emissions. Proper block machining (as mentioned earlier) and final assembly are very important elements in obtaining

Press-fit pins should never be assembled with a hydraulic press. The force required often scratches or galls the pin, resulting in a damaged piston.

Heating the small end of the connecting rod expands the pin bore and allows the pins to slide in easily. A pin-stop tool ensures the correct pin/rod relationship. Done right, this procedure won't harm the rod or the piston.

optimum ring seal. So is having the correct end gap. Rings that have too little gap can "go solid" when hot, damaging the rings and bore surfaces. A lesser evil is too much end gap. This allows a small portion of engine performance and economy to slip away into the oil pan as wasted gas pressure.

Piston ring sets are available in two basic types:

- Oversize or ungapped sets (+.005 inch, +.025 inch, +.035 inch, etc.) that must have the ends cut to obtain proper ring gap.
- Factory-gapped sets (standard, +.020 inch, +.030 inch, etc.) that have the "proper" end gap already in place. Common factory-gapped rings have the advantage of not needing the time-consuming and precision work required to obtain optimum end gaps. However, in order to be safely installed in a wide variety of engines, the end gaps on these rings are machined on the loose side. In contrast, oversize sets must be hand-gapped, but in doing so, it's possible to set the end gap to a minimum value that will optimize both reliability and performance.

If you purchased factory-gapped rings, they should require no additional work by your machine shop (other than making sure that the end gap is correct; see Chapter 7). If you opted for ungapped rings, you must either gap the rings yourself, or have your machine shop do it for you. If you have never gapped rings, we strongly urge that you have your machine shop do it. Here's why. Many shops own a precision tool such as the ABS gapper (see Sidebar "Setting Ring End Gap" on page 108), which quickly cuts a precision gap. Using this tool, a machine shop can do an extremely accurate job and charge a reasonable fee. If you use a file or hand-operated cutter, it can take hours to do the same job, and the result almost certainly won't be as accurate. Plus, you just may wind up buying an extra ring or two to replace the ones you've cut too wide.

Unless you have the experience and the proper equipment, take your block and rings to a machine shop that owns an ABS gapping tool and get the job done right.

Rod Machine Work

Connecting rods and the bolts holding the caps in place are probably the most highly stressed elements in your engine. If the rods pass Magnaflux inspection, you should consider having new bolts installed (such as ARP high-strength fasteners) and the big end of the rods should be resized. For improved stress resistance, consider having the beams of the rods ground smooth and the surfaces shot-peened. In many cases, it may be cheaper, or just a couple bucks more, to start with a new set of rods.

If your engine will be capable of producing more than 350 hp, you should also consider obtaining heavy-duty connecting rods. GMPP's "pink" rod is a stout piece that is widely used. Also, consider Crower's Sportsman rod. It doesn't require any clearance grinding, is made from 4340 material, and uses aircraft-quality bolts. Crower's machine work is top-notch, and the weight of both the big and small ends are so uniform that your machine shop may even give you a discount on balancing.

For all-out racing, there is a long list of modifications and specialty rods to choose from, including those from Carrillo, Competition Cams, Crower, Eagle, GMPP, and others. (For more information on high-performance rod selection and preparation, see sidebar "Rod Performance Tips" on page 40.)

Finally, many engine builders are curious about whether or not they should have their rods bushed to install full-floating pins. This modification is costly and will almost certainly produce no measurable increase in power. However,

Racing pistons are often subjected to a variety of special (and expensive) machine work, including dome contouring, special ring grooves, deeper valve reliefs, and lightening. However, most street and high-performance pistons require no additional machine work. The Speed Pro Hypereutectic pistons used in our engine buildup were installed virtually "right out of the box." The piston weights were so close that we even received a discounted price for the balancing.

Piston ring end gap is one of the most critical "clearances" in your engine. Unless you have the experience and proper tools, such as this terrific machine from Goodson, you may want to let your machine shop do the job for you. This tool does the job very quickly and accurately.

there is an advantage. The rods and pistons are much easier to assemble and disassemble since a hydraulic press and pin furnace isn't required. This is particularly helpful in a racing engine that is undergoing constant maintenance. The main disadvantage to floating pins (other than cost) is that the lock rings used to hold the piston pin in place occasionally work themselves out, which can cause severe cylinder bore wall damage. The bottom line is: Unless you're building a competitive race engine, stick with press-fit pins; they're reliable and less expensive, and they won't cost you any horsepower.

Crankshaft Machine Work

Your crankshaft may show such little wear that, providing it passed your inspection in Chapter 3, Steps 4 and 5 (on pages 52 and 53), and it passes Magnaflux inspection at your machine shop, it can be micro-polished and put directly back into service. Just as often, however, the journals must be reground to .010, .020, or .030 inch undersize. At the same time, the crank grinder usually corrects straightness, stroke, and indexing (so each journal has exactly the same stroke length, spaced 90 degrees apart), thoroughly cleans the crank, chamfers the oil holes, and micro-polishes the journals. For all intents and purposes, a crankshaft that has been through this reconditioning process can be considered in "new" condition.

If a crank is already .030 inch undersize, it's often believed to be "used up." In the past, bearing manufacturers added a thicker-surface Babbitt layer to the undersize bearings. The greater the undersize, the thicker the Babbitt. When the oversize was greater than about .030 inch, the Babbitt began to flake off under heavy loads. That has changed. New brand-name bearings (including Speed Pro, TRW, Clevite, etc.) have a uniformly thin Babbitt layer, using a thicker steel underlayer to allow for undersize journals up to .040 inch and even .060 inch. This design doesn't weaken the bearing. (Note: Some bearing manufacturers still use a thicker Babbitt layer on .060-inch oversize bearings; consult with the manufacturer before using this oversize). So, despite the long-held belief that .040-inch-undersize journals should never be used, they're acceptable with the new bearing designs. These options can save you a lot of money, especially if you own a good forged-steel crank that's already .030-inch undersize.

If you'll be using a manual transmission, ask your machine shop to remove the old pilot bushing from the flywheel end of the crankshaft (if you haven't already). If the nose of the crankshaft isn't tapped for a 7/16 NF bolt, make sure they do it for you.

There is a wide variety of special crankshaft machining and modification procedures that are performed for racing and heavy-duty use, including hard-chroming, Tuftriding, increasing fillet radius, cross-drilling the mains, and much more. If you're building a racing engine, discuss these possibilities with your machine shop. For more information on high-performance crank selection and preparation, see sidebar "Crank Performance Tips" on page 43.

Engine Balancing

As mentioned earlier, engine balancing is a procedure that you might want to postpone, at least until you have completed the pre-assembly fitting detailed in Chapter 7. If balancing is done before these checks are completed, and your

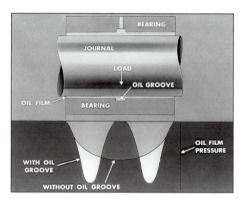

Many engine builders believe that reliability can be improved if ungrooved bearing shells are installed in the main caps (most modern main bearing sets include grooved bearings for the block and ungrooved shells for the caps). The results of oil-film-pressure research done by General Motors many years ago support this practice. When grooved shells are used, oil-film pressure is twice as high, greatly increasing the chance for metal-to-metal contact.

Connecting rods and the bolts and nuts holding the caps in place are probably the most highly stressed elements in your engine. Have new bolts installed (such as ARP high-strength fasteners) and the big end resized. For improved stress resistance, you can have the beams of the rods ground and shot peened.

THE MACHINE SHOP

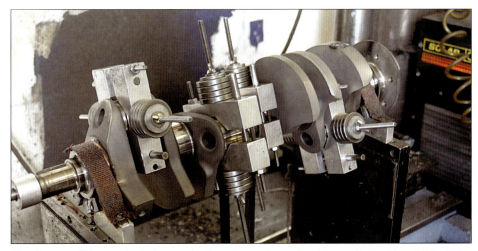

Crank reconditioning includes regrinding the main and rod journals to .010, .020, .030, or even .040 or .060 inch undersize. At the same time, the crank grinder often corrects straightness, stroke, index, thoroughly cleans the crank, chamfers the oil holes, and micro polishes the journals (right). For all intents and purposes, a crankshaft that has been through this reconditioning process can be considered "new." Balancing the crank after all the reconditioning is always a good idea.

pistons or other rotating components need additional machine work, the assembly may have to be balanced a second time.

The proper time for balancing is when all machine work is complete and everything fits properly. The balancing process involves grinding or machining the rods and pistons to a uniform weight, then balancing the crankshaft to the calculated rotating assembly weight (called "bob weight"). While there are several steps to this process, some of which are intricate and specialized, there are only a few facts you need to know about balancing to discuss it intelligently with your machinist.

The first important consideration is that internally balanced crankshafts should be balanced without the flywheel/flexplate or vibration damper attached. On an internally balanced crank, these external components have a "neutral" balance (have no out-of-balance weight). Maintaining this independent balance offers the advantage in interchangeability; a replacement flywheel or vibration damper can be directly installed without rebalancing the engine.

Many small-blocks, such as the 400, are externally balanced. It cost General Motors less money to manufacture a crankshaft with lighter counterweight. To "correct" for a light, out-of-balance crank, "weighted" vibration dampers and flywheels/flexplates are used. This transfers needed balance weight from the expensive crankshaft counterweights to the less-expensive external accessories. It all works just fine, but it makes balancing a bit more tricky. All externally balanced

You may want to postpone final balancing until you have completed the pre-assembly fitting (Chapter 7). If any components require additional machine work after balancing, you may have to pay for balancing a second time. Note how the rod on the right had a lot of grinding while the left rod did not.

cranks must be balanced with the vibration damper and flywheel/flexplate attached. Once they're balanced together, replacement parts cannot be installed without rebalancing the new components to the same "out-of-balance weight" as the old components (called transfer balancing).

Some engine builders have their externally balanced crankshafts converted to internal balance. In order to accomplish this, additional metal must be added to the counterweights, often in the form of "heavy" or "Mallory" metal. This is an expensive process, but it allows accessory interchangeability, which is a real asset on a racing engine.

In order to balance your engine, your machine shop must have the crank, rods, rod bearings, pistons, pins, pin locks (if used), and piston rings (so they can weigh and/or balance them). For externally balanced engines, they must also have the vibration damper, flywheel/flexplate, and clutch cover. While they don't need the external accessories for an internally balanced crankshaft, as I mentioned earlier, your engine will run as smoothly as possible if you have them independently "neutral" balanced.

Manifold Machine Work

Your intake manifold should fit tightly against the intake gaskets that seal the ports, and there should be sufficient clearance between the manifold and the valve rails on the block for the rubber gaskets or beads of silicone sealer to do their jobs. These two areas of fit are determined, more or less, by the angles milled on the intake surfaces of the heads and intake manifold. If the manifold is mismachined (more common than you might think) the intake runners might not seal. If the heads or block deck surfaces have been milled more than a minimum amount, the manifold's bolt holes

The intake manifold should fit tightly against the intake gaskets and there should be sufficient clearance between the manifold and the valley rails. By installing the heads with a couple of bolts and attaching the intake manifold to only one head, the alignment can be visually inspected. These, and other critical dimensions, are verified in Chapter 7, "Pre-Assembly Fitting."

may not align properly. Procedures to check the manifold fit are included in Chapter 7, "Pre-Assembly Fitting."

If, upon inspection, you find that the manifold-to-head contact surfaces are misaligned or other surfaces are mismatched, your machine shop can re-machine the manifold to fit your application. The best way to accomplish this is to return the block, heads, and manifold, and let them measure and calculate the required amounts of material to be removed (or at least verify your calculations).

Other Machine Shop Services

Well-equipped machine shops offer a wide range of additional services. Some of these "unusual" machine operations are used to repair rare or unique engines, others are "race-only" modifications, and some are part of normal shop practice. Here is a quick look at some of these procedures:

Install Cylinder Sleeves. This relatively costly process is used to repair one (usually) cylinder bore that has been damaged. The block is bored large enough so that a press-fit cylinder liner can be installed. In many cases, the existing bore is machined away entirely, exposing the liner to engine coolant. This repair process tends to weaken the block, since the deck surface is no longer securely supported by the bore wall.

O-Ring the Deck or Heads. It improves gasket seal on high-compression engines. A small groove is cut just outside of each cylinder bore. Copper or steel wire is inserted in the groove and allowed to protrude a specific distance above the surfaces. This raised ring around each cylinder applies additional sealing force to the gasket and is often the only way to prevent leakage with 12:1 or higher compression ratios, or on engines running higher boost pressures from turbochargers or superchargers.

If a groove wears in the hub on the vibration damper, either replace the damper or use a reconditioning sleeve. If you want to install the sleeve yourself, make sure the hub is completely clean. Coat the hub and sleeve with Red Loctite (usually provided). Install the sleeve using a press or a piece of wood to support the sleeve and drive it on with a hammer.

Check Rod/Piston Alignment. This is standard practice in most machine shops, and it's normally performed after the rods and pistons are assembled. The rod/piston assembly is installed on a fixture that verifies rod straightness and machining accuracy.

Special Piston Machining. Includes: machining domes to lower compression; cutting valve pockets to increase piston-to-valve clearance; drilling pistons for improved pin oiling; machining pin bores for special locks or short pins; machining the ring grooves for wider or unique piston rings. Most of these machine operations cost about $80 to $100 per set of eight pistons.

Angle-Mill Cylinder Heads. This is a specialized machining operation used primarily on racing engines. The idea is to reduce chamber volume and improve breathing, but when the angle of the head surface is altered, the intake surface must be machined to match. In addition, the cylinder bolt holes may need to be enlarged and/or spot-faced so the head bolts seat properly when tightened.

If the manifold-to-head contact surfaces are misaligned (not that uncommon), your machine shop can re-machine the manifold to fit your application. Return the block, heads, and manifold to them and let them measure and calculate the required amounts of material to be removed.

The thrust face on the block can be damaged when high valve-seat pressures or roller cams are used. Your machine shop can modify the block to accept a Torrington roller bearing (this one is available from Comp Cams), salvaging the block and virtually eliminating future wear.

Install Screw-In Studs. This should be done when valveseat pressure will exceed about 110 pounds. While you may want to do the installation yourself, unless you have the proper tools to ensure that the studs end up dead straight, rocker geometry and valvetrain life could be affected.

Install Exhaust Seats. As mentioned earlier, this machining process cuts out the existing seat and a cast-iron, nickel-cobalt, or hard-steel seat is pressed into its place. This modification is routine in most machine shops today, since unleaded gas (particularly if it's "oxygenated") has poor seat-lubricating properties, which reduces exhaust seat life on street-driven engines that lack hardened seats.

Install Helicoils. If a threaded hole becomes damaged, weakened, or stripped out, installing a Helicoil can return full bolt-holding strength. The process is simple: The old threads are drilled out, the hole is tapped with a special Helicoil tap, and the Helicoil insert is installed. Virtually any threaded hole can be Helicoil repaired, including spark plug holes.

Machine Cam Thrust Face. The thrust face on the block that contacts the upper cam sprocket is often damaged when high valveseat pressures or roller cams are used. The thrust face can be machined to accept a Torrington roller bearing (available from most camshaft manufacturers), salvaging the block and virtually eliminating future wear.

Sleeve Lifter Bore. Occasionally a lifter bore may wear or a block may come from the factory with an oversize bore. The block can be machined for a special sleeve to return the bore to standard size. Consider this procedure carefully, since the cost to repair a single lifter bore may exceed the cost of a used block.

Sonic Testing. Cylinder bore thickness can vary from bore to bore and from block to block. A thicker, more uniform bore can better withstand high cylinder pressures without distortion. This usually results in more horsepower. Sonic testing can reveal wall thickness without damaging the block. This procedure is usually performed on a group of blocks in an effort to select the best one, or on a single block to verify that it doesn't suffer from severe core-shift and/or thin cylinder walls.

Repair Vibration Damper Seal Surface. A groove sometimes wears in the sealing surface on the vibration damper. Either replace the damper or your machine shop can install a reconditioned sleeve, providing the damper is in otherwise good condition. In many cases you can find these sleeve kits at most parts stores and it is something you should easily be able to install.

Picking Up Your Parts

When you return to the machine shop to pick up your machined parts (and pay for them), you'll never have a more attentive audience or a better opportunity to benefit from the machinist's experience. Take as much time as they'll give you. Ask them how the work turned out. Carefully listen to what you're being told. Find out if they ran into any problems. Ask questions based on the information in this chapter. Don't be afraid to take notes.

Before you walk out the door with an armful of parts, carefully examine everything. Were all of the machine operations that you're paying for completed? Are all the parts really yours? Remember, the parts you dropped off should have had your identifying marks on them. And don't leave anything behind; compare your Work-A-Long Sheet, or the itemized list that the machine shop gave you when you delivered your job, with the items you're picking up.

Ask the machinists if they can offer any specific assembly advice based on the components you selected for your engine. Machine shop personnel see just about every mistake that can be made. Ask them to tell you what you should watch out for during cleaning, pre-assembly fitting, and final assembly.

Think about whether you need to buy any other items or accessories while you're there. Some machine shops offer parts, gaskets, assembly lube, gasket and bolt sealant, and other supplies at reasonable prices.

Finally, when everyone begins nervously gesturing at you and pointing toward the door, it's probably time to pick up your stuff, thank everyone for their advice, and go. Although putting your parts in your vehicle and driving home sounds just about as simple as life gets, some enthusiasts forget that heavy parts tend to roll around in a moving car or truck. Bring several small boxes, a couple of blankets for padding, and some rope to tie things down. Treat your parts like precision and delicate components—because they are!

Things To Do After You Pick Up Your Parts

The following step-by-step instructions guide you through parts preparation procedures that may not have been done by your machine shop. These steps should be performed before you begin component cleaning, as described in Chapter 6. Many machine shops include some or all of the following steps as part of their regular "shop practice."

Post-Machine-Shop Procedures

1 Prep Threaded Holes

If you haven't already, clean all threaded holes in the block, crank, heads, and other engine components. You can use bottoming taps or, even better, thread chasers such as these from Snap-on (part RTD42); they clean without cutting material from the threads and reducing holding strength. Also, lightly chamfer all threaded holes using a chamfering cutter in a drill motor.

THE MACHINE SHOP

2 Install Head-Locating Dowels

 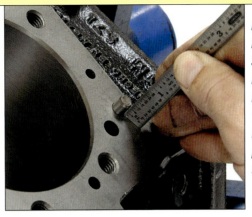

If the head-locating dowels are installed in your block, jump to Step 3. The correct dowel size is 5/16-inch diameter by 1/2-inch length. Drive each pin into the block with a 1/4-inch or larger punch and/or a brass hammer. The dowels should protrude 1/4 inch above the deck surfaces.

3 Drill Steam Holes When Using Non-400 Heads

If you will be installing non-400-ci heads on a 400-ci block, make sure that the six required steam holes are drilled in each head. If these holes are not drilled, hot spots will occur that can cause overheating, cracks, and blown head gaskets. (Note: If you are installing 400-ci heads—with the steam holes—on a non-400-ci block, do not drill steam holes in the block; they are not needed.) To drill these holes, use a 400-ci head gasket as a template. Make sure the gasket is properly aligned, and then transfer the steam hole locations to the heads with a center punch. Drill the three holes closest to the spark plugs with a 3/16-inch drill, perpendicular to the head surface. Then drill the remaining three holes (closest to the intake ports) with a 5/32-inch drill, angled at about 30 degrees away from the head bolt holes as shown. Be careful, as the drill breaks into the water jackets; it can easily "catch" on the non-uniform edges. Finish the job by lightly chamfering the holes.

4 Check Cam Bearing Oil Hole Alignment

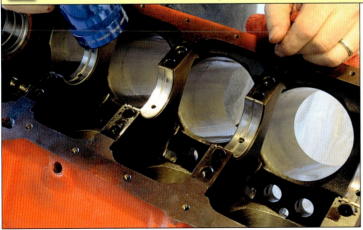

If the cam bearings are not installed, jump to Step 5. While it is not essential that the oil holes in the cam bearings line up with the main feed passages (except on the rear bearing of 1955 and 1956 small-blocks; see sidebar "Removing and Installing Cam Bearings" on page 46), some engine builders believe that there are benefits. One theory purports that due to the downward camshaft load, overall oil flow will be reduced because of reduced clearance at the feedholes. To check hole alignment, remove the main caps and inspect the feed passages. If you are able to see light through the passages, the bearing holes are lined up.

5 Front Oil Gallery Plugs

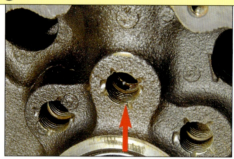

The stock cup-type plugs in the front of the main oil galleries have been known (on rare occasions) to pop out. This usually happens when starting a cold racing engine that uses heavyweight oil and a high-volume pump. Many engine builders recommend tapping the three front galleries for 1/4-inch pipe plugs. Run the tap in the galleries until only about four threads on the tap are visible. This depth will allow the plugs to screw into the galleries until they reach the "step," about 1/2 inch down the passage. Then they'll tighten up. Make sure that the center plug does not screw in far enough to restrict the connecting passage that feeds the front cam and main bearings (arrow). If it does, drill and tap the gallery for a larger 3/8-inch pipe plug. Run the tap in just far enough to allow the plug to tighten flush with the front of the passage. IMPORTANT: If you plan on using the factory cup-type plugs (and your gallery passages were not tapped), make sure you lightly deburr the ends of the galleries using a tapered reamer or a small file. This prevents gouging the plugs when they are installed during final assembly.

Performance Tip

6 Drill Cam-Thrust Lubrication Hole

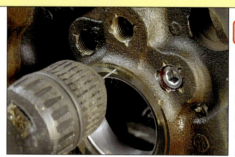

Many small-block experts drill a small hole in one oil gallery plug. Oil squirting from this hole lubricates the timing chain and upper-sprocket thrust face. If you're using a racing cam with high seat pressure (over 120 pounds), drilling an oil feed hole directly into the thrust face may be more effective. If you decide to perform these modifications (or have your machine shop do them), we don't recommend both at once, except on racing engines. Drill a .030-inch hole (a number 68 or number 69 drill) in ONE of the three oil gallery plugs (if the center gallery uses a large 3/8-inch pipe plug, drill this larger plug), and/or directly into the sprocket thrust face so that it intersects the oil feed passage. A hole this small is not easy to drill; you'll need a pin vise mounted in a drill motor, WD-40 or light oil, and plenty of patience. If you drill a gallery plug, mark it with machinist's dye so that it isn't mixed up with other plugs. If you drill the thrust face, make sure you pay extra attention to cleaning the oil passages (see Chapter 6, "Component Cleaning"), especially if the cam bearings are installed.

7 Deburr Crank Keyway/Install Keys

If your machine shop did not install the keys in your crank, use a small file to remove any burrs on the edges of the keyways. Slightly chamfer the rounded edge of the keys, and drive both keys into their slots with a 1/4-inch or larger punch. The keys must fit snugly in the crankshaft; if they go in without much effort, the crank should either be repaired or replaced. Remove any raised edges that may have been produced when the keys were installed. Finally, if your engine will be used with a manual transmission, the crank must either be fitted with a new pilot bushing, or be machined to accept one (either originally by the factory or by your machine shop).

CHAPTER 6

COMPONENT CLEANING

The interior of a running engine is an extraordinary place of dynamic motion. Hot, pressurized lubricant is forced through spaces only a few thousandths of an inch wide. These miniscule clearances separate soft metal bearings from spinning journals. Additional lubricant films prevent metal-to-metal contact between piston rings and cylinder walls, sliding over each other at unimaginably high speeds. Amazingly, all of this continues for years with little perceptible wear. But toss in just a teaspoon of "stuff" and, literally within minutes, bearings will be severely damaged, cam lobes will be on their way to destruction, and exhaust gases will begin leaking by marred ring surfaces. What's more, your engine block may have enough of this mystery material hidden away in recesses and corners right now to guarantee its destruction.

What is this powerful stuff? The compound is simple debris from machine operations, rust from the water jackets, dust, dirt, and other miscellaneous crud.

It should now be clear that the success of your rebuild depends on the cleanliness of the block and all other engine components before assembly. If you become impatient and don't spend enough time with the important matters in this chapter, you could easily cut engine life in half, or worse.

This assortment of brushes is ideal for cleaning blocks, heads, and crankshafts. Several companies offer cleaning kits that include most of the brushes required. Goodson offers a variety of brushes that can be ordered individually to suit specific cleaning requirements.

Tools and Supplies

The cleaning process illustrated in the following step-by-step instructions requires a few simple supplies, including solvent, a source of water, laundry soap, soft rags, and paper towels. In addition, a few specialized tools and supplies are needed to horoughly clean engine components:

Engine-Cleaning Brush Kit

Oil passages and small-diameter holes drilled in the block, crank, and heads often become hiding places for dirt and metal particles. An engine-cleaning brush kit, including long-stem brushes to reach deep into oil galleries, stiff-bristle brushes to work dirt out of cast-iron surfaces, and a large-diameter brush to clean cylinder bores should all be at hand during the cleaning process. Brush kits are available from Eastwood, Goodson, and other shop tool sources.

Carburetor Cleaner

You may also need a can of carburetor cleaner dip to remove crud from bolts and other small components. As an alternative, you can let your machine shop clean these pieces. But, even if you've taken the time to keep them organized in individual plastic bags, the machine shop will probably dump them all into one pile. Purchasing your own parts cleaner is a good idea and is something that will always come in handy.

Compressed Air

While you can clean the engine block and other components without compressed air, we really don't recommend it. After the block is thoroughly washed, it will begin to rust immediately, and the faster you can remove all traces of water and apply a rust inhibitor the better. This is where compressed air really pays off. Furthermore, it's almost impossible to get all the water out of bolt holes or oil galleries without compressed air, and rust will surely form in these passages if you don't act fast. If you don't own an air compressor, consider borrowing or renting one at least during the cleaning phase of your rebuilding project.

Pressure/Siphon Sprayer

This is another item that can help dislodge dirt and speed the cleaning process. These pistol-grip tools combine water pressure (from a hose pipe) with compressed air to really blast dirt from hidden corners of the block. Some incorporate a siphon feed that can draw liquid soap or solvent into the blast stream. Eastwood sells the pressure sprayer illustrated in the upcoming step-by-step instructions.

Sufficient Outdoor Space

Along with an engine stand, enough outdoor space to do the job properly is an absolutely essential requirement. A large, wetted-down concrete driveway is an ideal place, since it won't have dust and easily can be washed off when you're finished. In addition, the hard concrete surface makes rolling your engine stand around a lot easier.

Carburetor cleaner dip does a good job of removing crud from bolts and other small components. When parts are removed from carburetor cleaner, soak them in a bucket of hot water to dilute the potent chemicals in the cleaner. After a thorough soak, blow them dry with compressed air. Remember, always wear hand and eye protection (and a long-sleeved shirt) when using immersion cleaners.

Important Considerations

Most reputable machine shops do an excellent job of cleaning cylinder blocks, heads, and crankshafts after all the machine operations are completed. This "pre-cleaning" removes most contamination and makes the upcoming cleaning procedure easier and more effective. However, if your block hasn't been jet-sprayed, baked, or hot-tanked (and it doesn't need it), you may find it helpful to start the cleaning process at your local car wash. Blast off most dirt and grease, and thoroughly flush the water jackets. Then spray the block with ATF or WD-40 to prevent rust from forming while you transport it back to your house or shop. Finally, finish the cleaning process by performing the step-by-step cleaning instructions beginning on page 88.

It's always a good practice to pre-assemble your engine to ensure that all clearances are correct before you attempt final assembly (see Chapter 7, "Pre-Assembly Fitting"). If you're preparing the engine for pre-assembly rather than final assembly, a slightly less-thorough cleaning job is acceptable. However, virtually all of the same steps must be performed, because if any foreign matter comes in contact with bearings, pistons, lifters, the camshaft, or other engine components, they can be seriously damaged. The upcoming instructions have tips about procedures that can be abbreviated for pre-assembly cleaning only.

As mentioned earlier, block surfaces, internal passages, and (especially) cylinder bores will begin to rust as soon as you stop flushing the block with rinse water

Don't clean your engine and immediately begin assembly! Make sure you read Chapter 7, "Pre-Assembly"; it shows you how to perform important checks of internal clearances and component fit required before final assembly.

COMPONENT CLEANING

or even if the block is allowed to dry out during the washing procedure. Remember, the cleaner the block, the faster it will rust. Here are some ways to minimize this problem:

- Mix a very concentrated soap solution (about 1 cup of powdered soap per gallon of water). Thick solutions leave a heavy film on surfaces that tend to slow down rusting.
- Although hot, soapy cleaning solutions are most effective, the high temperature promotes rapid evaporation and rust. Use warm wash water instead and, after washing, thoroughly rinse the block with cold water before drying.
- If you have a siphon-sprayer, blast the block with solvent immediately after the final water rinse. Solvent is an oil-based material that has slight anti-rust properties.
- Have a friend immediately begin coating block surfaces (especially the cylinder bores) with oil and/or rust inhibitor as you blow it dry with compressed air.

Precautions

Although component cleaning is relatively straightforward, many home engine builders have fallen into some pitfalls that you can avoid. First, don't let solvent spill onto an asphalt driveway. It can soften and damage the surface. Use a drip pan under your engine stand to catch as much spillage as possible and dispose of it in an environmentally acceptable way (a good idea regardless of your driveway surface). Second, don't use toxic, powerful, or highly flammable solvents (especially gasoline). Do yourself a favor and stick with a standard, safe, parts-cleaning solvent. Finally, wear goggles (and wearing gloves to protect your hands isn't a bad idea either) during all of the cleaning steps. Soap and solvent will splash into your face, that's a given. Don't take chances; wear eye protection.

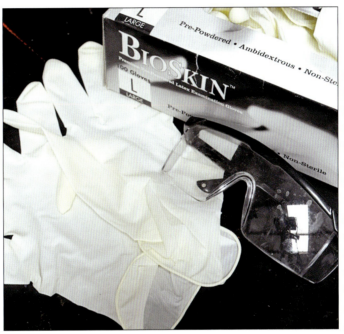

In addition to eye protection, gloves will protect your skin from the drying effects of solvent and strong soap solutions. These skin-tight latex gloves (available at most paint and hardware stores) are so thin that you can handle small parts with ease. Obviously, you'll need an alternative if you are allergic to latex.

 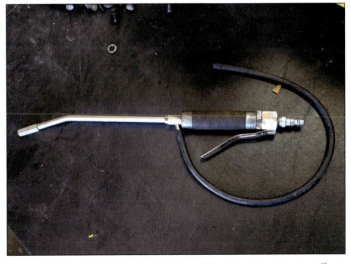

A pressure/siphon washer can speed up the cleaning process. Eastwood offers a pistol-grip tool that combines water pressure (from a hose pipe) with compressed air to really blast dirt from hidden corners of the block. It also has a siphon feed that can draw liquid soap or solvent into the blast stream.

REBUILDING THE SMALL-BLOCK CHEVROLET

CHAPTER 6

Blast Cabinet

Along with a parts washer, a blast cabinet will be one of your favorite tools in your shop. What may take hours of cleaning and grinding with wire brushes can be reduced to minutes, and without the mess, when you use a blast cabinet. Eastwood is one company that offers several blast cabinets in many shapes and sizes.

When choosing a cabinet, consider what size the parts are that you plan to blast. If you're planning to do wheels later, get a larger one. Also think about your shop layout, as a side-door cabinet may not work where you plan to install the blaster. Compressor volume will come into play, and most cabinets require 7 cfm at 80 psi.

These days there are also a variety of blasting mediums to use that range from glass beads to aluminum oxide or even aluminum pellets. These forms can be seen as aggressive and cause heat to add up in the parts, which in the case of body panels, is not welcome. Walnut shells and the now-common "soda" blasting are popular and do a good job.

Our blast cabinet was great when it came to cleaning items such as valve covers, the timing chain cover and other parts on our engine rebuild.

Component Cleaning Procedures

Before you begin cleaning, make sure all machine work and other preparations are completed. Furthermore, you should have purchased everything you need (including any special tools) to complete engine pre-assembly or final assembly soon after cleaning. Don't let cleaned parts sit around; they'll probably get dirty and start rusting.

Here are the cleaning supplies you should have at hand: 3 to 5 gallons of solvent, a source of water (preferably cold and hot), soap powder, a 5-gallon bucket, clean white rags, paper towels, compressed air, an engine brush kit, rust inhibitor (such as WD-40), plastic bags, and a quart of light oil or automatic transmission fluid (ATF).

88 REBUILDING THE SMALL-BLOCK CHEVROLET

COMPONENT CLEANING

1 Use Air and Solvent

If you haven't already washed the engine, the easiest way to do it is to mount it in the engine stand. Start the cleaning process by using compressed air to blow away any loose material, such as metal shavings or grinding debris. Concentrate air blasts in corners, bolt holes, oil passages, water jackets, and other block recesses. Next, begin washing the block with solvent and stiff-bristle nylon and wire brushes. A siphon-spray gun, such as this one from Eastwood, gets the block wet in a hurry and helps blast away dirt. As the solvent evaporates, rinse the surfaces with fresh solvent and continue scrubbing. If you're using a pressure sprayer, blast solvent into the water jackets.

2 Clean Hidden Spots

Dirt and other contaminants always seem to work their way into the difficult-to-get-at spots. Focus your efforts under the pan rails, in the cam gallery area, under the main saddles, and in the internal oil passages. Use the long stem brushes in your engine-cleaning kit to scrub the main oil galleries. If you have an air-powered drill, spinning the brushes helps remove debris (don't use an electric drill—unless it's cordless—there's a high electric-shock hazard). Work smaller brushes into main oil feeds and front and rear oil-pressure-sender passages. Use large brushes in lifter bores and oil drain-back holes. If the cam bearings aren't installed, scrub the annular oil passages machined in the block bores.

Draw the brushes in and out of the passages several times. Then remove the brush, clean the bristles in fresh solvent, blast solvent and/or air down the passage, and then work the brush into the passage again. Continue this process until the solvent on the brush head comes out clean (test it with a white rag). Use the various brushes in your cleaning kit and thoroughly scrub all passages, water jacket feeds, and bolt holes. Be careful when you blow out blind holes as solvent can spray back into your face.

REBUILDING THE SMALL-BLOCK CHEVROLET

CHAPTER 6

3 Clean Cylinder Bores

Now, turn your attention to the cylinder bores. Freshly machined bores contain metal particles, stone, and stone-binder embedded in the walls. You must remove as much of this debris as you can; the life of your engine depends on it! Start by wiping the bores with a solvent-soaked rag. Then scrub the walls with soft-bristle brushes and lots of clean solvent. Work the brushes back and forth, following the crosshatch pattern. Then vary your brush technique, and finally, scrub the bores with rags. Periodically wipe the bore with a clean, white rag and when very little dirt appears, spray the cylinder with a rust inhibitor and move on to the next bore.

4 Use Soap and Water

After solvent washing, prepare about 4 gallons of warm, concentrated soap solution (mix about 1 cup of soap per gallon of water). We suggest using warm (not hot) soapy water to minimize rusting. Liberally apply the soap solution using brushes, a large sponge, or if you have a siphon-sprayer, blast the block, oil passages, and water jackets. Rotate the block several times during cleaning to help loosen slag and dirt from the water jackets and other passages. As you scrub the block in the upcoming steps, make sure you keep it wet. If you let it dry out, it will begin to rust.

5 Scrub and Brush Surfaces

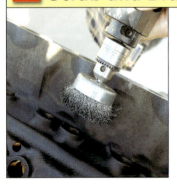 

As you did during the previous solvent cleaning, scrub all surfaces with stiff-bristle brushes, concentrating on hard-to-get-at spots that collect dirt. Don't wash the cylinder bores yet; keep them coated with rust inhibitor until the rest of the block has been thoroughly washed. Scrub all oil passages, lifter bores, and bolt holes with brushes. Continue washing and applying the soap solution until all dirt and debris has been washed away.

Important!

6 Inspect With Your Fingers

It's time to check your work. Start by blasting off the soap solution with water from your hose or pressure sprayer. After all detectable soap residue has been removed, spray external surfaces, especially the cylinder bores, with rust inhibitor (WD-40). When the block is "rust stable," you can begin inspection. Make sure your hands are completely clean, and then run your fingers over block surfaces in the valley area. If you can't feel or see any dirt or debris between your fingertips, move on to the corners of the valley, under the pan rails, and poke into every nook and cranny you can reach. If you find just one single particle of dirt, go back to Step 4 and repeat the cleaning process.

REBUILDING THE SMALL-BLOCK CHEVROLET

COMPONENT CLEANING

7 Clean For Pre-Assembly Fitting

If you're cleaning the engine for final assembly, skip to Step 8. If you're cleaning for pre-assembly fitting and the block has passed the previous test, you can: 1) blow off excess moisture or rust inhibitor with compressed air, 2) wipe the bores thoroughly with clean, oiled rags, 3) spray one final coat of rust inhibitor on other surfaces, and 4) place a plastic bag over the block, but don't seal the bag for at least 12 hours because moisture will continue to evaporate from internal and external surfaces for some time. Now skip to Step 15.

8 Scrub Cylinder Bores

Now that the interior block surfaces are clean, turn your attention once again to the cylinder bores. Warning: As you scrub the bores with soap and water in this step and rinse them in the next, do not let them dry out—they will begin to rust immediately! Scrub the first bore with brushes and rags using the warm soapy solution. Work on one bore at a time, and when you believe it is thoroughly clean, quickly wash it with water then spray it with rust inhibitor and move on to the next bore.

9 Final Rinse

Flush the block with lots of cold rinse water from a garden hose or pressure sprayer. Make sure you thoroughly flush the water jackets, oil passages, and all internal surfaces. Then use compressed air to blow off most of the water, but don't dry the block completely. While it's still a bit wet, spray it with rust inhibitor. Then, blow off all the remaining water, starting with bolt holes and water jackets and working out to oil passages and external surfaces. Periodically rotate the block and apply more rust inhibitor, especially to the cylinder bores and other freshly machined surfaces, including the lifter bores, and internal passages. Finally, wipe the cylinders with a clean rag saturated with ATF or engine oil.

10 Second Inspection

After the block is free of water, perform another finger inspection. If you find the slightest remaining dirt, grit, or other debris, jump back to Step 6 and try again. Note: It's not unusual to discover hidden dirt late in the cleaning process; it can sometimes take two or three cleaning sessions to remove it all. If the block passes your finger test, proceed to Step 11.

Detailing and Painting

Detailing

Some engine experts spend many hours grinding the interior surfaces of the block and heads, removing sharp edges, deburring and enlarging passages, and making sure everything is "perfect." To the racing professional, these steps can mean the difference between winning and paying the bills or losing and finding another job. Under these conditions, detailing is just another essential part of engine preparation—a few more of the hundreds of "details" that add an extra winning edge.

Although thousands of engines are built for street and high-performance use with only minimal consideration for component detailing, some enthusiasts gain a great deal of pleasure and satisfaction from performing the same precision detail work done by racing professionals. If you are willing to spend some time, have sufficient patience, and own the right tools, you can put the benefits of component detailing on your side.

Many of the most important parts of component detailing are covered in the step-by-step instructions throughout this book (including chamfering holes, removing sharp edges on valvesprings, etc.). However, specialized operations include:

Removing Casting Irregularities. When cylinder blocks and heads are cast, they can capture chunks of sand in a homogeneous mix of metal and sand, visible as porous "globs" on the surface. Portions can break free and scratch cylinder walls, damage oil pump gears, and score bearing surfaces. A high-speed grinder makes short work of sand inclusions or other casting "flashings."

Oil Passage Smoothing/Enlarging. Smoothing and enlarging oil passages can improve high-speed oiling (above 6,000 rpm). Passages that make sharp turns can usually be smoothed with long-shank carbide cutters and/or grinding stones. Undersize passages can be drilled with three-flute core drills (sometimes available in surplus stores).

Deburring. There are many places on the interior and exterior of block and head castings—and rotating components such as crankshafts, connecting rods, pistons, etc.—where sharp and rough edges can be smoothed. The benefits are fewer cuts and scratches on your hands and the elimination of stress points (called risers) that can otherwise promote crack formation, especially in high-RPM, high-HP applications.

Detailing Other Components. Many components that you purchase for your engine can be improved by "detailing" before installation. For example, the upper timing sprocket often has sharp edges where it contacts the front of the block. If not smoothed, the sprocket will begin to "machine" the block when the engine is started. By applying the same detailing procedures to all your engine components, you'll improve engine life and get the most for every dollar you spend on engine building.

Painting Your Engine

Detailing is more than grinding and filing. You can also detail your engine with paint. There are two common techniques used to paint engines:

- With minimal masking, you can paint the engine after it's assembled. You'll spend less than 30 minutes masking, but since bolts, core plugs, the vibration damper, and pointer, and many other components will all be painted the same color, the engine will look good, but not "detailed."
- If you paint each component individually before final

Detailing also means keeping a keen eye focused on every engine component. For example, sharp edges often exist on the upper timing sprocket. If not smoothed with a fine file, the sprocket can "machine" the block face when the engine is started.

COMPONENT CLEANING

assembly, you'll probably spend 2 hours or more masking and fussing over parts, but the engine will have a distinctly detailed look.

Whichever method you choose, you should select only the best fuel, heat, and oil-resistant engine paint. Top-quality paints are available in auto parts stores under the names Dupli-Color, Zynolyte, and others. Excellent paint is also available from Eastwood and Goodson. Their colors are bright and true, the paint covers in one or two coats, and because it dries so quickly, it's very run-resistant.

A final note on engine painting: paint will not stick to oily surfaces (since it's easy to get lubricant on component parts during assembly, this is another good reason to paint parts before assembly). Use lacquer thinner, acetone, or Goodson's SC-20 spray to remove all oil residues. Then carefully follow the instructions on the paint can, especially the recommended spray temperatures. If it's too cold, you'll be fighting runs and the paint will take forever to dry.

We're fans of the original Chevy Orange paint and choose that route with our fresh engine. It is up to you as to when you want to apply paint. An engine looks great when the hardware is not painted and shows attention to detail. We opted to paint ours in stages.

11 Final Bore Cleaning — Important!

This cleaning step again focuses on the cylinder bores. To remove as much embedded debris as possible, soak a paper towel with ATF, light oil, or WD-40, and thoroughly scrub a cylinder bore—and be aggressive! As you work contaminants out of the bore wall, they will show up as brown or black smudges on the towel. Regularly switch to freshly soaked towels, and when they start coming out clean, move on to the next bore. This procedure also forces lubricant into bore walls, minimizing the chance of rust and promoting initial ring lubrication.

12 Final Prep Before Storage

Spray a final coat of rust inhibitor on block surfaces and coat all cylinder walls with engine oil. Then place a plastic bag over the block but don't seal the bag airtight for at least 12 hours; moisture will continue to evaporate from internal and external surfaces for some time. The block is now ready for final assembly.

REBUILDING THE SMALL-BLOCK CHEVROLET

13 Clean Crankshaft

Begin cleaning the crank by flushing it with solvent (use a solvent tank with a built-in pump). Run your engine-cleaning brushes through the bolt holes in the rear flange and the nose. Brush solvent over all crank surfaces, being careful not to nick the journals. Run the brushes back and forth through all oil feed passages. After thoroughly flushing the crank with solvent, blast it with compressed air, making sure to blow out all oil passages. When you are satisfied that the crank is spotlessly clean, spray it with rust inhibitor and cover it with a plastic bag.

Professional Mechanic Tip

14 Clean Head and Manifold

The most difficult cylinder-head-cleaning problem arises because many machine shops use bead blasters to pre-clean heads and manifolds. While doing an excellent job, they also blast millions of miniature steel beads into the water jackets and small passages, hundreds of which remain lodged in place. Unfortunately, the slightest "bump" can free a few random beads. If you happen to bump the head during final assembly, loose particles—and they are hard to see—may find their way into the oiling system, potentially resulting in engine failure! The only solution is to first wash out all oil (that acts like a magnet for the beads) with solvent then soap and water, then blow the water jackets completely dry with compressed air. Next, "bang" the head on a clean surface (a flat, wood surface works well) several times to loosen the beads. Keep banging different surfaces and blowing the water jackets with air until no additional beads are knocked out of the casting.

15 Scrub Other Surfaces

Valveguides, especially those reconditioned with "threaded" inserts, must be thoroughly scrubbed with brushes and lots of solvent. The slightest remnant of metal particles or honing grit will cause rapid valveguide and valvestem wear. Lastly, cast surfaces of the head that come in contact with engine oil must be completely clean. Use the same techniques used to clean the block, and make sure to scrub all surfaces, bolt holes, valveguides, and water jackets. After a final rinse, spray with rust inhibitor and perform the finger test. If you find any dirt or blast beads, repeat the cleaning process. Store your clean components in plastic bags (but give 'em about 12 hours before you seal the bag).

16 Clean Other Components

Cleaning all of the other remaining engine components before assembly (or pre-assembly) is a time-consuming job, often taking a full day or two. You'll need plenty of clean solvent, a can of carburetor cleaner dip for particularly dirty pieces (such as bolts), a wire brush, and compressed air. After each part is cleaned and dries, spray as required with rust inhibitor, and place in a plastic storage bag. Finally, make sure all your tools are clean. Crud from dirty tools is just one of the endless ways that dirt can "sneak" into your engine rebuild.

Chemical Cleaning Aids

Solvent should be your first choice for removing dirt, grease, and oil from small parts. It is available in most hardware and paint stores; you'll often find it labeled as "paint thinner," with the words "multi-purpose degreaser" added. Other than soap and water, it is probably one of the safest chemical cleaners that readily cuts oil and grease. However, parts covered with flaking paint, varnish (such as carburetor parts), or burned-on carbon deposits may resist your best efforts with solvent. If you encounter any of these stubborn cleaning tasks, you can turn to a variety of additional chemical cleaners in two types: immersion and spray.

Immersion-type carburetor cleaner is probably the most powerful cleaner available to the home and professional shop. Despite its commonly-referred-to name, it is used to clean a lot more than carburetors. Typical cans of cleaner will have brand names including Johnson's Carburetor and Metal Parts Cleaner or TYME-1 Carburetor and Cold Parts Cleaner. An overnight soaking will usually remove all traces of oil, grease, varnish, and paint; in other words, almost anything!

Carburetor cleaner is safe for most types of metal, but it will destroy virtually all rubber and some plastic parts. Make sure you read and follow all the instructions on the can, especially those dealing with safety. Always wear rubber gloves and goggles. When you remove the basket from the cleaner, it is a good idea to lower it into a bucket of clean water. Let it soak for a few minutes. This weakens the cleaner and reduces your chances of coming in contact with the full-strength chemical.

Chemicals similar to immersion-type cleaner are available in spray cans. While not as powerful, they do an excellent job on small parts. Spray-type carburetor cleaner will slice through grease and grime. If allowed to soak in, it will even remove some carbon deposits and stubborn varnish. However, most spray-on cleaners won't do a very good job of removing old, cracking paint. Immersion cleaner, or better yet, a bead-blasting cabinet, handles this tough chore with ease.

If you need something to remove oil or grease and then disappear quickly, some spray carburetor cleaners are fast-drying formulas and work fine for this application. However, a better choice may be lacquer thinner or acetone; both are effective grease cutters and they dry very fast. But the best oil-busters are spray cleaners designed specifically for this job. One of the best is Goodson's SC-20. It removes oil, assembly lube, varnish, paint overspray, gum, and many other surface contaminants without scrubbing. It dries almost instantly.

A word of caution is in order. All of these cleaners are effective, powerful, and potentially dangerous chemicals. Don't get any of them on your skin, including solvent. Avoid breathing vapors. Follow directions and precautions on the containers. Think about safety and treat all chemicals with great respect. Your health depends on it!

For smaller parts you can use a little elbow grease to get them clean. Paint thinner is commonly used to clean parts. Be sure to work in a well-ventilated area and wear safety goggles and rubber gloves.

Many aerosol carburetor cleaners are available in parts stores. They consist of potent chemicals that remove dirt, grease, and oil. While not as powerful as immersion cleaners, they will remove some varnish and dried-on deposits.

CHAPTER 7

PRE-ASSEMBLY FITTING

At this point in the rebuild, you've probably purchased most, if not all, of the bolts, gaskets, sealants, and other parts required to assemble your engine. The major components have been machined. Everything has been cleaned thoroughly. Assembly tools are at hand. Unfortunately, now is the time that some individuals let their enthusiasm get the better of them. Even though you've carefully selected new parts and had the engine professionally machined, you still need to take the time to check and verify the critical clearances and compatibility of the components selected for your new engine. Don't skip ahead into final assembly!

The steps in this chapter are an essential part of the engine building process. If you skip them and jump to Chapter 8, "Final Assembly," you'll have overlooked procedures that are absolutely necessary to ensure the quality and reliability of your engine.

Read and perform all applicable step-by-step instructions in this chapter and carefully inspect everything before final assembly. In most cases, you'll find that your machine shop and parts manufacturers did an excellent job and everything checks out fine. However, you just may discover a problem that, if overlooked, could lead to a complete engine failure. Remember, as the engine builder, the final responsibility rests with you. When you personally confirm the quality of every part, it's almost a sure bet that your engine project will be a complete success and provide the top performance and reliability you desire.

Preparations and Supplies

Assembling an engine to measure important clearances and dimensions

Without checking critical clearances, some individuals jump into final assembly. Don't make this big mistake! Take the time to measure every critical clearance in your engine. The steps in this chapter are an essential part of the engine-building process. Without them, you cannot guarantee the quality and reliability of your engine buildup.

Bolt threads, bearings, cam lobes, and other components require lubrication during pre-assembly fitting. Perhaps the most versatile lubricant is petroleum jelly. While not as pressure- and temperature-resistant as other high-tech lubes, it is easy to use, inexpensive, and provides ample protection during the pre-assembly process.

requires most of the supplies and components needed for final assembly, including the block, heads, crankshaft, most fasteners, head gaskets, bearings, pistons, rings, connecting rods, camshaft and timing chain set, oil pump and pan, and all valvetrain components. Here's a list of some additional tools, supplies, and procedures you'll need for pre-assembly fitting:

Thin Assembly Lubricant in a Squirt Can. An acceptable lubricant for pre-assembly fitting is STP mixed one

REBUILDING THE SMALL-BLOCK CHEVROLET

part per four parts engine oil, or you can use straight engine oil. Applying it from a squirt keeps your components and your fingers clean. This thin assembly lube is only suitable for pre-assembly fitting and isn't recommended for final assembly (assembly lubes are discussed further in Chapter 8, "Final Assembly").

Petroleum Jelly. A fail-safe lubricant for fastener threads and general pre-assembly purposes (commonly sold as Vaseline). It produces uniform tightness for "standard-lubricated" torque specifications and won't overstretch fasteners.

ARP Thread Sealer and Assembly Lubricant. ARP, maker of specialty fasteners for automotive performance applications, offers two fastener lubricants. ATP Thread Sealer is Teflon-based with special lubricants added. It seals head bolts (and other fasteners that protrude into the water jackets) and provides optimum lubrication for uniform bolt torque. ARP Assembly Lubricant is a molybdenum-based lubricant that minimizes thread friction. Bolt torque values must be reduced when using this lubricant (bolt tightness, however, isn't reduced). See the torque charts on page 155.

Torque Wrenches. A torque wrench with a range from at least 5 to about 100 ft-lbs is required. Most wrenches won't cover this wide range with good accuracy. You'll probably need two: one with 1/4-inch drive (and/or a 3/8-inch drive), and one with 1/2-inch drive.

Light Checking Springs. During many of the inspections in this chapter,

These lightweight springs will make checking your valvetrain measurements much easier. Most cam companies, including Comp, Iskenderian, Crane, and others, offer them. These springs are strong enough to keep the valve closed, yet light enough to not put much pressure on the new lifters or cam lobes while you check your specifications.

you'll need at least two—and better yet 16—light valve-checking springs. These springs are used in place of normal valvesprings. They apply only enough pressure to close the valve, allowing you to perform many of the tests without worrying about damaging the camshaft. Light springs are available from Comp, Crane, Iskenderian, and others.

Degree Wheel. In order to check cam timing, you'll need a degree wheel and the hardware to mount it to your crankshaft. Almost every cam manufacturer offers degree wheels.

Offset Cam Bushings. Again, these are available from most camshaft manufacturers. A multi-keyed lower sprocket or some other method of varying cam timing can be used. However, many cam and cam drives won't require timing changes.

Bench Vise with Soft Jaws. A firmly mounted bench vise with about 6-inch jaws will make several pre-assembly steps much easier. A pair of soft jaws (brass, aluminum, or rubber) is essential for holding items that should not be marred, such as your connecting rods.

Rod Bolt Protectors. Lengths of 3/8-inch rubber hose or plastic protector boots are absolutely essential to prevent damaging the crankshaft during pre-assembly fitting. Goodson offers inexpensive protectors.

All Machine Work Completed. Block should be bored, honed, and optionally decked and align-bored. Valveguides, valves, and all other valvetrain components should either be new or rebuilt. The crankshaft and the connecting rods should be reconditioned.

Cam Bearings Installed. The cam bearings must be installed in the block before you can accomplish any camshaft fitting, valvetrain measuring, or timing.

Everything Thoroughly Cleaned. You should have performed all the applicable cleaning steps described in Chapter 6. Everything should be cleaned, placed in plastic bags, and ready for installation.

Generous Supply of Clean Rags. Rags can be purchased from home and business supply warehouses. Have plenty of "lint-free" cotton rags on hand to keep dirt off your hands and precision components.

Throughout the pre-assembly steps in this chapter, you'll be working with the same precision parts that will be installed in your engine during final assembly. If they're damaged from improper assembly techniques, the reliability and performance will suffer. Prevent these problems before they occur by taking your time. Review the assembly advice presented in

Torque wrenches are essential for both fitting and final assembly. This 1/2-inch-drive Snap-on torque wrench will go up to 175 ft-lbs, which is more than enough for our engine buildup. A smaller 3/8-inch torque wrench with a range of about 5 to 75 ft-lbs is a good model to have as well. Adding a 1/4-inch-drive wrench that measures in-lbs will fill most of your mechanical needs.

Chapter 8, "Final Assembly," and keep dirt out of your engine! Perform pre-assembly fitting in the same "clean room" environment that you'll use for final assembly.

Precision Tools

Pre-assembly fitting will check two major areas: the accuracy of factory and purchased machine work, and the operational compatibility of various engine components. This includes checking bearing clearances, critical bore diameters, cam fit and timing, valvetrain function, and much more.

Some of these dimensions can be checked without expensive dial indicators and precision micrometers. But when you realize that all precision measurements require "instruments" at least as precise as the dimension under test, it's no surprise that some surfaces and components can only be tested with specialized and somewhat costly measuring tools.

However, before you grab for your wallet in panic, you should consider several things:

First, not all of the following steps/inspections may be required for your engine (for example, if you're installing a stock cam in a street engine, piston-to-valve clearance checks are optional). You should carefully read all of the following steps and make a list of the tools required for your specific project.

Second, some measurements allow substituting a common, inexpensive tool in place of an expensive one, providing you're willing to accept a reduction in measurement accuracy. These options are discussed in the step-by-step instructions.

Third, even if you need an expensive measuring tool, that doesn't mean you should run out and buy it. If you can't borrow it from a friend, or rent it from a parts shop, or if you're unfamiliar with precision tools (see sidebar "Using Precision Tools" on page 49), you can choose to have a professional engine builder perform some or all of the pre-assembly checking for you. While it will cost you some money, it may be cheaper than buying an expensive micrometer you'll never use again, plus you'll benefit from the advice of an experienced (hopefully) engine builder.

Special Considerations

Every engine is as unique as each engine builder. Because of the components chosen and the machine work performed, your engine may require special procedures in order to complete its assembly.

For example, if you have selected a hydraulic camshaft for your engine, you must make special preparations in order to perform some of the valvetrain checks. The inner cup on hydraulic lifters (where the pushrod rides) is "spongy" when not fed with pressurized oil. This compressibility will lead to errors when measuring valve lift and piston-to-valve clearance. The most common solution to this problem is to obtain a pair (or more) of solid lifters with exactly the same pushrod cup heights as the hydraulic lifters supplied with your cam.

As an alternative, some experienced engine builders disassemble a pair of hydraulic lifters and install a machined spacer or a short stack of washers that prevents the cup from compressing during valvetrain tests.

In either case, discuss the situation with your machine shop; they may have a set of "checking" lifters you can borrow for pre-assembly fitting (they'll be used with light-pressure checking springs so they don't "wear in" on the cam lobes).

If the piston pins in your engine are retained with a press fit (the rods have not been machined for floating pins), the rods and pistons must be assembled by your machine shop before you can perform pre-assembly fitting. Optionally, you can obtain one or more .0015-inch undersize "dummy" pins (again, often available from your machine shop). These pins, used for pre-assembly fitting only, can be assembled and disassembled by hand. They're particularly helpful if you suspect that the valve pockets, piston dome surfaces, etc., may need additional machine work (common when running high-compression ratios and high-lift cams).

Many precision tools can be used for pre-assembly fitting, but before you grab for your wallet in a panic, you should know that many checks can be done with inexpensive tools. Here the deck height is being checked with a straightedge and a feeler gauge. Carefully review all of the following steps and make a list of the tools required for your specific project.

While you can measure valvespring installed height and perform most cylinder head checks without a spring tester, measuring seat pressure and variations from spring to spring are important. Goodson offers a couple different spring testers from the professional model to the hobbyist.

PRE-ASSEMBLY FITTING

The first components checked in the pre-assembly inspection are the cylinder heads. Since all reconditioning and valve grinding should be completed, make absolutely sure you keep the valves organized and/or identified for proper reassembly. If the springs have been set up by your machine shop, make sure you also keep the retainers, springs, and spring shims in order. If press-on-type valve seals have been installed, they must be removed to perform some of the steps. Unfortunately, once removed, they should never be reused, since the sharp edges on the valvestem often damage the sealing surfaces. Because of this, only install new seals when you reassemble the heads (check with your machine shop for specific advice and replacement seals).

Final Tips

Remember to keep everything—including your hands and tools—clean. Mount your block on an engine stand near your workbench and think over everything carefully before you act. If you run into problems performing the upcoming steps, or you find that any of your components are outside of acceptable specifications, discuss the problems with your machine shop before you continue with pre-assembly. As we've mentioned before, reputable shops will (or at least should) bend over backward to make sure you're completely satisfied with the services you've purchased from them.

All measurements made during pre-assembly fitting should be recorded on your Work-A-Long Sheet for future reference. When you've completed your engine-building project, your Work-A-Long Sheet will become a valuable, permanent record of vital engine statistics that would otherwise be lost to memory. Do yourself a favor—keep your Work-A-Long Sheet accurate and up to date.

Finally, if you're building a stock- or mild-performance engine, you should find the pre-assembly steps in this chapter (and the information in previous chapters on parts selection and machine work) adequate for your purpose. However, if you're building a high-performance or racing engine, you may find the additional information in *Engine Blueprinting*, by Rick Voegelin, and *Chevy Performance, Vol. I* and *Vol. II*, by John Baechtel, of great help to you.

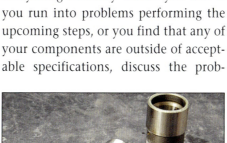

If you're installing a hydraulic cam, you can't use the hydraulic lifters for the pre-assembly checks that follow. The plungers in the lifters will compress and give false lift and valve timing readings. Many builders will swap in a set of solid lifters (left photo) with the same pushrod cup height. Some engine builders disassemble two lifters and replace the springs with spacers or washers (arrow, right photo) to lock the plungers in the "up" position.

Step-by-Step Pre-Assembly Fitting

1 Before You Begin

As mentioned earlier, most of the tools and components required for final assembly will be needed for pre-assembly checking. All machine work (except, possibly, decking) should be completed. The cam bearings should be installed. Everything should be thoroughly cleaned. You need assembly lube in a squirt can (use straight engine oil or a 1:4 STP/engine oil mix). You also need a few precision tools such as feeler gauges, Plastigauge, micrometers, a degree wheel, and a dial indicator set. (Though they would be nice to own, a dial bore gauge, burette, and valvespring tester are probably not tools that you're going to have in your garage. They may be available for rent.) Read all of the following steps before you begin. Based on how many of the following steps you intend to perform (we recommend performing all pre-assembly steps), make a list of the specific tools, equipment, and supplies you need to complete the process.

REBUILDING THE SMALL-BLOCK CHEVROLET

2 Check Valveguide Clearance

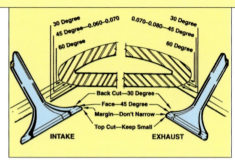

If your heads have been set up by your machine shop, keep the valves, retainers, springs, and spring shims tagged and organized to ensure proper reassembly. The heads should be disassembled and the guide-mounted valveseats should be removed. Make sure they are completely clean and no lubricants remain on the valvestems or in the guides. Guide clearance can be checked with hole gauges and micrometers or by the "wobble" method. Move the valves about 1/4 inch off their seats. Then wiggle the heads side-to-side. You should feel virtually no wobble. If you have a dial indicator, head wobble should measure under .010 to .015 inch (that translates to about .003 inch or less guide clearance). Guide clearance greater than this will cause excess oil consumption and premature seat failure. In Step 3, you'll inspect and test the quality of the valve and seats.

3 Check Valveseat Quality

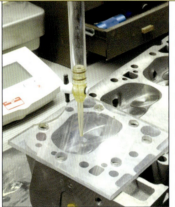

Most machine shops use layout dye (bluing) or lapping compound on the valves/seats to verify concentricity, seat width, and position. Since lapping embeds grit in the valveseats, we recommend using only blue or red layout dye. First, apply a thin coating of dye to the seats and valve faces. When thoroughly dry, press the valves against the seats and twist them with a lapping stick for about 3 to 5 seconds. Check the critical dimensions, and if everything is okay, wipe the valves and seats clean. Next, install a set of light checking springs and spark plugs. Pour enough solvent into the combustion chambers to cover the valves. Look for leaks into the ports or down the valvestems with a high-intensity light source. Top-quality valve seats won't leak a drop!

4 Measure Clearance

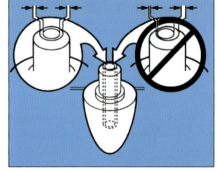

If your heads use valvestem seals that press onto the valveguides, they will only seal properly if the outside of the guides are concentric with the valvestems. Check for machining marks on the guides; better yet, verify their concentricity with dial calipers. If any type of press-on or stem-umbrella seal is used, install them on the intake and exhaust valves/guides of the number-1 cylinder. Now open each valve to the maximum valve lift indicated on your cam card (use a dial indicator or machinist's rule). There should be at least .070-inch clearance between the bottom of the retainers and the top of the seals or guides. If it's close to the minimum, you should check all remaining valves.

PRE-ASSEMBLY FITTING

5 Verify Valvespring Seat Pressure

All valvesprings should provide the seat pressure recommended by the cam manufacturer. To check or set up this important spec, you'll need a valvespring tester and a Goodson spring-height micrometer or a snap-gauge (a machinist's rule can be used but with less accuracy). First, measure the spring installed height on one valve; make sure you use the matching retainer and any installed spring shims (here it measures 1.704 inches). Next, completely compress and relax the valvespring at least 10 times to allow it to stabilize. Then compress the spring to the measured installed height (retainer must be in place for dual springs). The indicated seat pressure should be within ±10 percent of the cam manufacturer's specs. Repeat this process for all of the remaining valves and springs.

6 Calculate Compressed Spring Clearance

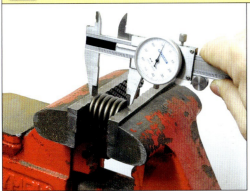

Installed Spring Height	= 1.107
- (Maximum Valve Lift)	= -0.500
Compressed Spring Height	= 1.204
- (Solid Height)	= -1.090
Compressed Spring Clearance	= +0.114

Only after seat pressure has been established and/or verified, can compressed spring clearance be checked. First, measure and record the spring installed height, as you did in Step 5 (it's 1.704 inches in our example). Now calculate the compressed height by subtracting the maximum valve lift, indicated on your cam card, from the measured installed height (if you're using non-standard rocker ratios, make sure you adjust the maximum valve lift accordingly). Next, fully compress a spring until it is solid (retainer must be in place for dual springs). Measure and record this solid height, sometimes called stack height (ours is 1.090 inches). Finally, subtract the solid height from the compressed height to find the compressed spring clearance. The result should be at least +.100 inch for optimum reliability. Check the rest of the valves and springs.

7 Measure Rod and Main Bore Sizes

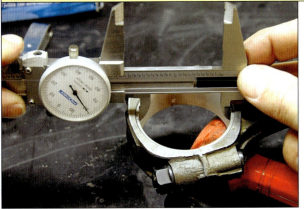

Engine Application	Rod Bore (inches)	Rod Bore Tolerance (inches)	Main Bore (inches)	Main Bore Tolerance (inches)
Small Journal Crank	2.1250	+0.0002 / -0.0003	2.4910	+0.0006 / -0.0004
Large Journal Crank	2.2250	+0.0002 / -0.0003	2.6410	+0.0006 / -0.0004
400 ci Crank	2.2250	+0.0002 / -0.0003	2.8410	+0.0005 / -0.0004

Checking rod and main bearing bore diameters verifies bearing shell crush (holding force). You need a 2- to 3-inch outside micrometer and an inside micrometer set or a dial-bore gauge (snap gauges can be used, but with less accuracy). If you don't have these instruments, make sure a qualified engine builder performs these inspections for you and skip to Step 8. First, carefully set the outside mics with the supplied standards. Lubricate the bolts and torque the main and rod caps. Hold the rods by clamping the full face of the big end in a vise with soft jaws. Mic each main and rod bore several times. All bores should be within spec, have no more than .0002-inch taper, and be no more than .0007-inch out of round. When you have completed your measurements, remove the main caps from the block and loosen all of the rod caps.

REBUILDING THE SMALL-BLOCK CHEVROLET

CHAPTER 7

8 Check Crank Straightness

If the crankshaft is not straight, bearing clearances measured in the upcoming steps will not be accurate. Fortunately, checking crank straightness is easy, requiring only a dial indicator set. First, install the front and rear main bearings in the block (you don't need the main caps for this test). Lubricate the bearing shells and front and rear crank journals with assembly lube, and then carefully set the crank into the block. Position your dial indicator to read off the center main. (Make sure the indicator pin does not fall into the crank oil hole.) Rotate the crank and read the total runout on the dial indicator. Street engines with main clearances less than .003 inch should have no more than .002-inch runout. You should not tolerate more than .0008-inch runout in a high-speed racing engine. Also, check the runout on the front sprocket and rear seal surfaces (maximum acceptable is .002 inch).

9 Measure Main Bearing Clearances

Engine Application	Main Bearing Clearance
Stock Street	.002 - .0035 in
Hi-Po Street	.0025 - .0037 in
High-RPM Racing	.0032 - .004 in
Many racing mechanics use the tried-and-true rule of 0.001-in clearance for each inch of shaft diameter as the minimum operating clearance. Multiply this amount by 1.5 to determine maximum bearing clearance.	

Checking main bearing clearance can be done with the same precision tools used in Step 7. You can also install the crank in the block and use Plastigauge with reasonable accuracy. To use micrometers: Install the bearings in the block and main caps and tighten to full torque. Subtract the inside bearing diameters (measured 90 degrees from the parting lines) from the crank journal diameters to obtain bearing clearance. To use Plastigauge: Install all the bearing shells but do not lubricate them or the crank. Set the dry crankshaft onto the bearings and do not rotate the crank! Place strips of Plastigauge along the center of the journals, install the caps, and tighten to full torque. Then remove the caps and compare the width of the plastic strip to the Plastigauge chart. See Sidebar "Using Plastigauge" on page 103 for tips on improving accuracy.

10 Install Crank

Now, install all the main bearing shells (no rear main seal). Make sure no Plastigauge remains on the crank. Lubricate the new bearings and main journals with assembly lube, and set the crank in the block. Install the rear main cap and tighten the two bolts finger tight. Then strike the rear of the crank two or three times with a softhead hammer to seat the thrust bearing. Install the remaining caps and tighten all bolts to full torque. The crank should turn freely; if it does not, the block is warped and needs align boring.

11 Check Thrust Endplay

Crank fore-and-aft thrust clearance can be checked with a dial indicator or a feeler gauge. To use a dial indicator: Position a dial indicator on the front of the block and position the plunger on the nose of the crank, as shown. Pry the crank forward and back with a screwdriver and note the dial reading. To use a feeler gauge: Pry the crank fully back and, while maintaining a slight rearward pressure on the crank, insert a feeler gauge between the crank thrust face and the bearing thrust flange. Start with a .003-inch gauge and step up in one-thousandth increments until the gauge won't slide in. An acceptable clearance is .007 to .010 inch.

PRE-ASSEMBLY FITTING

Using Plastigauge

Plastigauge Clearance Indicator consists of a 12-inch length of plastic "string" in a paper package. It comes in three thicknesses that check overlapping clearance ranges: green for .001 to .003 inch, red for .002 to .006 inch, and blue for .004 to .009 inch. It's used by cutting a short piece and placing it on the bearing or crank journal. When the cap is tightened and then removed, the plastic strip has flattened to a width precisely determined by the bearing clearance. By comparing the width of the strip at its widest point with the scale printed on the package, clearance can be measured, often to within .0005 inch.

Check Main Clearance

Since Plastigauge measures the space between the bearing and the journal, the crankshaft and the main saddles in the block must be straight. So the first step in measuring main bearing clearances should be a check of crank straightness (see Step 8 on page 102). If crank runout is more than .001 inch, follow the technique described in "Additional Plastigauge Tips."

Install the bearing shells in the block but do not lubricate them or the crank (lubricant takes up space and will affect your measurement). Set the dry crank into the block and do not rotate it. Cut short strips of Plastigauge and apply them to the journals, using a thin smear of Vaseline to hold them in place. Install the caps, tighten to full torque, remove them, and compare the width of the Plastigauge strip to the scale on the package.

Check Rod Clearance

Checking rod bearing clearance with Plastigauge requires additional steps because the rods tend to twist on the crank journals when the caps are tightened, and the caps are often removed with a few light hammer blows to the bolts or nuts. Both of these effects can apply extra "crush" to the Plastigauge strips and cause inaccurate readings.

Use this technique for measuring rod-bearing clearance: Apply short strips to the bearing shells in number-1 and number-2 rods, not the caps. Then rotate the crank so the front throw points directly away from the block. Note: To prevent the crank from turning farther, lay a piece of rope-type rear main seal in the rear cap (remove the neoprene seal) and tighten the rear cap just enough to "lock" the crank in place. Install both rods (using bolt protectors). Insert two feeler gauges between the rods to prevent them from twisting. Next, tighten all four nuts (don't let the crank turn), and with the feeler gauges still in place, loosen all the nuts. Remove the rods and read the bearing clearances. Continue checking clearances with the second crankthrow (using number-3 and number-4 rods).

Additional Plastigauge Tips

Here are three more helpful ideas:
- Don't Stretch Plastigauge. Cut it into short strips with scissors.
- Keeping Plastigauge From Tearing. Keeping a very thin smear of Vaseline to the journal and bearing often keeps the plastic strip in one piece.
- Compensating for Crank Runout Greater than .001 Inch. Measure only two journals at a time and space them two journals apart. For example, install bearings in number-2 and -4, or -3 and either -1 or -5 saddles and caps.
- Remove All Remnants. Remove all traces of Plastigauge before you recheck clearances or before assembly.

To obtain the most accurate rod-bearing clearance readings with Plastigauge, apply strips to the bearing shell in the rod rather than the cap. When you tap the bolts or nuts to loosen the cap, it won't affect the reading. Use a pair of feeler gauges, or you can make a special tool like the one pictured here, to prevent the rods from twisting on the journal as the nuts are tightened and loosened.

Cut Plastigauge into short strips with scissors. If you tear pieces with your fingers, you can easily stretch the plastic material, causing excessively large readings.

12 Camshaft Fitting

Apply a thin film of engine oil on the cam bearings and journals. Install a long bolt or this Goodson "handle" to help support the cam. Begin installing the cam in the block, rotating it as you go. If the bearings have been installed properly, the cam should turn freely as it enters each successive bearing. If the cam fits properly, proceed to Step 13. If the cam binds up, remove it and look for shiny high spots on the bearings; they can sometimes be removed by careful scraping with a bearing knife. If you don't see distinct high spots, the cam may be bent; have your machine shop check it in a lathe or V-block fixture. If the cam is not bent, the bearings in the block may be undersize or out of alignment.

13 Install Keys and Lower Sprocket

If the cam fits properly, remove it and oil the cam journals and lobes with assembly lube, then reinstall it in the block. If the keys are not installed in the crank, see Step 7, on page 84. With the keys installed, lightly lubricate the crank nose, and then install the sprocket with the large interior chamfer facing toward the block. Some lower sprockets have multiple keyways (often labeled with a circle, square, and a triangle or other similar marks). Align the sprocket on the ZERO keyway mark (usually labeled with a 0). Drive the sprocket on with a crank socket or a brass drift using light hammer blows.

14 Install Upper Sprocket

Rotate the crank so the keyway points to approximately 2 o'clock, and then rotate the cam so that the dowel pinpoints to approximately the 3 o'clock position. Install the upper sprocket and timing chain. Make sure the timing marks line up as shown. IMPORTANT: With the keyway on the crankshaft pointing to the 2 o'clock position and the camshaft dowel pin close to the 3 o'clock position, the timing marks on the upper sprockets should line up. If they don't, the sprockets are aligned to the wrong marks.

15 Check Cam Drive Clearance

Some wide timing chains may scrape against the block or the chain cover. Check block clearance: Press the upper sprocket against the block face and rotate the crank. Look for chain contact of less than .030-inch clearance. Mark the tight points and remove the upper sprocket (not the cam). Stick strips of duct tape over the cam bore and around the main journal to keep grinding debris away from the bearings. Draping rags over the block and crank also helps. Grind only enough to provide the necessary clearance. Wipe everything clean and recheck clearance. Check cover clearance: When sufficient block clearance is obtained, install the chain cover (without a gasket) and rotate the assembly. If the chain contacts the cover, you should locate a deeper replacement cover, such as the aluminum cover (offered by a variety of companies such as Milodon) or install a narrower timing chain set. IMPORTANT: If you have to grind the block, we recommend that you disassemble and thoroughly re-clean everything. Then reassemble the engine to the same point.

PRE-ASSEMBLY FITTING

16 Piston Orientation Rules

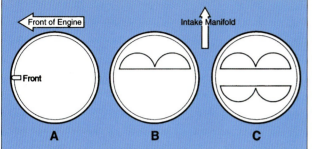

The following rules dictate how to properly install pistons in your engine. Piston Rule 1: If the pistons have a "front" stamp, notch, or other front-indicating mark (piston A), this mark must always face the front of the block. Piston Rule 2: If the pistons have a single pair of valve reliefs (Piston B), the pistons must be installed so that the valve reliefs are closest to the intake manifold. (If the pistons have four valve reliefs and no "front" mark or notch [piston C], they can be installed upside down in any cylinder and assembled with any rod.)

17 Special Racing Pistons

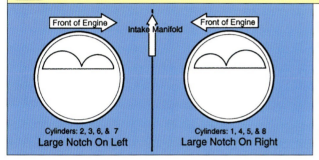

Pistons with non-equal valve reliefs come in sets composed of four of one type (larger reliefs on the left–dome oriented down) and four "mirror" pistons (with larger reliefs on the right). An additional rule applies to these pistons. Piston Rule 3: Make sure that pistons with large reliefs on the left are installed in cylinders number-2, number-3, number-6, and number-7. Pistons with large reliefs on the right must be installed in cylinders number-1, number-4, number-5, and number-8.

18 Number/Mark Pistons

Abiding by the rules above, mark each piston with a felt-tip pen indicating the cylinder number you've chosen and an arrow pointing to the front of the block. Also, write the cylinder numbers on the deck surface just above the bores. These numbers make pre-assembly and final assembly much easier. IMPORTANT: If the pistons are already numbered, or if the pistons and rods have been assembled, make sure the numbering on the pistons and/or rods does not violate any piston orientation rule.

19 Orient the Piston

Rod Rule 1: All odd-numbered rods/pistons (number-1, number-3, number-5, and number-7) should be assembled with the rod bearing locking tangs pointing DOWN and the front arrow pointing to the LEFT. Rod Rule 2: All even-numbered rods/pistons (number-2, number-4, number-6, and number-8) should be assembled with the rod bearing locking tangs pointing DOWN and the front arrow pointing to the RIGHT. Also, pay attention to the chamfered edge on the rods. The side with more chamfer should face the crankshaft. The additional chamfer allows clearance on the fillet of the crankshaft.

20 Assemble Rod and Piston

Oil the pin bores in the rods and pistons lightly. Then, following all the applicable orientation rules, assemble (or check the assembly of) all rods and pistons. If you have press-fit pins, proceed to Step 21. For floating pins: You don't need to install the pin lock rings for pre-assembly. However, you should check pin endplay on at least one piston (preferably the entire set). Use snap-ring pliers for standard pin locks, while Spirolox can be worked in one loop at a time with a probe or small screwdriver. Make sure the lock rings are fully seated in the pistons. Then check pin endplay with either feeler gauges or vernier calipers. Endplay should be .001 to .008 inch; clearance outside this range can force the locks out during engine operation!

21 Check Piston-to-Wall Clearance

Checking piston-to-cylinder wall (also called "skirt") clearance can be done with micrometers, or you can use feeler gauges with very little, if any, loss in accuracy. To use micrometers: Use an outside mic to measure a piston skirt at the position indicated by the manufacturer. Then measure the minimum bore diameter in the matching bore. Subtract piston diameter from bore diameter to obtain skirt clearance. To be certain of your figures, repeat the measurements several times for each piston. To use feeler gauges: Insert a piston upside down in its bore with feeler gauge strips between the skirt and the bore. Start with feeler strips .001- to .002-inch too thin and increase in .001-inch steps. When the piston just becomes snug in the bore, the skirt clearance is .001 inch less than the gauge thickness.

22 Measure Ring End Gaps

Before you begin, review sidebar "Setting Ring End Gap" on page 108. If you're using rings that haven't been gapped by your machine shop, they should be labeled with their respective cylinder numbers. Standard ring sets have the proper gap built in and should not need modification, but all rings should be checked before final assembly. First, make sure all rings have been deburred. Insert a ring into its respective bore a uniform distance down from the deck surface (you can use a piston with ring installed in the second ring groove as a tool). Visually inspect the end gap; the ends of the rings should be parallel. Measure the gap with feeler gauges; it should fall within the manufacturer's specs (supplied with your rings). Repeat this process for all remaining top and second rings. Then install the oil rails just to make sure they have plenty of end gap (.017 to .060 inch or even more is acceptable).

PRE-ASSEMBLY FITTING

Ring End Gap Recommendations	
For 5/64 and 1/16-in Ductile Iron Top Rings and .043 and .031 Pressure Back Head Land Top Rings (all figures in inches)	
Using Special Fuels	
Supercharged/injected nitro engines	.022-.024 in
Supercharged/injected alcohol engines	.018-.020 in
Using Gasoline	
Supercharged/injected gas engines	.022-.024 in
Oval track rectangular rings	.018-.020 in
Oval track head land rings	.024-.026 in
Oval track pressure back rings	.020-.022 in
Pro/Stock, Comp Eliminator, Modified Prod., etc.	.018-.020 in
Super stock	.018-.020 in
Stock	.016-.018 in
Street engines	.016-.018 in
For Regular (Plain) Iron Second Rings (all figures in inches)	
Using Special Fuels	
Supercharged/injected nitro engines	.014-.016 in
Supercharged/injected alcohol engines	.012-.014 in
Using Gasoline	
Supercharged/injected gas engines	.012-.014 in
Oval track	.012-.014 in
Pro/Stock, Comp Eliminator, Modified Prod., etc.	.012/.014 in
Super Stock	.010-.012 in
Stock	.010-.012 in
Street engines	.010-.012 in

Note: These Speed Pro end gap recommendations will be appropriate in most cases. They stress that this chart should be used as a guide to normal ring fitting, and that the ideal end gap may be different for specific combinations. If you're ever in doubt, check with other engine builders or add .002 in to the recommended gap. Racers with plenty of experience often close up the gaps from .002 to .004 in, but you have to be willing to sacrifice a motor if you guess wrong.

23 Measure Rod Bearing Clearance

Engine Application	Rod Bearing Clearance
Stock Street	.0017-.003 in
Hi-Po Street	.002-.003 in
High-RPM Racing	.0025-.0035 in

Many racing mechanics use the tried-and-true rule of 0.001-in clearance for each inch of shaft diameter as the minimum operating clearance. Multiply this amount by 1.5 to determine maximum bearing clearance.

Checking rod-bearing clearance can be done with precision tools or you can use Plastigauge with reasonable accuracy. If you're using Plastigauge, skip to Step 24. To use micrometers: Install bearings in the rods without any lubricant, tighten the caps to full torque in a vise with soft jaws. Use an outside micrometer to measure the diameter of one rod journal. Measure the rod bearing diameter (90 degrees from the parting lines) on a matching rod. Bearing clearance is found by subtracting rod journal OD from rod bearing ID. Measure the remaining seven journals then skip to Step 25.

24 Measure Rod Bearing and Side Clearance

Rod Material/Application	Rod Side Clearance
Stock Steel	.008-.012 in
High-RPM Steel	.008-.015 in
Aluminum Racing	.032-.060 in

The above rod side clearances are appropriate for most applications listed above. However, some rod manufacturers recommend specific side clearances or do not recommend machining their rods to change side clearance. Check with your rods' manufacturer for specific recommendations.

Plastigauge will produce accurate readings only if you follow the guidelines outlined in sidebar "Using Plastigauge" on page 103. First, read (but do not perform) Step 26 for information about component assembly. Then perform the procedures indicated. Refer to the chart in Step 23 for rod-bearing clearance recommendations. Rod side clearance can be measured simply by noting the thickness of the feeler gauge that you insert between the rods. After checking side and bearing clearances on the first journal, check each of the remaining journals, one pair of rods at a time. When finished, skip to Step 26.

Setting Ring End Gap

Properly setting the end gap on oversize (gappable) ring sets can be a tedious, error-prone process. However, done precisely, it almost certainly will improve horsepower, reliability, and fuel economy; and it will extend engine life. Done incorrectly, it can take the fine edge off an otherwise excellent engine or, in the worst case, result in severe ring damage and greatly shortened engine life.

Properly gapping rings places two demands on the engine builder:

- The precise amount of material (exact to the thousandths of an inch) must be removed from the end of each ring,
- The resulting gap must be parallel and have no sharp edges that can scratch the bore.

Filing while holding the ring in a vise is one common practice but even with experience, it's easy to ruin a ring or two (although most machine shops will sell individual replacement rings at a reasonable price).

Goodson offers a terrific tool that uses a rotating "table" and a dial indicator that make gapping rings the precision process it should be. In fact, using this tool makes it possible for an experienced builder to gap all 16 top and second rings in about 15 to 30 minutes. With only a little care, each ring gap will be exactly the right width and dead parallel.

However, the Goodson Ring Gap Machine Tool isn't something that the non-professional builder is going to have, or even buy for that matter. We strongly recommend that you have your rings gapped by one of the shops that use a similar type of ring-gapping tool.

The ring-gapping tool from Goodson uses a rotating "table" and a dial indicator that makes gapping rings a precision process. It's easy to remove exactly the right amount of material when using such a precision tool.

For piston installation, a good-quality ring tool is important. There are specific-diameter rings available, which seem to work best with their tapered sleeve, yet they are not very universal for the hobbyist. We used this set that is supplied with a few different diameter sleeves and a set of special pliers to lock and hold the sleeve in position.

25 Measure Rod Side Clearance

Rod side clearances can be measured with vernier calipers before the rods and pistons are installed. If you don't own vernier calipers, side clearance will be checked later with feeler gauges; skip to Step 26. Set the rods from the first crankthrow (number-1/number-2) side by side. Use vernier calipers to measure their combined width. Next, measure the width of the crank journal; make sure your calipers are positioned on the journal thrust faces. Subtract the width of the rods from the journal width to determine side clearance (see Step 24 for clearance specs). Perform the measurements two or three times to verify accuracy. Then, measure the side clearance of the remaining three crankthrows.

PRE-ASSEMBLY FITTING

26 Install Number-1 and Number-2 Rods/Pistons

Locating TDC requires a degree wheel, mounting hardware, and a piston-stop tool. Start by installing the bearings for the number-1 and -2 rods/pistons, and then lubricate the bearings and the front crank journal with assembly lube (make sure you're familiar with the rod/piston installation procedure in Chapter 8). Lubricate the cylinder bores and piston skirts with engine oil lightly, place protectors over the rod bolts, and install both rods/pistons (without rings) in their respective bores. When both rods/pistons are installed, torque the caps to full torque. Rotate the crank carefully; if it "hangs up," STOP! Refer to Step 33.

27 Find TDC

Move the number-1 piston so that it's as visually close to TDC as possible. Attach a degree wheel to the crank nose and fabricate a firmly mounted pointer (coat-hanger wire works okay) that points to the TDC mark. Move the piston down the bore and attach a TDC stop tool over number-1 bore (this one is from B&B Performance) and tighten the stop bolt. Slowly turn the crank clockwise until the piston contacts the stop; note the reading on the wheel (a china marker works well). Turn the crank counter-clockwise until the piston again stops, and note this reading. The two readings should indicate the same number of degrees before and after TDC. Adjust the pointer and/or degree wheel until repeated tests produce the desired result. (Note: The TDC mark accuracy on the vibration damper will be established during final assembly.)

28 Measure Piston-to-Head Clearance

If the distances between the flat surfaces of the cylinder heads and the pistons are less than about .050 inch at TDC, the pistons may contact the heads. This piston-to-head clearance is the sum of the deck clearance and the compressed head-gasket thickness. Deck clearance is measured with a dial indicator, or feeler gauges and a machinist's straightedge. Bring number-1 piston to TDC. Rock the piston to one side of the bore and hold it there. Measure the deck clearance as shown. Rock the piston to the other side and repeat the measurement. Average these measurements and add the result (or subtract if the piston is above the deck surface) to the compressed head-gasket thickness to determine piston-to-head clearance.

REBUILDING THE SMALL-BLOCK CHEVROLET

CHAPTER 7

29 Domed Piston-to-Head Clearance

Performance Tip

This step is required if your pistons have high-compression domes, otherwise, proceed to the next step. First, install the left cylinder head (number-1 cylinder) without a head gasket. Then remove number-1 rod cap but leave the rod—and its half bearing—in place. While holding the rod against the crank journal, carefully bring number-1 piston to TDC. Attach a dial indicator as shown, make sure the bearing is firmly seated in the rod and against the journal, zero the indicator, then push the rod/piston toward the head and note the reading. This distance plus the compressed head gasket thickness is piston-to-head clearance. If it is less than measured in Step 28, the dome is closer to the head than the flat surface of the piston (minimum acceptable is .050 inch). When you're finished measuring, replace the rod cap and remove the indicator and cylinder head.

30 Prepare to Degree the Cam

Lubricate the diameters and faces of two lifters with engine oil and install them in the intake and exhaust lifter bores of number-1 cylinder. Mount a dial indicator on the block, with the plunger riding on the edge of the lifter, parallel to the lifter bore. Apply slight downward pressure with your finger to make sure the lifter is riding on the cam lobe. Then rotate the crank until the lifter is in its lowest position.

31 Degree the Cam

Refer to the timing card supplied with your cam and locate the valve timing specs for the intake valve and the lifter rise at which the timing points are measured (usually .050 inch). Slowly rotate the crank clockwise (normal rotation) until the lifter raises precisely the indicated amount. Note the reading on the degree wheel. Continue rotating the crank (clockwise) until the lifter returns to the same tappet lift, but on the closing side of the lobe (if you miss it, back up and come at it again, always from the clockwise direction). Compare these opening and closing figures with those on the cam card. Repeat the same check of exhaust lobe timing. Ours opened at 26 degrees, just as its card noted.

32 Degree the Cam CONTINUED

In most cases, the cam should be installed so the measured valve timing matches the cam card. If you need to alter cam timing, you can use offset bushings or keys, multi-keyed lower sprockets, or an adjustable cam gear like this one from Comp Cams (see Sidebar "Cam Drives" on page 131). When you are confident that the desired timing is established, note any required offset bushing, key, or keyway position on your Work-A-Long Sheet. Bring the number-1 cylinder to precisely TDC on the power stroke (both lifters on the base circle), then remove the degree wheel and mark the keys, bushings, and sprockets with your own identification marks. This will be extremely helpful during final assembly. Now remove the two lifters and set them aside.

PRE-ASSEMBLY FITTING

33 Check Assembly Clearance

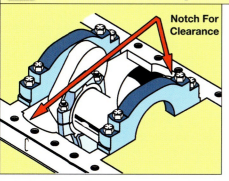
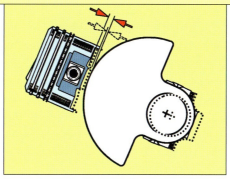

Install all remaining rods/pistons using the same techniques described in Step 26. If you're rebuilding a stock engine, you shouldn't encounter any rotating-assembly interference. However, if any special or heavy-duty parts are used, you should check for free crank rotation by carefully turning the crank at least two full turns. If the crank becomes hard to turn or "hangs up," don't force it! Take your time and look for interference. Common sources: rod bolt contacting cylinder bore or pan-rail edges, small end of a connecting rod rubbing on the underside of the piston dome or at pin boss, connecting rod beam/bolt area contacting a cam lobe. Less common sources: piston skirt contacting a counterweight, crank counterweight contacting the block, particularly at the rear. Read Engine Blueprinting by Rick Voegelin if you need to modify the block or any other components for clearance.

34 Miscellaneous Measurements

Several other measurements can now be performed. The first is determining true compression ratio. For instructions on performing compression-ratio measurement and the tools required, see sidebar "Measuring and Calculating Compression Ratio" on page 114. If you haven't checked rod side clearance, insert a feeler gauge between each pair of rods on each crank journal (see Step 24 for clearance recommendations). You can also verify the accuracy of rod-journal "indexing" on your crankshaft. First, double-check the accuracy of your TDC pointer on cylinder number-1 (Step 27). Then use your piston stop tool on, alternately, cylinders number-3, -5, -7; you should exactly locate the 90-, 180-, and 270-degree marks on your degree wheel. Finally, an overall check of machining accuracy can be performed. By comparing the deck height on all cylinders (using degree-wheel indexing), you will simultaneously test the uniformity of stroke, journal index, rod length, piston pin height, and deck machining. Variations of up to ±.005 inch are generally acceptable.

35 Inspect Rocker Geometry

While many engine builders do not bother to perform the following valvetrain tests, we recommend you do the following checks on at least cylinder number-1. If it passes with plenty of room to spare, you can optionally test the remaining cylinders. However, if things look "tight" or questionable, you must test all the remaining valves. Install the head without a gasket.

REBUILDING THE SMALL-BLOCK CHEVROLET

36 Inspect Rocker Geometry CONTINUED

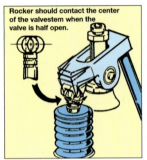
Rocker should contact the center of the valvestem when the valve is half open.

Oil and reinstall the two lifters for cylinder number-1. If you're using a hydraulic camshaft, you must use two solid or modified lifters with the exact same cup height. Install the pushrods, rockers, and pivot balls. Use two standard 3/8-inch NF nuts, rather than self-locking nuts, and adjust the rocker arms to the correct clearance. With the lifters on the base circle of the cam, set the specified intake and exhaust clearance for solid cams and zero clearance for hydraulic cams (be careful, don't pre-load the checking springs open, even slightly). Turn the crank and observe the rocker contact point on the valve tip move from the inside across the middle to the outside of the valve tip. With proper rocker geometry, the contact point should be in the middle of the valve tip when the valve is halfway open.

37 Miscellaneous Measurements

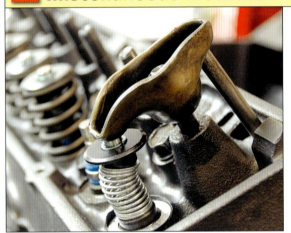

With the valvetrain assembled on number-1, several other measurements can be performed. First, double-check that the retainer has at least .070-inch clearance to the top of the guide or the press-on valve seal at maximum lift. Make sure the rocker does not contact the retainer when the valve is closed. Verify that the rocker slot has adequate clearance with the stud (at least .040 inch) at maximum lift. Finally, you can mount a dial indicator on the retainer, and compare true valve lift to measured lifter rise to determine actual rocker ratio.

38 Check Piston-to-Valve Clearance

Piston-to-valve clearance (PTVC) can now be checked. Rotate the crank clockwise (engine rotation) to bring the number-1 piston to TDC during valve overlap (both valves open). Press down on the intake rocker until you feel the valve contact the piston. Release the rocker (make sure the pushrod drops back into the cups in the lifter and rocker arm) and rotate the crank 2 or 3 degrees after TDC. Open the valve again. Repeat this procedure until you locate the point at which minimum clearance occurs (about 10 degrees ATDC). When you feel you're close, use a dial indicator or feeler gauges to measure the exact minimum value. If you move the crank too far, back up before TDC and approach it again (always moving the crank clockwise). Repeat this procedure for the exhaust valve (exhaust PTVC should occur before TDC). You should not run an engine that has less than .100-inch clearance on the intake valve and .080-inch on the exhaust. If PTVC, or any other valvetrain clearances, are close to minimum safe values, check all remaining cylinders to ensure reliability.

PRE-ASSEMBLY FITTING

Performance Tip

39 Verify Oil Pump Driveshaft Length

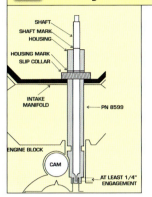

There are several different oil pump driveshaft lengths, and only one will work properly in your engine. If you have replaced the shaft, especially with a high-performance part (strongly recommended; see sidebar "Oil Pumps: Blueprinting and Modifying" on page 44), perform the following check. Install both heads, the manifold, and the distributor (all without gaskets). Tighten the distributor hold-down bracket. With the block upside down, lower the pump driveshaft into the rear main cap. Rotate the shaft and make sure it drops into the distributor drive-gear slot. Now set the pump on the main cap. Try to move the pump shaft up and down. If the shaft length is correct, it should fully engage the drive tangs and have .010- to .040-inch free play. When you have completed this inspection, remove the distributor, manifold, and both cylinder heads. MSD offers a 3-in-1 Tool, which helps check the oil pump driveshaft depth, as well as the distributor shaft slip collar (if you're using one). Another great feature is that it acts as an oil pump priming drive for pre-lubing.

40 Check Oil Pump/Pickup Clearance

Install the oil pump on the rear main cap (and the windage tray, if used). Rotate the crank a couple of turns to make sure nothing contacts the pump or tray. Now lubricate the end of the pickup tube and the oil pump counter-bore, then install the pickup using an installation tool such as this one from Goodson. Set the oil pan on the block; it should sit flush (without a gasket). If it is held off the block, rotate the crank to determine if the pan is hitting the rotating assembly or a stationary object like the oil pump/pickup or windage tray. If the pan fits properly, temporarily remove it and pivot the pickup up so it will contact the pan. Then install the pan and force it down flat against the block surface. Remove the pan and carefully rotate the pickup down another 1/4 inch; mark this position. (See sidebar "Oil Pumps: Blueprinting and Modifying" on page 44 for info on welding the pickup and preparing the pump for final assembly.)

41 Check Intake Manifold Fit

Set both cylinder heads on the block again, but this time with head gaskets in place. To prevent damaging the gaskets, do not tighten the bolts; just snug them down to about 5 ft-lbs. First, set the manifold on (without gaskets) and bolt it to one head using a couple of bolts. Inspect the space between the manifold and the intake surface on the other head. It should be parallel; if it isn't, the manifold or cylinder heads have been miss-machined. Now, reinstall the manifold with both gaskets in place (leave off the end rail gaskets). Use a flashlight and align the boltholes in the gaskets, cylinder heads, and intake manifold. Try installing a bolt in each corner; they should screw in easily. Tighten them finger tight. Check the spacing between the manifold and block rails; you should have between .060- and .120-inch clearance. Discuss any fitting problems with your machine shop.

REBUILDING THE SMALL-BLOCK CHEVROLET

CHAPTER 7

Measuring and Calculating Compression Ratio

Compression ratio is the measurement of how many times the inducted charge is squeezed into a space one-half again as large. Within limits, the higher the compression, the higher the power output. However, it's "the limits" that make setting and calculating compression so critical. For example, most unleaded fuel will detonate with higher than about 10:1 compression. You'll never know the actual compression—despite the "advertised" compression of the pistons—until you measure and calculate it yourself.

In its simplest form, compression ratio is calculated by dividing the volume enclosed in the cylinder when the piston is at bottom dead center (BDC) with the volume enclosed at top dead center (TDC). The only tricky part to this process is measuring these volumes. To calculate compression ratio, the following volumes must be measured or calculated: the swept volume of the piston, the displaced volume of piston dome and valve notches, the head gasket volume, and the volume in the combustion chamber.

Calculating the swept volume of the piston is quite straightforward. The following formula calculates the volume of a simple cylinder.

$$\text{Volume (in CCs)} = \frac{(D^2) \times 51.49 \times S}{2}$$

Where D = bore diamerter and
S = stroke length (in inches)

This formula also includes a factor that converts the "inches" of bore and stroke to the cubic centimeters (cc) of volume that are much more convenient and compatible with the remaining measurements.

The displaced volume of the piston dome and valve notches is more complex. The dome can be raised, causing an increase in the compression ratio, or it can be dished, lowering the compression ratio. Even if the piston has no dome (a flat top), it can "pop out" above the deck surface at TDC or end up below the deck. If the piston has valve notches, they will always reduce the compression by some amount. The combination of all these factors is the "displaced dome volume."

Fortunately, there is a relatively easy way to measure this variable. By moving the piston a precise amount down the bore from TDC (often 1/2 or 1 inch) and sealing it with grease or Vaseline, you can fill the space with water dispensed from a burette. With the bore covered by a plastic plate (also sealed with Vaseline), the volume can be measured to within .1 cc. By comparing this volume with the calculated volume of a cylinder of the same height (1/2 or 1 inch), the difference is the net volume displaced by the piston dome. A sample calculation uses the same formula as before, except the distance the piston is lowered in the bore (1/2 inch) is substituted for the stroke:

$$\text{Volume (1/2 inch down)} = \frac{(4.030)^2 \times 51.49 \times .5}{2}$$

$$= 4.060 \times 51.49 \times .5 = 104.53 \text{ (CCs)}$$
$$= 104.53 \text{ (calculated)} - 99.8 \text{ (measured)}$$
$$= 4.72 \text{ (positive displaced dome volume)}$$

The measured volume using the burette on 99.8 cc is subtracted from the calculated volume of 104.53 cc. In this case, the result is positive, indicating that the displaced dome volume of 4.73 cc will increase the compression ratio.

The gasket manufacturer often provides the volume in the compressed head gasket. If it isn't provided, you can calculate it by using the same volume formula, except this time substitute the compressed gasket thickness (.035 inch in our example below) for the stroke and the inside gasket circle (4.100 inches) for the bore. Here's the calculation:

$$\text{Volume (head gasket)} = \frac{(4.100)^2 \times 51.49 \times .035}{2}$$

$$= 4.203 \times 51.49 \times .035 = 7.75 \text{ (CCs)}$$

The final volume is the space in the combustion chamber. It is measured using the water/burette method. Make sure the valves are sealed (a little grease on the valveseats helps) and the spark plug is installed. Use a plastic plate to seal the head surface. Typical chamber volumes run from under 60 cc to over 800 cc.

Now that all of the enclosed volumes have been measured or calculated, it's just a matter of adding (or subtracting) them and doing the final division to determine compression ratio. Here's the formula:

PRE-ASSEMBLY FITTING

$$CR = \frac{C - (P) + G + V}{C - (P) + G}$$

Where CR = compression Ratio
C = Combustion Chamber Volume
P = Displaced Dome Volume
G = Compressed Head Gasket Volume
V = Swept Volume in the Cylinder

Let's plug in some numbers for the 350 we're building in this book.

$$CR = \frac{78 - (-4.2) + 7.57 + 727.5}{78 - (-4.2) + 7.57}$$

$$CR = \frac{89.77 + 727.5}{89.77}$$

$$CR = 9.1:1$$

There is only one confusing part to this process. Note that the formula requires subtracting the displaced piston dome volume from the numerator and denominator. However, our engine has a negative dome volume (flat-top pistons with valve reliefs that rests below the deck surface at TDC), and if you remember math class, two negatives make a positive. Therefore, the rule is: negative dome volumes are added; positive dome volumes are subtracted.

Here is one more example using a 302-racing engine with positive dome displacement:

$$CR = \frac{68 - (+7.1) + 7.57 + 627.2}{68 - (+7.1) + 7.57}$$

$$CR = \frac{68.47 + 627.5}{68.47}$$

$$CR = 10.2:1$$

Using a dial indicator, the piston is lowered 1/2 or 1 inch down the bore. This volume is subtracted from the calculated volume to measure displaced dome volume. The value indicates dome, valve pocket, and deck height volumes.

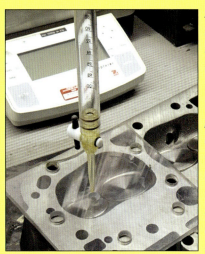

A burette is used to measure the volume of space in the combustion chamber as well as the volume of the cylinder when taking domed pistons or valve reliefs into account. For the combustion chamber, both valves must be closed and a spark plug installed. A plastic plate seals the head surface as you fill it with a liquid.

42 Final Pre-Assembly Checks

If any of the accessories, drive pulleys, or belts have been modified or adapted to your engine, now is a good time to attach them and make sure everything fits as intended. If you have installed a new set of connecting rods, cylinder heads, valves, or any other components that could be mixed up before final assembly, make sure everything is numbered and identified. After you have completed all pre-assembly checks, completely disassemble the engine. If any final machine work must be performed to the block, cylinder heads, pistons, etc., repeat relevant pre-assembly steps to make sure clearances are still acceptable. Re-clean everything for final assembly, making sure to perform the final bore cleaning steps in Chapter 6, "Component Cleaning," that were skipped during pre-assembly.

REBUILDING THE SMALL-BLOCK CHEVROLET

CHAPTER 8

FINAL ASSEMBLY

This chapter shows you how to professionally assemble your engine. Not included in this chapter are measurements, tolerances and checks of bearing clearances, cam timing, and other critical dimensions. Important issues of parts selection, machine work, cleaning, and pre-assembly component fitting were detailed in the previous chapters. Do not assemble your engine unless you have performed all the appropriate steps in those chapters. The reliability of your engine, and a good chunk of your wallet, is riding on it!

Even when all of the required preparation is done, don't undertake final assembly until you recall the basics of successful engine building. You can never remind yourself too often to take your time, read everything thoroughly, and think ahead. Don't let your excitement get the better of you. After all, watching your engine come together with shiny, new parts is exciting! Make sure you take the time to be 100-percent sure of everything. Then, just to be safe, check it again. Measure twice, install once. If you come across something that you don't feel right about, ask your machine shop or do more reading and research.

When you begin assembly, don't invite a bunch of friends over to watch. Don't turn the volume on your favorite radio up to "11." Don't roll the TV into your shop. Don't start assembly when you're tired. And save the celebratory beers for when you're all finished. Assembling an engine requires your full attention. Experts with years of experience often trace mistakes to interruptions and distractions. Don't let a "stupid" mistake happen to you. Keep your attention focused on the job at hand.

Tools and Supplies

Assembly requires many of the same tools used during disassembly and pre-assembly checking. However, several additional tools and supplies are needed for final engine assembly.

Thick Assembly Lubricant. An acceptable lubricant for final assembly is STP mixed 1:1 with engine oil. Applying it from a squirt-can will keep components, and your fingers, clean.

Petroleum Jelly. A fail-safe thread lubricant for fasteners and other general assembly purposes (commonly sold as Vaseline) produces uniform tightness for "standard-lubricated" torque specifications and won't over-tighten and pull threads. Torque specs included in the upcoming step-by-step instructions

Watching your engine come together with shiny new parts is exciting! However, don't let your excitement get the better of you. Make sure you take the time to be 100-percent sure of everything. Then, just to be safe, check it again. If you have doubts about anything, ask your machine shop for advice.

FINAL ASSEMBLY

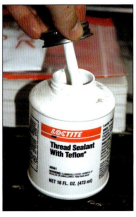

ARP offers assembly lube and a separate thread sealer (they even include in it some applications such as their rod bolts). Assembly lube reduces friction when tightening bolts so be sure to use their recommended torque spec. Thread sealer (shown here from Loctite) will be needed on bolts that protrude into water jackets to help seal the engine.

Goodson offers inexpensive protectors that prevent damaging the crankshaft during final assembly. You can also use short lengths of 3/8-inch rubber hose.

assume that petroleum jelly or a similar lubricant is used on threads and bolt head contact surfaces.

ARP Thread Sealer and Assembly Lubricant. ARP, maker of specialty fasteners for performance applications, offers two fastener lubricants. 1) ATP Thread Sealer is Teflon-based with special lubricants added. It seals head bolts (and other fasteners that protrude into the water jackets) and provides optimum lubrication for uniform bolt torque. 2) ARP Assembly Lubricant is a moly-based lubricant that minimizes thread friction. Bolt torque values must be reduced when using either of these lubricants (bolt tightness, however, isn't reduced). See the torque chart on page 155.

Anti-Seize Compound. Applied to bolt threads in the exhaust system, it will prevent "frozen" and broken fasteners when the engine is disassembled in the future.

Camshaft Break-In Lube. Some types of molybdenum-disulfide (black) cam break-in lubes are too "dry" to prevent lifter/lobe scuffing. Add a little GM Engine Oil Supplement or STP to these moly lubes—not enough to make them "runny"; just enough to give them a distinctly "wet" appearance.

Silicone Rubber Adhesive. Available everywhere as Silicone Gasket or Silicone Sealer. CRC and Permatex offer it in a convenient dispenser that doesn't clog up.

Weather-strip Adhesive. This fast-drying adhesive holds specific gaskets (such as pan gaskets) in place until they're tightened.

Loctite. There are two types of Loctite used during engine assembly: Blue and Red. Both act as a thread-locking compound; however, they're for different applications. Blue should be used on bolts that will be removed for service at some point in your engine's life. The Red Loctite is intended for permanent installation of retainers. Do not use this compound on fasteners unless instructed.

Complete Gasket Package. All engine gaskets, including head gaskets from Fel-Pro, Mr. Gasket, and SCE, will have everything you need. If piston-to-head and piston-to-valve clearances were close to minimum safe values when checked in the previous chapter, make sure to use head gaskets no thinner than those used during testing.

Set of "Core" and Oil Passage Plugs. Can be purchased as a kit (from Milodon or others) or individually. Make sure you also get the large "core" plug used at the rear of the cam.

Rod Bolt Protectors. Lengths of 3/8-inch rubber hose or plastic protector boots are absolutely essential to prevent damaging the crankshaft during final assembly. Goodson and other manufacturers offer inexpensive protectors. You may feel that if you're just careful you won't need these, but trust us, cover the rod bolts.

Bench Vise with Soft Jaws. A firmly mounted bench vise with about 6-inch jaws will make several engine assembly steps much easier. A pair of soft (aluminum or plastic) jaws is essential for clamping items that should not be marred, such as connecting rods.

Rod Installation Tool (optional). A tool that attaches to a rod bolt and guides the rod down the bore when installing the pistons is very helpful. B&B Performance offers an inexpensive Pro model, or you can make one yourself (see Step 44 on page 38).

Torque Wrenches. It's best to have two sizes available: a 3/8-inch drive with a range to about 100 ft-lbs, and a large 1/2-inch drive wrench with a range to about 200 ft-lbs.

Internal Snap Ring Pliers. If your pistons and rods use floating (not press-fit) pins and standard lock rings, you'll need to use snap ring pliers for assembly. Don't try to insert a snap ring without the proper tool; you could easily damage the piston and/or the snap ring (not to mention fling one across the garage).

Ring Compressor. The recommended type (very strongly recommended) is a taper-bore compressor available from B&B Performance. In addition, adjustable taper-bore compressors are available from

REBUILDING THE SMALL-BLOCK CHEVROLET

CHAPTER 8

Additional assembly aids include silicone sealer, anti-seize, Loctite thread-locking sealant, and High Tach gasket adhesive. Silicone gasket adhesive (left) helps build a leak-free engine. It is available from Permatex and CRC in non-clog dispensers. Permatex Anti-Seize (right) prevents "frozen" exhaust manifold and header bolts.

Goodson. You can use a steel band compressor, but it must be a single-wrap band model that is compressed with special "pliers." Though we don't recommend it, use care when using a multi-wrap band compressor that is tightened with a square "key" (they're notorious for breaking rings).

Vibration Damper Installer. The vibration damper should be installed with a special tool, available from B&B Performance and other sources. Do not drive it on with a hammer or pull it on with the crank center bolt. Do it right! Buy this tool before you begin assembly. It's something that you'll use again, on your next engine project.

Pre-Oiling Tool. Another must-have item. The B&B Performance Pro model works great, and MSD Ignition offers one that also helps you set the distributor gear depth (if your deck surfaces have been modified). You'll also need a 100-psi pressure gauge and 1/8-inch pipe fittings to install it in the pressure access at the rear of the block.

Engine Oil and Filter. At least enough oil and filters for initial fill-up and one oil change (after initial break-in). Do not use synthetic oils during break-in.

Miscellaneous. The following items may need to be rebuilt, replaced, or purchased to complete your engine build-up: distributor, coil, spark plug wires, carburetor, choke, bi-metal actuator, EGR valve, PCV valve and hose, oil pressure sender, water pump, thermostat, belts, hoses, and antifreeze.

Final Assembly Tips

Before you begin your final assembly, here's a short "top ten" list of important things that should be completed. If any machining or cleaning step was overlooked, make sure to thoroughly re-clean the component(s) before proceeding with final assembly.

- Block and other components detailed and (optionally) painted.
- Front oil gallery passages deburred or tapped to accept new plugs.
- All threaded holes cleaned with tap or "chasing" tool and/or repaired.
- Cam bearings installed in block (and cam degreed).
- All machine work on block, heads, crankshaft, and other components completed.
- Rotating assembly balanced.
- All pre-assembly checks completed.
- Rods and pistons assembled (for pressed pins only).
- Bores scrubbed with oiled paper towel until spotless.
- All components, including fasteners and small parts, cleaned, stored in plastic bags, and ready for final assembly.

One final thought before you begin: if you run into problems, don't just forge ahead, hoping everything will turn out fine. Stop, locate, and understand the problem, then correct it before you proceed, even if that means taking everything apart and re-cleaning (again!). While the thought of all that "wasted" time may be hard to stomach, you'll be more than pleased when the engine is installed and running great. You'll soon forget the long hours of preparation if everything works out fine; you'll never forget the frustration if your rebuilt engine runs badly or malfunctions.

Step-by-Step Final Assembly

1 Prepare for Assembly

Do not begin final assembly until you have completed all of the step-by-step instructions in previous chapters, especially those in Chapter 6, "Component Cleaning," and Chapter 7, "Pre-Assembly Fitting." Make sure you've read the information presented earlier in this chapter on tools, supplies, and other final-assembly preparations. All components, including fasteners and small parts, should be cleaned, stored in plastic bags, and labeled for easy identification. If you haven't painted your engine, take a look at Sidebar "Detailing and Painting" on page 92.

FINAL ASSEMBLY

2 Assemble Cylinder Head

If your cylinder heads are assembled, skip to Step 4. First, thoroughly lubricate the valveguides with assembly lube. Work the valves in and out of the guides and make sure the lubricant has completely penetrated every crevice in the guides. Double-check valve numbering to make sure the correct valves are installed in their matching chambers. If guide-mounted seals are used on your engine, squirt some assembly lube in the "cups," then slide the seals over the valvestems and onto the guides (using the thin protective sleeve supplied with the seals).

3 Detail Valvesprings

The ends of the coils on most new valvesprings have sharp edges that have been known to "machine" their way into cylinder heads and retainers. When this happens, metal particles are released into the oil, and in some cases, springs have cut their way completely into the water jackets. Perhaps one of the best-kept "secrets" of engine assembly, taking the time to deburr the spring coils is a simple task that improves valvetrain reliability. First, remove any inner springs and flat-wound dampers. Use an abrasive wheel or a small high-speed grinder to smooth off all sharp edges on both ends of all springs. Make sure all abrasive particles are completely removed with solvent and compressed air before you reassemble the inner springs and dampers.

4 Assemble Cylinder Head CONTINUED

Now, install a retainer, spring, and matching spring shims over their matching valve. Note: Do not install shims thinner than .030 inch in direct contact with the spring coils unless they are made from hardened spring steel. Compress the spring, and if your valves have a second stem groove, lubricate a rubber O-ring seal and install it on the valvestem. Install a pair of split-locks and slowly release the valvespring compressor tool. Verify that the locks have seated in the retainer. Repeat the procedure for the remaining valves.

5 Install Rear Water Jacket and Gallery Plugs

Before you mount the block on an engine stand, install the six rear block plugs. Start by smearing a thin layer of silicone sealer on the edges of the two water jacket (core) plugs and the bores in the block. Drive in the core plugs using a large socket with an OD of about 1/8-inch smaller than the ID of the plugs (a 1 1/16-inch socket often works). Stop when the edge of the plug lines up with the center of the chamfer in the block. If the core plugs are retained with safety screws, apply silicone sealer to the threads and install the screws. Next, apply silicone sealer to the threads on the three oil gallery plugs (apply none to the threads in the block). Install and tighten the plugs to 20 ft-lbs. Wipe excess silicone from all plugs.

REBUILDING THE SMALL-BLOCK CHEVROLET

CHAPTER 8

Bolt Torquing Techniques

Properly torqued fasteners are essential to a secure mechanical assembly. Apply too little torque and there will be insufficient clamping force to prevent gasket leakage, or fasteners may loosen and back out completely. Over-torquing can warp components, pull threads, and damage fasteners.

Accurate torque readings are only possible when the threads are clean, undamaged, and lubricated. While some mechanics install bolts dry, we recommend that all fastener threads and head contact surfaces are lubricated before bolts are installed and tightened. Lubrication allows fasteners to screw in easier, prevents thread seizure, and most important, reduces variations in bolt stretch, the true measure of "tightness." But various lubricants have various bolt stretch effects, so a lubricant that generates uniform, predictable thread friction is needed. Vaseline is often chosen because it is widely available and does not contain any of the slippery synthetics or moly compounds that can radically change torque requirements from commonly published values. Use other lubricants, such as ARP assembly lube, that contain these moly compounds only when you know their precise effect on bolt torque. ARP has published unique torque tables calibrated for fasteners using their lubricants (see "Torque Specifications" on page 155 and sidebar "ARP Fasteners" on page 127).

Torque specifications are listed as a range or a single number. If a range of values is given, attempt to torque to the upper limit (but never above it). In either case, if the torque reading levels off before you reach your target value, do not continue turning the fastener. Remove it and examine both the male and female threads. If the threads in the bolt hole appear undamaged, install a new fastener and try again. If the threaded hole is damaged, it must be repaired (see sidebar "Thread Repair" on page 53).

When more than one fastener holds a single part, such as with cylinder heads, intake manifolds, etc., bolt torque should be applied in several steps, following a specific tightening sequence. If no sequence is specified, use a crisscross pattern. In all cases, applying torque in increasing steps is essential to obtain long-term sealing reliability.

Using "known" lubricants and the proper torque tables when tightening fasteners is the mark of the real professional. Leave "home-brew" thread lubricants or "the-tighter-the-better" techniques to the rank amateur. Since proper torquing technique greatly reduces the chances of damaging the block and other engine components, it can save you a lot of time and money, too.

Petroleum jelly is often chosen as a thread lubricant because it is widely available and does not contain any of the synthetics or moly compounds that can radically change torque requirements from commonly published values.

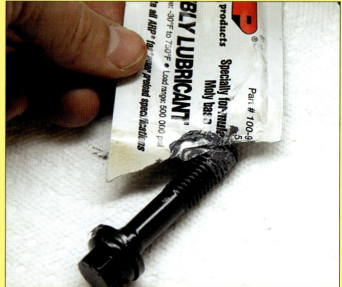

If you use a very "slippery" thread lube, such as this one from ARP, standard published torque specs will be too high. ARP developed its own torque table (see page 155) that must be followed.

FINAL ASSEMBLY

6 Install Rear Cam Plug

Apply a uniform, thin film of silicone sealer to the edge of the cam plug. Apply no silicone to the bore in the block. Don't use excess sealer; it can work its way into the cam bearing. The plug is shallow and must be carefully aligned when it is driven into the block. Drive the plug in using a large socket (again, about 1/8-inch smaller than the ID of the plug). The edge of the plug should end up 1/32 inch below the machined surface; if it's much deeper than that, it may contact the rear of the camshaft.

7 Install Cup-Type Oil Gallery Plugs

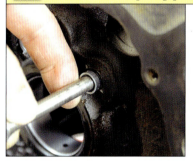 

Install the block on your engine stand. If your machine shop tapped the front of the oil galleries for 1/4- or 3/8-inch plugs, jump to Step 8. The 1/2-inch (type P5) front gallery plugs press fit into the front of the oil galleries. Note: If a .030-inch hole was drilled in one of the plugs (see Step 6, page 84), install that plug in the center oil gallery. No sealer is required on these plugs. Use a 5/16-inch straight-shank punch (no larger), and drive each plug in until it seats against the step in the gallery passages (deepest portion of plug will rest about 1/4 to 3/8 inch below the surface). To be on the safe side, place two to four chisel marks in the edge of each bore to keep the plugs in place. Jump to Step 7.

8 Install Screw-In Gallery Plugs

Install a 1/4- or 3/8-inch pipe plug (depending on the size of the tap used) in each of the main oil galleries. No silicone sealer is required. If a .030-inch hole was drilled in one of the plugs (see Step 6, on page 84), install that plug in the center oil gallery. Torque the 1/4-inch plugs to 20 ft-lbs and the 3/8-inch plug to 40 ft-lbs.

9 Install Remaining Block Plugs

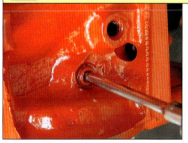  

Using the same technique as illustrated in Step 5, on page 119 (for installing gallery plugs), install the remaining seven water jacket core plugs in the block. Apply silicone sealer to the threads of four 1/4-inch pipe plugs, and install: 1) one plug in the oil gallery passage located in the side of the block, near the oil filter mount; 2) install a second plug in the oil passage at the top rear of the block; and 3) install the final two plugs in the water drain holes near the oil pan rails on each side of the block. Torque all plugs to 20 ft-lbs. (A 1/8-inch pipe plug will be installed in the oil-pressure sender takeoff in Step 64, page 139.)

REBUILDING THE SMALL-BLOCK CHEVROLET

CHAPTER 8

Important!

10 Install Oil Passage Plugs

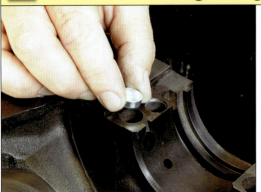

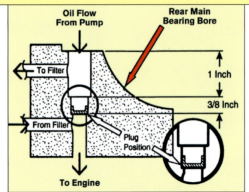

! If the cup-type plug in the oil passage under the rear main cap is in place, jump to Step 10. If you removed this plug as instructed during disassembly, install a new plug in the passage now. The plug is the same type used in the front of the oil galleries (1/2-inch, type P5). Apply a little assembly lube to the OD of the plug and drop it into the bore; it will fall about 1 inch down and then stop. Use a 3/8-inch straight-shank punch and drive the plug in another 3/8 inch. Warning: If you drive this plug in more than 1/4 inch, you can restrict engine oil flow. If you leave this plug out, engine oil will not pass through the oil filter.

11 Install Main Plugs

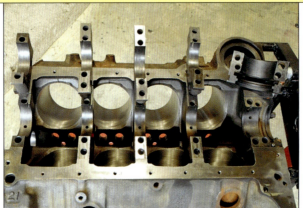

Make sure the main bearings, the block bores, and the caps are spotlessly clean. Install the bearing shells in the block and caps by pressing them firmly in place with your fingers, rocking them back and forth to make sure they are fully seated. Install grooved bearing shells in the block; non-grooved shells in the caps. Bearings for number-1 through number-4 are interchangeable; number-5 is a wide bearing with a thrust face. When all bearings are firmly seated, proceed to Step 12.

12 Install Neoprene Rear Main Seal

Early small-blocks used a rope seal for the rear main. When using a rope seal it is important to let the seals soak in engine oil and to really work the seal into the block and cap. Be sure to review the instructions with the new seal. (There are conversion seal kits available also.) If you have a two-piece seal, apply a very thin film of silicone sealer to the backside of both seal halves; install them in the block and main cap (seal "lip" must point inward). We offset the seal halves just a little. Apply a small amount of silicone to the mating edges of the seal and the adjacent block and cap surfaces, as shown. Make sure there's a shallow "bead" of silicone in the corners of the block (arrows). Now jump to Step 14.

FINAL ASSEMBLY

13 Install Crankshaft

Generously lubricate the main bearing shells in the block (and the cam bearings, while they're still accessible) with assembly lube. If your engine uses a two-piece rear seal, apply a thin coat of assembly lube on the seal surfaces in the block and cap; too much will mix with the silicone sealer on the ends of the seal. Lightly lubricate the seal surface on the crankshaft. Then carefully lower the crank into the block, rotating it slightly as you set it in place.

14 Install Rear Main Cap

Apply assembly lube to the bearing in the rear main cap. Make sure the cap and block mating surfaces are clean, and then install the cap on the block. Tap the cap lightly with a softhead hammer to fully seat it in the block registers. Refer to sidebar "Bolt Torquing Techniques" on page 120, for information on lubricating and tightening fasteners, and then lubricate the main cap bolt threads and heads with thread assembly lube. When you are sure that the main cap is properly seated, install the bolts and tighten them finger tight. Then strike the rear of the crank two or three times with a softhead hammer to seat the thrust bearing against the block.

15 Install Remaining Main Caps

Install the remaining main caps, then lubricate and install the remaining main bolts (if you will be using a windage tray, you must install studs in the three center caps). Make sure all the caps are in the correct location and not turned end-for-end. N

The following torque values are for normal grade-8 fasteners lubricated with petroleum jelly; for other fasteners and lubes, refer to the torque chart on page 155. Torque all the main bolts in 25-ft-lb steps to 75 ft-lbs (65 ft-lbs for outer bolts on 4-bolt caps). With the bolts tight, the crank should turn freely; with rope-type rear seals, about 15 to 25 ft-lbs is required to rotate the crank.

16 Lubricate One-Piece Rear Main Seal

Perform this step if your engine uses a one-piece rear main seal; otherwise, skip to Step 18. Smear a thin coat of silicone seal on the outside of the seal and install the seal in the appliance with a hammer. Apply a thin film of silicone sealer to one side of the appliance gasket. Set the gasket against the block surface. Apply another film of silicone sealer to the mating surface on the appliance. Finally, lubricate the seal and crankshaft, and carefully position the appliance against the block, making sure the seal does not "fold" backward. Install two short and two long 1/4-inch mounting screws and torque them to 8 ft-lbs.

17 Assemble Floating Pins and Connecting Rods

If your rods and pistons use press-fit pins and are already assembled, skip to Step 19. First, make sure the pin bores in the rods and pistons are well oiled with assembly lube. Then assemble the pistons and rods following the piston and rod orientation rules described in Chapter 7, "Pre-Assembly Fitting," Steps 16 through 19, on page 105. Use internal snap-ring pliers to install standard Tru-Arc lock rings, while Spirolox should be worked in—one loop at a time—with a small probe or screwdriver. Important: Install Tru-Arcs with the open ends pointing up or down only and make sure the flat side (with the sharp corners) faces out. Never use old, damaged, or weak lock rings. Make sure all lock rings are fully seated in the grooves in the pistons.

18 Install Three-Piece Oil Ring

Gently clamp the number-1 piston/rod in a vise with soft jaws. The valve pockets should face away from you (pockets face toward you on even-numbered pistons); the front arrow should always point to the left. Install an oil-ring wavy expander with the ends facing directly away from you. Make sure the ends butt and that they do not overlap. Install the first oil rail by inserting one end just below the expander and wrapping it around the piston. Position the rail gap about 45 degrees to the left. Then install the upper rail and position its gap about 45 degrees to the right. Make sure the expander ends still butt and have not overlapped. If the ring is properly installed, it should slide smoothly in the groove with only slight drag. After you're finished inspecting the ring, make sure the ring orientation matches the drawing in on page 156.

19 Install Compression Rings

Refer to the instructions included with your ring set to determine which rings are the second rings and which are the top rings. Also, find out which side of the ring should face up. Most rings have the word "top" or a dimple that should face up, but some are not marked. Don't guess! Find out, even if it means a call to the ring manufacturer. Now install the second ring. You can expand it with your thumbs, or you can use a ring-expanding tool. Position the gap facing directly toward you. Finally, install the top ring and position its gap facing directly away from you. Note: You can install the top and second rings with your thumbs by just prying the end-gap apart (like an expanding tool) or you can "wrap" the rings around the piston (as shown on the right), similar to installing oil-ring rails.

20 Install Rod Bearings

Make sure the rod bearing halves, the rod bore, and the cap mating surfaces are spotlessly clean. Install a bearing shell in the rod by pressing it firmly in place with your fingers. Then install another bearing shell in the rod cap.

21 Protect Crank Journals

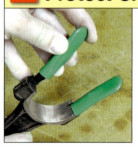 

Before the rod/piston can be installed, two important steps must be taken to prevent damaging the crank. First, install protective sleeves or short lengths of 3/8-inch rubber fuel hose on both rod bolts. Second, rotate the crank so the rod journal you're working on (in this case, the number-1 journal) is close to the BDC position.

FINAL ASSEMBLY

Professional Mechanic Tip
22 Use Ring Compressor

There are two types of ring compressors that are known for ease of use and reliability. The first, and by far the better, is a one-piece taper-bore sleeve that is designed to fit a specific-size bore and piston. These are available from Goodson and other tool sources. You can also use a steel-band compressor, and there are also multi-wrap band compressors that work, but use care as they are known for breaking rings.

23 Lubricate Pin/Piston

Before you continue, make sure the pin and pin bores have been thoroughly lubricated with assembly lube. Then lubricate both rod bearing shells and the matching crank journal. Thoroughly lubricate the cylinder bore with engine oil using a clean, lint-free rag. Then, obtain a 6-inch-diameter plastic container and add about 2 inches of engine oil. Dip the piston and ring package into the oil to thoroughly saturate the rings, grooves, and skirts. Remove the piston and let the excess oil drip off.

24 Prepare to Install Piston

Double-check the end-gap location of all rings (refer to Step 30, on page 127), and then carefully install the ring compressor over the ring package. If you're using a band-type compressor, compress the rings until the band is snug. If you're using a taper-bore compressor, slide the compressor over the skirt until the top of the compressor is flush with the top of the piston. Make sure the rings don't slip out of the grooves as they start to compress.

25 Install Piston

Slide the rod in the piston (side-to-side) toward the rear of the engine (slide even-numbered rods toward the front of the engine); this gives the maximum clearance to the crank counterweight.

Slide the piston into the bore. Make sure that you are installing the correct piston, and that it's correctly oriented "up" or "down." Hold the ring compressor seated flat against the deck surface and firmly (but not hard!) tap the piston into the cylinder with a hammer handle. If the piston "hangs up," STOP! Review Step 26 for help in solving problems.

Critical Inspection
26 Possible Ring/Piston Installation Problems

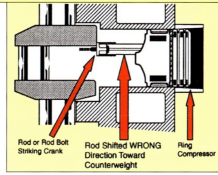

If the piston stops as you are tapping it into the bore, look for the following problems: 1) Ring has "popped out" (arrows) between the compressor and the block (start over, holding the compressor firmly against deck surface). 2) Rod or rod bolt has contacted the crank or block (make sure the crank is at BDC and the rod is slid to one side, away from the crank counterweight). 3) Wrong size taper-bore ring compressor. 4) Ring end gaps not set properly (see Step 22 on page 106).

27 Continue Piston Installation

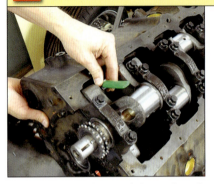 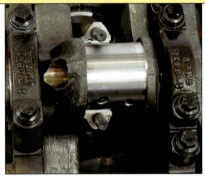

When the ring package has fully entered the bore and the ring compressor has been removed, reach around and hold the big end of the rod while you continue to tap the piston down the bore. As the rod approaches the crank, make sure that the rod properly aligns with the crank journal (you may have to twist the rod slightly or slide it side-to-side). Take your time and carefully tap the piston until the rod bearing seats against the crank journal. (If you are installing a second rod on the crank journal, make sure that the rods don't contact one another as the second rod approaches the crank.)

28 Install Rod Caps

Before you continue, make sure that: 1) the bearing shell in the rod has not slipped out of position, 2) the numbering stamped in the rod matches the correct installation sequence, and 3) the bearing-tang side of the rod faces away from the engine. Remove the protective sleeves from the rod. If you haven't already, lubricate the bearing shell in the rod cap with assembly lube. Also, apply thread lube to rod-bolt threads and install the cap and nuts (cap and rod mated tang to tang). Torque the rod bolts in 10-ft-lb steps to the manufacturer's recommended torque (usually 35 ft-lbs for 11/32-inch bolts, 45 ft-lbs for 3/8-inch bolts, and 75 ft-lbs for 7/16-inch bolts).

29 Check Rotating Torque

Check the torque required to rotate the crankshaft after each rod/piston is installed. It should not increase more than about 5 ft-lbs per piston/rod. If the reading is much higher, there are possible problems such as improperly installed rings, pistons in wrong bores, or improper bearing or rotating clearance. Find out what's wrong and fix it before you continue. With the bottom end fully assembled, it shouldn't take more than 35 to 40 ft-lbs to rotate the crankshaft. (If your engine uses a rope-type rear main seal, it may take as much as 45 to 55 ft-lbs.)

30 Check Bore Wall

Rotate the crank two turns and position the piston that was just installed at BDC. Inspect the cylinder wall for scratches by feeling the bore with your fingernail. While you may see faint vertical marks (sometimes caused by the top ring end gap), they pose no problem unless you can feel an indentation in the bore with your fingernail. If this happens, remove the rod/piston and look for a broken ring or improperly deburred ring ends. A deep scratch in the bore wall can hurt engine performance; if you find one, you may have to consider taking the block back to your machine shop for inspection and consultation.

FINAL ASSEMBLY

ARP Fasteners

The full name of this company is Automotive Racing Products but to just about every automotive enthusiast, they are simply known as ARP or "the place where you go to buy bolts."

ARP offers a wide selection of high-grade primary fasteners, main-bearing cap bolts, rod bolts, and head bolts for most major V-8 engines. They also sell specialty studs for main caps, cylinder heads, and other applications. For certain engines, they offer complete engine kits in either chrome-moly steel or stainless steel that include primary fasteners—with either bolts or studs—and many of the secondary bolts for external accessories.

ARP's products are available through most retail speed shops and auto-supply houses. The do not sell direct, but they will send product information and literature if you call (see the Source Guide on page 160).

Rocker arm adjusting nut kits include a 12-point head and Allen locking screws that make adjusting valves a breeze. Plus, they don't damage rocker stud threads like stock, self-locking nuts.

ARP is known as the leader in fastener hardware and accessories such as thread sealers and compounds. They have high-strength bolts for nearly every application. We opted for their 12-point intake bolt kit for our project.

In addition to a wide selection of high-grade primary fasteners for main-bearing caps, rod bolts, head bolts, etc., ARP also sells complete engine kits in either chrome-moly or stainless steel that include many of the secondary bolts for external accessories.

31 Verify Ring End-Gap Locations

Front of Engine

Cylinders 1, 3, 5, 7

Cylinders 2, 4, 6, 8

Intake Manifold

1—Oil Ring Expander And Top-Ring Gaps
2—Oil Ring Scraper-Rail Gaps
3—Second-Ring Gap

Use these optimum ring end-gap locations for all cylinders. Jump back to Step 18 on page 124 and repeat the installation steps for the remaining rods/pistons. Remember: On the even-numbered cylinders (number-2, -4, -6, and -8) make sure to clamp the piston in Step 18 so that the valve notches face toward you while the front arrows point to the left as you install the rings.

Torque Fasteners

32 Recheck Rod/Main Bolt Torque

After you have installed all pistons and rods, recheck the torque on all rod bolts by starting at the front of the engine (number-1 cylinder) and moving toward the rear, one rod at a time. Similarly, recheck the torque of all main bolts.

REBUILDING THE SMALL-BLOCK CHEVROLET

CHAPTER 8

33 Install Dipstick Shield

If your engine uses a dipstick shield that extends between the crankshaft counterweights, insert it in the passage in the side of the block from the deck surface end. Use a 3/8-inch punch to gently seat it in the end of the passage; the tube should protrude from the pan rail surface about 2½ inches.

34 Install Oil Pump/Pickup

Before you install the oil pump on the rear main cap, install the driveshaft. If you are using a stock-type driveshaft, use a new plastic sleeve and "snap" it on the driveshaft and pump. If you're using a high-performance replacement shaft (strongly recommended), a permanently attached steel collar (that does not "snap" together) replaces the plastic sleeve. Turn the pump and driveshaft upside down and lower them onto the rear main cap (no gasket is required between the pump and cap). Lubricate the threads and install the single 2⅜-inch-long, 7/16-inch attaching bolt. Torque to 65 ft-lbs. If your oil pump pickup screen was not installed in Chapter 7, now is the time to bolt it in place.

35 Install Oil Filter Adapter

Set the oil filter adapter in the block. There are three types of oil filter adapters; yours may look different from the one pictured here. The adapter can be installed with the pressure relief valve either facing toward or away from the crankshaft. No gasket is used between the adapter and the block. Locate the two 1/4- or 5/16-inch bolts, lubricate the threads, and torque 1/4-inch bolts to 7 to 8 ft-lbs and 5/16-inch bolts to 13 to 15 ft-lbs.

36 Prepare the Cam for Installation

The following "journal-by-journal" installation and lubrication procedure will keep break-in lube on the cam lobes instead of all over your hands. Rotate the engine right-side up. Attach a "handle" to help you support the cam (use the Goodson tool, a 4-inch or longer bolt, or temporarily install the upper sprocket). Lubricate only the two rear cam journals (number-5 and -4) with assembly lube. Then generously lubricate the four rear lobes and the distributor drive gear with cam break-in lube (refer to "Tools and Supplies" on pages 116–118 for information about break-in lube).

37 Install Camshaft

Begin installing the cam, twisting it slightly, and keeping it centered in the bores as you go. Stop when the number-4 journal enters the block. Apply assembly lube to the next cam journal and break-in lube to the next four lobes. Continue installing the cam, journal-by-journal, lubricating as you go (don't forget to lube the fuel-pump lobe just before the cam is fully installed). Try to prevent the cam from "banging" against the bearings as you slide it in; this will keep as much cam break-in lube on the lobes as possible.

FINAL ASSEMBLY

38 Install Cam Drive

Both crank keys and the lower sprocket should already have been installed (if not, see Chapter 5, "The Machine Shop," Step 7, page 84). Rotate the crank so that the keyway points to approximately 2 o'clock, and rotate the cam so that the dowel pins point to approximately 3 o'clock. Lubricate the thrust surfaces of the upper sprocket and block with assembly lube, and saturate the timing chain with engine oil (right). Refer to your Work-A-Long Sheet (and the marks you applied during pre-assembly) and install the correct offset bushing and/or lower keyway configuration (see Chapter 7, "Pre-Assembly Fitting," Step 32, on page 110). Then install the upper sprocket and timing chain. Make sure you align the timing marks and any additional marks applied during pre-assembly fitting.

39 Secure Upper Sprocket

Before you proceed, take a moment to double-check the timing marks (refer to Step 38). When everything is properly aligned, apply Red Loctite to the three attaching bolts and install them in the upper sprocket. If you are using an offset bushing or a cam thrust bumper, you must install a lock plate (this one is from Goodson) to prevent the bushing or bumper from coming out of place. Torque all three bolts to 20 ft-lbs.

Air Flow Research

The awesome power output of current racing engines can be attributed largely to detailed studies of airflow through the cylinder head and manifold. This type of development is now fairly widespread, but a unique Los Angeles company was one of the earliest vanguards in this esoteric science. Today, Air Flow Research is one of the best known and most widely respected developers of high-flow cylinder heads in the country.

The Air Flow Research 195 aluminum heads actually have smog-legal status for street-use vehicles through 1994! They flow much better than stock cast pieces and offer many strength and durability improvements, plus they weigh only about half of a set of stockers.

AFR produces a wide variety of complete cylinder head castings, finished assemblies, cams, intake manifolds, and a variety of accessories for both racing and street applications. Their "195" aluminum heads are terrific upgrades plus they are CARB for use on street cars through 1994 models. That's great news for anyone interested in building a super street engine! The "195s" offer a long list of improvements over production heads and are ideal for operating from 2,000 to 6,500 rpm. Some of the features include the addition of 3/4-inch-thick deck surfaces (so strong they work great with blower and nitrous applications), heat-treated T6 aluminum, special chamber design in 68 or 72 cc, and much more. You can even get models with center-bolt valve covers (1987 and up).

AFR 195s are available with 68- or 72-cc chambers that can be enlarged or reduced upon request. The heads even offer additional mounting holes for accessories.

REBUILDING THE SMALL-BLOCK CHEVROLET

CHAPTER 8

40 Install Timing Chain Cover Seal

Smear a thin coat of silicone sealer inside the seal bore in the timing chain cover. Place a piece of wood under the cover for support or position it on the edge of your workbench. Use a small piece of wood over the seal and drive the seal into the cover. Make sure the seal starts straight in its bore. Continue hammering until the seal is flush with the front of the cover. Before you continue, make sure the cover is free of wood particles or other debris.

41 Install Timing Chain Cover

First, make sure the gasket face of the timing chain cover is flat; tap down any "high spots" with a hammer. Apply a thin film of weather-strip adhesive to the block face to hold the gasket in position. Slide the gasket over the two alignment dowels and press it against the block. Apply a thin film of silicone to the gasket surface. Install the cover and all the bolts and lockwashers (if your cover uses a removable ignition timing mark, refer to your Work-A-Long Sheet for the proper bolt location). Torque all bolts to 6 to 8 ft-lbs. Note: Some small-blocks (pre-1961) used an oil slinger inside the front cover.

Camshafts and Lifters

There are a variety of camshafts and lifters offered with three distinct different groups: hydraulic, solid, and roller. These cam designs must be used with their matching lifters. You can't run a solid lifter with a hydraulic cam or vice versa.

Hydraulic lifters are the most common on street cars and the most affordable. They're quiet and for the most part, never require service or adjustment, as they self adjust, to an extent. The lifter fills with oil and adjusts to its operating parameters by having oil fill inside the lifter. The oil pushes the lifter plunger up to take any play out of the valvetrain. A check valve inside the lifter closes and traps the oil inside, kind of creating a solid lifter.

Mechanical or solid lifters are not self adjusting, therefore, require maintenance by you! There must be a valve lash adjustment made by backing off a nut or screw on the rocker arm. This clearance, referred to as valve lash, allows for a clicking and clatter noise to emit that would annoy most anyone besides a racer. Solid lifters are found on race engines due to their high-RPM operation and solid response.

Roller lifters come in both mechanical and hydraulic designs. As the name implies, a roller lifter features a roller, or wheel, that rides on the cam lobe. This design reduces friction between the two and allows for exotic, high-lift, steep lobes on the cam. Complete solid roller setups are regarded as race-only setups, but there are many hydraulic roller systems offered for the street. In fact, many late-model engines were equipped with hydraulic roller cam systems!

When it comes time to choose your cam and lifters, contact Crane, Comp, Crower, or Iskenderian to talk with their technicians. They will ask you a lot of questions about your engine, transmission, rear-end gearing, torque converter, and weight of the car. Be prepared to give them accurate answers to all of their questions and you'll have the right cam recommended in minutes.

Shown here is a standard flat tappet hydraulic lifter (top) and a hydraulic roller lifter. Standard hydraulics are more popular due to their lower cost, quiet operation, and proven record. Roller hydraulic cam and lifter combos are becoming more popular due to use in stock engines. They are also quiet and maintenance free, plus the roller design lessens friction between the cam and lifter.

REBUILDING THE SMALL-BLOCK CHEVROLET

FINAL ASSEMBLY

42 Install Vibration Damper

Special Tool Required

Install the vibration damper with a special tool. Don't use the crank centerbolt as you could end up pulling the threads out of the crank. And don't drive it in with a hammer! Thoroughly lubricate all threads on the installation tool and screw it snugly into the crank. Lubricate the oil seal surface on the damper with assembly lube and position it on the end of the crank. Slide the roller bearing and thrust washer against the damper and begin tightening the nut. Stop when the damper is fully installed.

Cam Drives

The stock chain and sprockets used to drive the camshaft in production engines is adequate for everyday applications. However, over the life span of a normal engine, the timing chain will stretch and the sprockets will wear. This wear will often retard cam timing and cause unpredictable variations at high engine speeds. The chain and gears should be inspected and/or replaced during every rebuild. Also, never reuse an original nylon-tipped upper sprocket (the authors recommend never using nylon sprockets at all). While they may look reusable, they often chip, crack, and can rapidly fail.

If you elect to upgrade, the most common choice is an all-metal double-row sprocket and chain. This design is often called a "double-roller" chain. Several aftermarket sources produce heavy-duty cam drives, including Milodon, Speed Pro, Comp, Crane, Iskenderian, and others. All of these specialty kits have all-metal upper and lower sprockets, and the lower sprockets are often broached with multiple keyways. The few extra dollars spent for one of these rugged timing chains buys a lot of additional reliability.

A limited adjustment of cam timing is possible with these specialty drives by indexing the lower sprocket on one of the alternate keyways. This usually provides a ±4-degree timing change. If you wish to advance or retard the cam more (or less) than this pre-set amount, the most common method is to use offset bushings. They are installed by first drilling the drive-pin hole in the upper sprocket oversize. A bushing can then be installed in either the advance or retard position. When offset bushings are used, a cam locking plate must be installed to hold the bushing in place during engine operation.

Many racing engines are fitted with systems that eliminate the chain and sprockets and drive the cam through a combination of meshed gears. These gear-drive systems provide highly precise cam timing and offer the ultimate in durability. Most are expensive and quite noisy; a few produce much less noise and are suitable for street applications. Check with your machine or speed shop for specific recommendations.

This is a stock replacement. Note that there are no ways of indexing the cam gear. Do yourself a favor and step up to a good-performance timing gear and chain.

This Comp Cams timing chain and gear set features a double roller chain plus an adjustable upper gear through an elliptical adjusting screw so you can easily advance or retard the cam's position.

REBUILDING THE SMALL-BLOCK CHEVROLET

CHAPTER 8

43 Install Crank Pulley

Refer to your Work-A-Long Sheet to determine whether the pulley-attaching bolts are coarse thread or fine thread (verify they are correct by screwing them into the damper but only with your fingers). Install the lower pulley, making sure that its locating ridge fits into the damper centerbore. Install the three pulley bolts and tighten them to 30 ft-lbs. Finally, install and tighten the centerbolt to 60 ft-lbs (use a little Blue Loctite on all fasteners).

44 Establish TDC Mark Accuracy

Move the number-1 piston down the bore (turn the crank using the crank centerbolt) and attach your TDC stop tool. Slowly turn the crank clockwise until the piston contacts the stop; mark this point on your damper. Turn the crank counterclockwise until the piston again stops; mark this point. True TDC lies exactly halfway between the two marks (use a ruler or dividers to find midpoint). We installed a timing tape from MSD on our TDC mark. This tape will also help us set the mechanical advance in the distributor. To determine which size tape you require, measure the diameter of the balancer and choose the corresponding tape.

45 Prepare to Install Heads

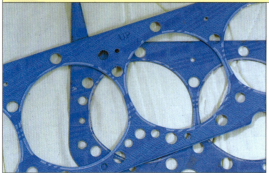

Both head-alignment dowels in each deck surface should be installed (see Chapter 5, "The Machine Shop," Step 2, on page 82). Steel-shim head gaskets: A variety of techniques are used. Some experts apply a very thin film of silicone sealant around the bolt and water holes (if you apply too much it will ooze out and close off small water passages). Others spray or coat the gaskets with heat-resistant aluminum paint. Composition gaskets: Most head gasket manufacturers (including Fel-Pro and SCE) strongly recommend that their gaskets be installed dry, without any additional sealant whatsoever. Whatever method you use, make sure the head and deck surfaces are perfectly flat and clean.

46 Install Gaskets and Heads

Install a head gasket on the left deck surface (look for any orientation marks, such as "TOP" or "TOWARD HEAD"; on Fel-Pro gaskets, the "Fel-Pro" name faces up—arrow). Steel-shim gaskets should be installed with the sealing ridges up. Firmly lock the wheels on your engine stand. Install the left cylinder head. Head bolts enter the water jackets and require a special installation technique to prevent water leaks into the engine. Apply silicone sealant or ARP thread sealant to the first 1/2 inch of the threads on each head bolt. Then install all 17 bolts: 8 short along the bottom, 2 medium on each end of the head, and 7 long in the remaining holes. Repeat this procedure for the right cylinder head.

132   REBUILDING THE SMALL-BLOCK CHEVROLET

FINAL ASSEMBLY

47 Torque Bolts in Proper Sequence

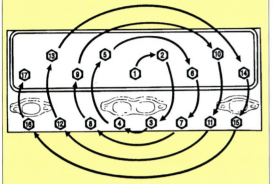

Make sure the cylinder heads are installed on the correct sides (you stamped an identification mark on the front of each head during disassembly). Following the helical tightening sequence illustrated in the diagram, torque all bolts to 25 ft-lbs. Then repeat the process in 20-ft-lb steps until you reach the full 65-ft-lb torque. After all bolts in both heads are tight, check each bolt one final time. Make absolutely sure you haven't missed any!

48 Install Lifters and Pushrods

If you are reinstalling used lifters, the same lifter must be returned to its matching bore. Generously lubricate the cam contact surface with break-in lube. Apply assembly lube to the outside diameter of the lifter and insert it in the block. Using the same technique, install the remaining 15 lifters. Then apply assembly lube to the pushrod cup in each lifter. Now, install all 16 pushrods, making sure they are fully seated in the lifters. Finally, apply assembly lube to the pushrods and guide slots or guideplate contact points in the heads.

49 Lubricate and Install Ball-Pivot Rocker Arms

 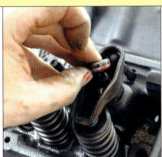

If you are reinstalling used rocker arms, the same rocker and matching pivot ball must be returned to its original location. Apply assembly lube to the pushrod cup and valve tip contact points. Squirt a little more lube on the rocker arm surfaces that contact the valves and pushrods, and then slip the rockers over the studs. Apply lube into the rocker-pivot sockets. Then lubricate and install all pivot balls. Slide them down over the studs until they seat in the rocker arms.

50 Install Rocker Arm Locknuts

Lubricate the threads on all the studs with assembly lube. If you are installing self-locking nuts (they should be new; old nuts may not stay tight) lubricate the threads, screw the nuts on until they are hard to turn, and then tighten them about three additional turns. If you are installing nuts that lock with setscrews, lube the threads and screw on the nuts until they just begin to tighten. Repeat this lubrication/installation procedure for the remaining 15 rocker arm nuts.

51 Adjust Intake Valves

Rotate the engine clockwise and watch the exhaust valve on the particular cylinder you want to adjust. If you're unsure of which valve is the exhaust valve, look at the exhaust manifold or header; the exhaust valve will line up with it and the exhaust port. As an aid, you may mark the head as illustrated. When the exhaust valve begins to open, stop and adjust that cylinder's intake rocker arm. Gently rotate the intake pushrod with your fingers while tightening down the rocker arm retaining nut. When you first feel a slight resistance at the pushrod, and there is no up and down movement, you are just starting to compress the spring inside the lifter. From this point, turn the retaining nut an additional 1/4 to 3/4 turn. Lock the nut into position. The intake is now adjusted properly.

CHAPTER 8

🟥52 Adjust Valves

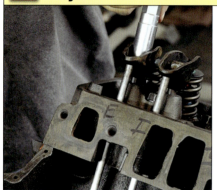

You will need a breaker bar or a large 1/2-inch-drive ratchet and socket to rotate the engine by hand via the bolt on the front of the crankshaft. This is much easier if the spark plugs are removed. Rotate the engine clockwise and watch the exhaust valve on the cylinder that you want to adjust. If you're unsure which valve is the exhaust valve, look at the exhaust manifold or header; the exhaust valve will line up with it. When the exhaust valve begins to open, stop and adjust that cylinder's intake valve. This is the point in the rotation of the camshaft when the intake valve is closed and the lifter is directly opposite the cam lobe.

To adjust the valves, loosen the retaining nut on the rocker arm to remove any tension from the pushrod. If the lifter is filled with oil, wait a minute or two for it to return to a neutral position. If you give it time, the spring inside the lifter will move the pushrod seat up against the retaining lock. You don't need to wait if you are installing new lifters that are not oil filled. You can start adjusting right away.

Gently rotate the intake pushrod with your fingers while tightening the rocker arm retaining nut. You are just starting to compress the spring inside the lifter when you first the feel slight resistance at the pushrod. Turn the retaining nut 1/4 to 3/4 turn from this point. Lock the nut into position. The intake is now adjusted properly.

Turn the engine again by hand and watch the intake valve that you just adjusted. It opens fully and then begins to close. When the intake valve is almost closed, stop and adjust the exhaust rocker arm on that same cylinder. This is the exhaust valve's spot on the base circle of the cam. Adjust the exhaust rocker in the same manner as the intake.

Both valves on this cylinder are now adjusted, and you can move on to the next cylinder. Follow the same procedure.

In summary, adjust the exhaust valve just as the intake closes, and adjust the intake just as the exhaust valve begins to open.

Crower Equipment

Crower Cams & Equipment Company, Inc. originally gained their renown from high-lift "cheater cams" favored by early hot rod enthusiasts and has since expanded its product line to include a complete spectrum of racing and performance products. If there's anything that bolts into or onto an engine, Crower has used their considerable ingenuity to make a better one. Moreover, they were one of the first specialty firms to experiment with totally fabricated "one-off" racing engines.

Their camshaft line is diverse. In addition to a wide range of solid, hydraulic, and roller cams, they offer mushroom-hydraulic profiles (that don't require block machining), roller-hydraulic profiles for street and racing, cams for endurance racing using large diameter (.874 inch) lifters, race-only roller cams with valve lifts over .630 inch, and much more. Camshaft technology is obviously a big part of the Crower product line.

In addition to their impressive line of cams and valvetrain components, Crower has gained a solid foothold in the specialty connecting rod and crankshaft business. Crowerods encompass a variety of configurations from their Sportsman rod through billet titanium rods for the ultimate race engines. Crower also offers cranks using genuine factory forgings to their fully machined billet-steel Ultra-Light cranks. While most

Our small-block was built with Crower's Sportsman rods. They are forged from 4340 chrome-moly steel and are equipped with premium-grade hardware.

of these cranks are regularly stocked for various engines, they will custom build a crank for virtually any application. The Crower catalog is chock full of their extensive line of cams, valvetrain components, rods, crankshafts, and much more for most popular engines.

Rocker Arms

High valvespring seat pressures and extreme opening rates put a severe strain on rocker arms. Production ball-mounted rockers should be limited to maximum engine speeds of about 6,000 rpm and valvespring seat pressures of less than 120 pounds. Specialized rocker arms will be required for valvetrain loads above these limits. Keep in mind, though, that these guidelines are somewhat arbitrary: manufacturer recommendations or specific experience may indicate different limits for specific applications. However, before you buy a set of expensive rockers, consider an inexpensive first step. The valvetrain can be "beefed up" to a level adequate for most performance street applications by installing screw-in studs, like those manufactured by ARP, and heavy-duty stamped-steel rockers from Comp Cams or other manufacturers.

Numerous companies offer roller-tip and/or needle-bearing rockers made of aluminum and special steel alloys. These designs vary in quality (avoid "offshore" manufactured rockers), but the best will operate at engine speeds exceeding 9,000 rpm. However, the small "needle" roller bearings used in some of these rockers are, by nature, vulnerable to long-term stresses. While they will withstand the tremendous loads of racing operation, most are not suited for long-term use in street engines. Nonetheless, many street builders use them—probably as a sign of status. If you are tempted to use needle-bearing rockers on the street, make sure you use sensible seat pressures and inspect/replace the rockers on a regular basis.

Racing valvetrains are often fitted with heavy-duty rocker studs, special locking-type adjusting nuts, pushrod guideplates, hardened pushrods, and other accessories. Rocker stud tie-bars, often called stud girdles, are commonly used in racing engines to reduce stud flex and firmly lock the adjusting nuts in place.

Changing the stock rocker arm ratio can increase valve lift and opening rates. However, high-rate rockers add considerable stress to the valvetrain and should only be used with appropriate matching components (discuss high-ratio rockers with your machine shop and/or cam manufacturer before you buy).

All-out racing valvetrains for the small-block now incorporate specialized shaft-mounted rocker arms. These systems require modification to the topside of the cylinder head but they are strong, durable, reliable—and expensive! Despite the "exotic" nature of these assemblies, some are suitable for long-term operation.

While there are many "exotic" components that are required for racing and high-RPM use, carefully selected valvetrain parts correctly assembled and adequately lubricated will meet most heavy-duty requirements. The Speed Pro special rockers, balls, and pushrods, combined with the easy-to-adjust ARP locknuts, make a durable valvetrain for street performance.

Another great upgrade is a set of roller tip rocker arms. These rockers bolt in place and feature a roller shaft on the tip that pushes the valves open. This produces very smooth control of the valve opening. Also, these rockers are available in different ratios that will increase the valve opening without having to change the camshaft.

53 Prepare for Oil Pan Installation

 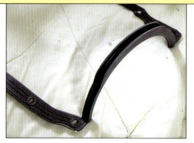 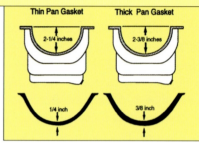

Rotate the engine bottom-side up (the engine is now quite heavy so be very careful). There are three basic types (left) of pan gaskets: 1955-1975 use 1/4-inch rubber end gaskets; 1976-1985 use thicker 3/8-inch rubber end gaskets; and 1986 and later use a one-piece pan gasket that uses integral 3/8-inch-thick front and rear seals. You can now also get a one-piece pan gasket for the 1976-1985 systems (middle). If you are uncertain whether your engine uses thick or thin end gaskets, measure the distance from the pan rail to the lowest point on the front pan lip and compare it with the diagram (right). Finally, determine the proper orientation of the long pan-rail gaskets, and then mark "F" or "FRONT" on them with a felt-tip pen.

54 Begin Oil Pan Installation

First, wipe off any oil from the pan rails and front cover and rear main-cap grooves. Then smear a thin layer of weather-strip adhesive or silicone on the block rails and gaskets. When the gasket adhesive has set up (takes about 3 minutes), make sure to orient the long gaskets properly ("F" or "FRONT" forward) then press them against the block. Remove any excess silicone sealer that may have squeezed out of the rear main cap. Apply a small bead of silicone along the full length of the end-gasket grooves in the timing cover and rear main cap.

55 Continue Oil Pan Installation

Apply four small "blobs" of silicone sealer between the rubber end gaskets and the pan rail gaskets. Then press the rubber gaskets in place in the front cover and rear main cap grooves, overlapping the ends onto the rail gaskets, as shown.

56 Complete Oil Pan Installation

Next, apply a small continuous bead of silicone sealer on top of both the rubber end gaskets and the rail gaskets (every surface that will contact the pan). Lower the pan onto the block and install four 5/16-inch bolts, two at each end of the pan; tighten finger tight. Install the remaining 14 1/4-inch bolts and star lockwashers. Tighten all bolts in several increasing stages; final torque is 8 to 10 ft-lbs for the larger bolts and 6 to 7 ft-lbs for the smaller bolts. As the gaskets compress, the bolts will loosen. Retorque all fasteners until they remain tight. Do not overtighten and cause the gasket to squish out of position.

FINAL ASSEMBLY

57 Install the Starter

The small-block that we've rebuilt is equipped with a 153-tooth flexplate, compared to the 168-tooth model that was originally installed. This means a different starter is required. We went with a gear-reduction starter from Powermaster. These models are much smaller and stronger than a traditional starter. Once the starter is installed, check the mesh between the starter's pinion gear and the flexplate. When engaged, there should be .020- to .030 inch between the valley of the starter gear and the tip of the flexplate tooth. You can check this with a standard paperclip. Check the clearance in at least three positions.

58 Install Mounts/Brackets

Refer to your Work-A-Long Sheet (and photos taken during disassembly) for this step. First, install the starter and torque the bolts to 35 ft-lbs. Note: Some installations require installing the starter after the engine is replaced in the vehicle. Next, locate the left and right motor mounts or mounting brackets. They should have been identified with a stamp (remember, the engine is upside down and "right" and "left" appear switched). Install the brackets/mounts and tighten to 35 ft-lbs.

59 Install Fuel Pump Pushrod/Support Plate

Rotate the engine so the fuel pump pushrod bore is level. Lubricate each end of the fuel pump pushrod with break-in lube. Squirt some assembly lube into the pushrod bore, then slide the rod into the block. You can lock the rod in position by gently installing a 1¼-inch-long bolt through the second hole from the bottom of the block. With the rod held in place, apply a thin film of weather-strip adhesive on the gasket surface of the block, then place the gasket in position. Apply a thin film of silicone on the gasket. Position the pump support plate and install the two lower 1/4-inch bolts. Carefully line up the two larger holes and tighten the small bolts to 8 ft-lbs.

60 Install Fuel Pump

If the fuel pump won't be in the way during engine installation, install the pump now. Apply a thin film of silicone sealer to both sides of the fuel pump gasket, install the pump, and tighten the two bolts to 30 ft-lbs. Don't forget to remove the long bolt you installed to hold the pump rod in place! Also, you'll need to install a short bolt with a bit of silicone sealer on the threads to prevent engine oil from leaking out of the hole.

Moroso

Like most successful specialty businesses, Moroso was started by a racer that had a good idea. Dick Moroso began fiddling with oil pans that helped improve oil systems and performance and the company has since become a leader in the aftermarket industry.

It is easy to overlook the importance of the lowly oil pan and pump, but it only takes a few seconds without oil for an expensive engine to become history. A stock pan is adequate for a pure-stock rebuild but a heavier gauge and well-designed pan is always a good idea.

However, if your project engine is going to weather some heavy-duty action, a surf through the Moroso website or catalog will give you plenty to look at. They offer a huge array of deep- and wide-sump pans (when ground clearance is a problem) that increase oil volume and/or keep the sump oil further away from the rotating assembly. Their systems will match the performance of your engine with the lubrication it constantly requires.

Since we were swapping a different engine into our car, we needed a new pan. The Moroso oil pickup screen bolted right in place on the pump saving us from having to weld it, and the pan fit great, both on the engine and in the car. Don't overlook your oiling system!

Moroso is known for their oil pans as well as a long list of performance components and accessories including spark plug wires. Since our engine was going into a different vehicle than it came from, the oil pan needed to be replaced. The longer sump section (bottom pan) wouldn't clear the crossmember, but the new Moroso pan will have no trouble fitting.

This Moroso oil pan features a hinged oil-control panel. On hard acceleration, oil flows to the rear of the pan, but on deceleration, oil flows forward, which could limit the amount of oil in the sump area. The hinge of this pan closes on deceleration to keep the oil in the sump for constant lubrication.

61 Install Dipstick Tube and Oil Filter

If you are installing a new dipstick, it will fit snugly in the block. Apply a little silicone sealant to the tube surface. Then insert a 5/16-inch bolt into the tube and tap the bolt to seat the tube in the block. If the tube fits loosely, apply weather-strip adhesive to the tube, press it in place, and let the adhesive set up. Note: You may have to reposition the tube later to provide clearance for the exhaust manifold, spark plugs, etc. Install the new oil filter. We recommend pouring half a quart of oil into the filter to help prime the engine quickly. Spread some of the new oil on the O-ring seal and spin the filter onto the block.

62 Pre-Oil Engine

Before you rotate the engine right-side up make sure the drain plug in the pan is tight. With the engine upright, pour about 4 quarts of oil into the pan through the distributor hole to minimize "washing" break-in lube off the cam. Install a pre-oiling tool, which can be an old distributor shaft, and connect a 100-psi pressure gauge to the oil gallery takeoff at the rear or front of the block. Install a 1/8-inch pipe plug in the other, unused, pressure takeoff. Use an electric drill in clockwise rotation to turn the pump. Pressurize the system for about 30 seconds. Continue with Step 62.

FINAL ASSEMBLY

63 Continue Engine Pre-Oiling

The entire valvetrain will usually pre-oil with the crank in one position. However, if a rocker or two refuses to oil, turn the crank a half turn and run the drill another 30 seconds. If all is right with the valvetrain, every rocker will eventually receive oil. When all rockers have oiled, return the crank to TDC with the number-1 cylinder firing (intake and exhaust lifters on cylinder number-1 on the base circle). Remove the pre-oiling tool, and remember, don't turn the engine upside down again!

64 Prepare to Install Intake Manifold

You can install the manifold on the front and rear valley rails using two methods: 1) use rubber gaskets supplied in your rebuild kit, or 2) use a bead of silicone adhesive. If you use the rubber gaskets, apply a layer of weather-strip adhesive to the front and rear valley rails on the block. Position the correct gaskets on each rail and let the adhesive set up. If you decide to use silicone (preferred method), lay a 1/4-inch-diameter bead of silicone along the full length of each gasket rail. Regardless of which method you use, apply a thin film of silicone sealant to the water passage holes at each end of both heads (use none around the intake ports). Refer to your Work-A-Long Sheet or the instructions with your gasket package to determine the proper heat-rise passage configuration.

65 Begin Manifold Installation

We used a set of SCE gaskets for the intake because of their embossed seal around the intake runners. Position the intake gaskets on the heads and apply another thin layer of silicone around the water passages. If you are using rubber valley-rail gaskets, make sure the gaskets properly interlock with the valley-rail gaskets (arrow). Apply a bead of silicone sealer along each end-rail gasket, and apply a little extra "blob" in the corners, where the rubber and composite gaskets meet. If your intake manifold uses a shield to cover the heat-riser passage, reinstall it now (apply a drop of Red Loctite to the threads of each screw).

66 Complete Manifold Installation

Now, carefully position and lower the intake manifold onto the engine; don't slide it around or you may dislodge the gaskets. Install all bolts (must be no longer than 1¼ inches or some will interfere with the pushrods!). Following the torque-sequence drawing, tighten the bolts in 5-ft-lb steps to 30 to 35 ft-lbs. As the gaskets compress, the bolts will loosen slightly. Continue retorquing until fasteners remain tight.

REBUILDING THE SMALL-BLOCK CHEVROLET

CHAPTER 8

67 Install Water Pump

Apply a thin film of silicone sealant to the water passages on the block. Position the gaskets and then apply a thin film of sealant to the gasket surfaces. Position the water pump and install the appropriate bolts and brackets; refer to your Work-A-Long Sheet and the photos you took during disassembly for help in locating and attaching accessory-mounting brackets. Note: The lower-right bolt (as viewed from the front of the engine) enters a water jacket and should have silicone sealant or ARP thread sealant applied to the thread. Torque all bolts to 30 ft-lbs.

68 Install Valve Covers

Apply "high-tack" weather-strip gasket adhesive to the gaskets and contact surfaces of both valve covers. When the adhesive has set up, position the gaskets in the covers and hold them until the adhesive locks them firmly in place. Then apply a thin layer of silicone sealant to the gasket surfaces and set the covers on the cylinder heads. Make sure the covers are installed on the correct heads (see your Work-A-Long Sheet and photos for help), and then install the bolts and support washers. Just tighten the bolts snug (about 5 ft-lbs); any tighter might damage the gaskets or covers.

69 Install Thermostat/Housing

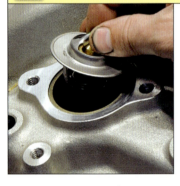 

Install the thermostat in the intake manifold with the temperature bulb pointed down (opening temperature is usually stamped on it). Apply a thin film of silicone sealant or gasket adhesive to the manifold surface, set the gasket in place, then apply another thin film of silicone to the gasket. Install the thermostat housing and bolts (refer to your disassembly photos for proper bolt types), and torque to 30 ft-lbs. If using an aftermarket housing with a rubber O-ring gasket as shown, sealer will not be necessary.

Important!

70 Installation Considerations

The remaining steps in this chapter install components and accessories that, if performed now, may make installing the engine in your vehicle more difficult. Because of the virtually unlimited possibilities, we suggest only that you reinstall the engine in the same state of assembly as when it was removed. Perform the balance of assembly after the engine is installed. Make sure that any open access holes, such as spark plugs, carburetor, water inlet and outlet, distributor, exhaust ports, etc., are covered with duct tape during engine installation. This will keep out dust and errant nuts and bolts.

FINAL ASSEMBLY

71 Install Exhaust Manifold

Apply anti-seize to the exhaust-manifold bolt threads. Then attach an exhaust manifold (make sure it's the correct side; check your marks) with only two outside bolts (leave them loose). Slide a gasket between the manifold and the head (metal side of composition gasket goes toward manifold). Start all the remaining bolts with your fingers, then tighten and torque all bolts to 20 ft-lbs. Finally, increase the tightness of the four inside bolts to 30 ft-lbs. Repeat this process for the other manifold. If your vehicle uses a smog pump, apply anti-seize to the injector tube fittings, then install and tighten both injector lines.

Important!

72 Position Crank Correctly

The crank must be set on exactly TDC of the compression stroke for cylinder number-1. If the crank has been rotated since Step 52 on page 134 (or you're not sure that it's positioned correctly), remove the left valve cover, and rotate the engine clockwise until the number-1 exhaust valve opens fully then almost completely closes. Check the mark on the damper; it should be close to TDC. Rotate the crank one more revolution clockwise until it again comes to exactly TDC. At this position, both intake and exhaust valves are closed and the number-1 cylinder is at TDC, just at the ignition point. Reinstall the valve cover.

73 Prepare to Install Distributor

Apply a little gasket adhesive to the bottom of the distributor and to one side of the gasket, and after it has set up for a minute or so, press the paper gasket in place. Next, rotate the oil pump shaft with a screwdriver until the notch points to the number-7 intake valve (or approximately the 10 o'clock position). Before you install the distributor, liberally apply the break-in lube on the gear. Have the rotor installed before you drop the distributor in place.

74 Install Distributor

As you lower the distributor housing into the engine, remember that it will engage to the helical gear on the cam, which will turn the rotor about 45 degrees clockwise. Many installations position the rotor pointing directly forward for a good starting point. Remember, you can make nearly any cap terminal number one. If the oil pump drive does not engage, the housing will not drop down into position (as shown). Wiggle the housing and if it doesn't drop into position, remove the distributor, rotate the pump drive slightly with a long screwdriver, and try it again. When the housing drops against the manifold, note the position of the rotor. When you install the distributor cap, the terminal that the rotor points toward is number-1. Install the distributor hold-down clamp.

CHAPTER 8

Ignition Components

Your new engine isn't going to go anywhere without a reliable and powerful spark. The ignition is an extremely important system on your car. It has to accurately fire each spark plug at exactly the right moment in each piston's power stroke.

There are several ignition companies in the aftermarket that offer distributors, coils, wires, and ignition systems, including Crane, Mallory, ACCEL, and MSD to name a few. All of them provide quality performance ignition components for a variety of applications. Here are a few parts you'll need and what you need to look for:

Distributor

A distributor is an incredible part of the ignition. It triggers the ignition, alters the timing to match load and RPM, plus it distributes each spark that comes out of the coil to the correct cylinder. You'll see breaker point triggers, but they require maintenance so upgrade to an electronic version such as a magnetic pickup, optical trigger, or Hall Effects Switch. Also, be sure to get a distributor that has an adjustable mechanical advance so you can tune it to match your engine's needs. For street cars, a vacuum advance is a good economical accessory.

Coils

The coil is responsible for stepping up its low supply voltage with a very high output voltage. This is done through inducing the voltage and current through from one set of windings to another. Coils come in all shapes and sizes, but you don't have to buy a 60,000-volt coil. Most engines will never require that kind of voltage. Simply pick one from a company that you trust.

Spark Plug Wires

There's more to plug wires than you may think! First and foremost, get a set that is spiral or helically wound. This design produces a sort of filter or choke that prevents radio noise or other electronic noise from interfering with other electronics on your car. Also, look for a lower resistance conductor and one with a good, durable sleeving and quality crimped ends.

Ignition Control

You've no doubt heard of an MSD 6A or Crane HI6 ignition control. These "boxes" will work with your stock or existing distributor and coil and will provide a very powerful spark. Actually, not just a single spark, but multiple sparks! Under 3,000 rpm most of these Capacitive Discharge ignitions will fire the spark plug numerous times on one cycle. This ensures combustion and results in improved starting, a smooth idle, and quick throttle response.

MSD Ignition offers a full line of performance ignition components. Their MSD 6 Series ignition controls are their most popular and can be used on most anything with a distributor. The 6 Series delivers high-voltage capacitive discharge sparks and at a lower RPM it will fire the same plug multiple times to ensure combustion (hence, MSD—multiple spark discharge). They also offer a variety of rev limiters, timing controls, and accessories.

The rugged construction of this MSD distributor is matched by its high-speed reliability. Their distributors feature a maintenance-free magnetic pickup and an easy-to-adjust mechanical-advance assembly.

FINAL ASSEMBLY

75 Install Ignition Wires/Spark Plugs

Align the rotor with a mark on the engine to determine where the number-1 will be (it is okay to rotate the distributor housing to position the vacuum advance where you want it). Once you establish which terminal will be number-1, mark the housing. Next, install the distributor cap and note which terminal on the cap aligns with the rotor terminal. Now, moving in a clockwise rotation install the spark plug wires beginning with number-1 and the following in this order; -8, -4, -3, -6, -5, -7, and -2 (the firing order of a V-8 Chevy). Route the wires through clips and supports so that they stay clear of hot exhaust manifolds. Finally, gap the spark plugs to the factory recommended spec, then install and torque them to 25 ft-lbs.

76 Install Carburetor

The carburetor you install should be in new, like-new, or just-rebuilt condition. Install a fresh base gasket on the intake manifold. The best gaskets are made from thick, heat-insulating material, with hard inserts at each bolt hole. The non-compressible inserts prevent distortion of the throttle plate, a common cause of throttle sticking and fuel/air leaks. Install the carburetor and torque the fasteners to 7 to 8 ft-lbs.

77 Install Remaining Accessories and Fittings

Install topside accessories, including the choke bi-metal spring and housing, the oil-pressure sender, vacuum takeoff fittings, EGR valve, and all connecting vacuum lines. Install a new rubber grommet in the (usually LEFT) valve cover and press in a new or clean PCV valve. Install a new 3/8-inch hose between the PCV valve and the carburetor. Also, install a length of vacuum line between the ported vacuum takeoff on the carburetor to the vacuum advance canister on the distributor. Refer to your Work-A-Long Sheet and disassembly photos to make sure you've properly reinstalled all components. If you choose, you can now also install remaining front-mounted accessories, including the air conditioning compressor, alternator, AIR pump, power steering pump, and all pulleys and support brackets. Install all remaining hoses, including AIR-injection hoses (if so equipped) and the fuel line to the carburetor (make sure you install a new fuel line).

78 Install Flywheel or Flexplate

Remove the engine from its stand with your cherry picker and install the flywheel or flexplate on the crank flange. Apply Blue Loctite to the bolt threads and install all six bolts and star-type lockwashers. Torque the bolts to 60 ft-lbs. To prevent the engine from turning, insert a screwdriver between the ring gear and starter. If you are installing a flywheel, be sure that you have installed a new pilot bushing in the crankshaft. Also, keep all oil and grease off the flywheel and clutch surfaces.

Distributor Rebuilding

An engine rebuild is not complete until the distributor is reconditioned for peak performance. Distributor designs vary considerably, but here are a few hints and tips you may find useful.

Disassembly

Begin by removing the rotor. Then remove the centrifugal advance balance springs and the counterweights from the top of the breaker points (if equipped). Then check the shaft for excessive "wobble" by installing it in your vise (or lathe) and measure with a dial indicator. If the side-to-side movement is more than about .002 to .003 inch for a breaker point, or more than .005 inch for a breakerless system, new bushings should be installed. In either case, remove the centershaft by driving out the roll pin in the helical gear with a pin punch (keep track of the location of the thrust and spacer washers). Then remove the advance plate from the centershaft. Next, remove the breaker plate from the housing (may have a snap ring holding it in place). Remove the vacuum advance and any remaining wires. Finally, remove the felt washer and/or plastic cover over the top bushing. Thoroughly clean all metal components in carburetor cleaner. If necessary, install new bushings and/or locate a new drive gear if it shows signs of wear.

Reassembly

First, lubricate the bushings with assembly lube. Reinstall the plastic cover and felt washer, then install the vacuum advance and breaker (stator) plate. Lightly lubricate and reassemble the centrifugal advance mechanism onto the centershaft, install the shaft in the housing, and slide on the lower thrust and spacer washers. Reinstall the helical gear and roll pin. Make sure the pin is snug in the gear. If it installs without much resistance, locate a new roll pin. Lubricate the breaker points (if used). Finally, install a new rotor and cap.

Adjustment

When fully assembled, take the distributor to your machine or local tune-up shop to have the advance mechanisms and dwell (for points) tested on a distributor machine. The most effective advance curve will vary depending on the type of application (car weight, type of transmission, rear-end gearing, etc.). Note: To maintain a "smog-legal" setup, ignition advance must follow factory specs. The curve can be altered by varying the springs and counterweights and, if necessary, a different advance canister (or an adjustable canister) can be installed.

Every distributor rebuild should include removing the shaft to inspect the bushings and shaft itself for wear. You'll need a pin punch to drive out the roller pin. Keep track of thrust and spacer washers for reassembly.

Firmly clamp the housing and check shaft side-to-side motion with a dial indicator.

FINAL ASSEMBLY

ARP supplies instructions with their flexplate bolts (and other hardware kits). It is important to note that they do not require a washer, as with standard bolts. Be sure to read any instructions prior to installing the parts!

79 Double-Check Everything

Now's the time to look over your notes, photos, and even reread the assembly steps in this chapter to make sure nothing was overlooked. Examine your engine carefully and compare it with the photos and notes you made during disassembly. Make sure all vacuum hoses and wires are reconnected properly. Go over Steps 69 through 74 to make certain that the ignition system is properly timed so the engine will start up quickly. Finally, double-check the oil level and make sure the drain plug in the pan is tight. This completes final assembly.

Holley Replacement Parts

The Holley name has been associated with automobiles since the 1900s. In the early years, the Holley Carburetor Company established their reputation through the millions of OEM carburetors they supplied to Detroit auto manufacturers. Today, they are most widely recognized for their incredibly diverse line of high quality replacement carburetors, intake manifolds, fuel injection, and fuel system accessories.

Since 1955, Holley has grown to dominate the market for performance carburetors, based on the runaway success of the innovative model 4150 4-barrel. This design—upon which most modern Holley carbs are still based—was supposedly developed in a legendary southern racing shop with one objective in mind: build a carb that is easy to tune at the racetrack. Regardless of legend, to say that the 4150 was a success is an understatement. Today, virtually every carbureted racing engine in this country is fitted with one or two Holley 4150s (or direct derivatives).

We selected many Holley fuel-system components and accessories for the engines built in our facility. Just some of the items we used include "smog-legal" carburetors, Holley Custom Shop modification and customizing services, electronic-carburetor conversion kits, manifolds, fuel pumps, AIR pumps, chrome accessories, dash-mounted fuel consumption instruments, and much more.

Holley products are available at speed shops and auto parts stores nationwide. Holley Replacement Parts publishes a catalog that illustrates their extensive line of replacement and performance products and services.

The Holley model 4150 carburetor is easy to tune, reliable, and available in many sizes and types. It is hard to imagine a V-8 engine that would not run great with a Holley carburetor.

For a street car with a carburetor, a mechanical fuel pump will do just fine. If you have electronic fuel injection or more of a race engine, Holley offers a great line of durable and strong electric fuel pumps.

REBUILDING THE SMALL-BLOCK CHEVROLET

CHAPTER 9

INSTALLATION, BREAK-IN AND TESTING

Congratulations! Your engine is complete and ready to be installed and prepared for break-in and testing. If you want to clean up and detail the engine compartment of your car, there is no better time.

Installing the Engine

Before you begin, remember that maneuvering a heavy engine into a tight engine compartment often requires more hands and muscle than most of us can muster on our own. If you can persuade a friend or two to help out, the job will be a lot easier. Before you get started, review Sidebar "Shop Safety," on page 28. It's easy to get caught up in the excitement of completing your engine project. Never take chances or become impatient. Keep your mind focused, and if you feel yourself starting to rush, take a break for a few minutes.

While the installation is usually straightforward, there are some details to keep in mind. If you are re-installing an engine into the chassis from which it was removed, the job will be a lot less difficult if you have detailed notes, sketches, and/or photos to refresh your memory. It may be several days, weeks, or even months since you removed the engine, and it's easy to get some details confused, especially in late-model engine compartments that may be overflowing with electronics and complex emissions systems.

The first step is to obtain a method of lifting the engine into the chassis. The most common technique is to use a "cherry picker" hoist. If you rent one, make sure that the hoist is rated to lift at least 750 pounds or, even better, 1,000 pounds. Most V-8 engines weigh at least 600 pounds, often more, and an "over-rated" lift will provide an added measure of safety. It is also important that the lift arm and the engine suspended beneath it will rise high enough to clear the fenders (or other obstacles). This is, incidentally, another important consideration when you purchase a hoist.

The maximum lift-over height will also depend on the type of apparatus used to connect the engine to the hoist. Inexpensive methods of "grasping" the engine include a simple length of chain about 24 inches long, or an "attaching point" bolted to the intake manifold in place of the carb. Another common type is simply a steel cable (or chain) with a moveable loop for attaching to the hoist. These engine "chains" are available from Good-son. A third type (the handiest and, unfortunately, the most expensive) has a long adjusting screw to move the attaching point back and forth. This allows the user to easily vary the balance point and/or tilt the engine when it is lowered into place. This type of lift adapter is available at some rental and tool stores; it is also available from Goodson.

In some cases it may be better to leave the carburetor and distributor out of the engine during the installation. A distributor cap can easily get broken or throttle linkage can get tweaked during the process. If you do remove them, be sure to cover the holes in your clean, new engine with duct tape to avoid dropping dirt grime or other debris inside. Also, before you remove the distributor, note the rotor's position, as well as the housing in the block.

Once the engine is lowered into the engine compartment, it can be carefully positioned on the engine mounts. In most cases, the cushion mounts should be bolted to the engine before it is lowered into place. When the cushion mounts on the engine interlock with the chassis, the engine mount through-bolts can be slipped in place and tightened. Some engines, particularly on trucks, have an

INSTALLATION, BREAK-IN AND TESTING

adaptor bracket attached to the engine. The cushion mounts are bolted to the chassis before the engine is lowered into place (see Step 58, on page 137). Then the mounts are attached to the engine adaptor brackets when the engine is installed.

The engine can be installed with the transmission attached or still in the car. If you choose to install them together, be sure that the cherry picker can handle the extra weight, and be prepared to play with angles as you lower the drivetrain into the engine bay. If they are separated, make sure the clutch/flywheel/flexplate are attached to the engine (or that the torque converter with a new front seal is installed in the automatic transmission) before the engine is lowered into place. Whatever the case, once the engine is in position, the rear of the engine can be attached to the transmission, or the rear motor mount (on the transmission tailshaft) can be bolted down.

With the engine and transmission in the chassis, the driveshaft, shift and clutch linkage, and exhaust system can be attached. If no modifications have been made or specialty equipment used, these steps are simply the reverse of disassembly procedures. However, when the engine or auxiliary systems have been modified, you may have to fabricate or improvise some of the installation procedures. Most of these difficulties can be overcome with patience, careful thought, and common mechanical techniques, but in some cases (exhaust system modifications being the most common) the chassis may have to be transported to a specialty shop to have the work completed. If this is a possibility, or a certainty, check the rental yards to locate a trailer or towing dolly that can be used to transport the chassis.

The external accessories, such as alternator, power steering pump, A/C compressor, AIR pump, etc., can now be bolted into place and fitted with new drive belts (check your notes). Finally, the electrical, coolant, and fuel connections can be completed

Starting Your New Engine

The time has come to get your new engine fired up for the first time. Appropriate initial startup of is imperative to its performance and longevity. The first 20 to 30 minutes is when the rings seat in the cylinder bores and the cam and lifters all break-in together. It is important to be prepared to fire up the engine and let it run for at least 30 minutes.

Filling the cooling system in a "dry" engine requires special attention.

Step-by-Step Engine Installation

1 Install New Motor Mounts (if applicable)

Since we were installing a small-block in place of an inline 6-cylinder, we needed new engine mounts. YearOne Restoration Products had the set of small-block mounts we needed for our 1964 Chevelle. The original mount (left), is taller and is positioned differently than the standard small-block mount.

2 Secure Engine Mount Bolts

The new engine mounts bolted right in place on the chassis, although getting to the bottom nuts in the chassis took a little articulation.

3 Gather Hardware

This is the hardware you need to install the engine. Two long engine-mount bolts, three torque-converter-to-flexplate bolts, and five bell-housing bolts.

4 Install Torque Converter

Whether your transmission is already in the car or you plan to connect it to the engine out of the car, you'll need to install the torque converter. It is imperative that the converter slide onto the transmission input shaft all the way. There are several steps on the shaft that the converter needs to slide over. If not, the converter bolts or the flexplate will not align properly.

Note that we have a floor jack under the transmission to help angle it properly.

REBUILDING THE SMALL-BLOCK CHEVROLET 147

CHAPTER 9

5 Secure Engine to Hoist

Mount a chain to the engine using the holes on the front and back of the cylinder head. It is best to position the engine so the rear of the engine is slightly lower than the front. This generally helps out when you're lowering the engine into position with the transmission. It is also recommended to install an old set of spark plugs because one or two will get broken during the install.

6 Lower Engine Into Car

It is best to have a couple sets of eyes when lowering the engine into the bay. Having a pal over to control the cherry picker is a huge help. Use extreme caution and do not reach or guide in the engine by reaching below the engine! Also use care and keep an eye on other wires and hoses as the engine is lowered into position.

7 Align Transmission

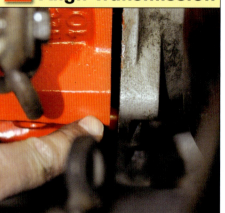

As the engine gets closer to being in position, you'll need to align the transmission. The engine has two locating dowels that help in making the big connection. As the engine and transmission align, it's a good idea to install one of the bellhousing bolts and start the threads—don't tighten it, just start the threads to hold it steady. This will give you the opportunity to start a couple other bolts.

8 Align Motor Mount Bolt Holes

With the transmission loosely connected, align the motor mounts. Sometimes you may need to use a screwdriver to wiggle into the mounts and negotiate the bolt holes to align. Once in place, install the mount bolts on both sides.

9 Align Torque Converter and Flexplate

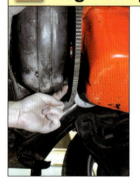

With the bellhousing bolts installed and the mount bolts in place, crawl under the car and align the torque converter with the flexplate. Be sure that the converter bolts are the correct ones for your converter (some are fine thread, some coarse thread, some may be metric). Install all three bolts (Blue Loctite is recommended) and tighten them at even intervals with a final torque to the manufacturer's specs.

REBUILDING THE SMALL-BLOCK CHEVROLET

INSTALLATION, BREAK-IN AND TESTING

As the block fills, pockets of trapped air can sometimes overheat and damage new components. Removing one of the manifold plugs or sensors will help push air out of the engine as the water fills. Once the water level tops off, reinstall the plug, hose, or sensor.

Here's a tip: don't add antifreeze yet. Wait until the engine has been running long enough for you to make sure that there are no water leaks or other engine problems that might require draining the cooling system (usually a few hours or about 100 miles).

Here's another tip: if you have installed a new set of aluminum heads, you may want to add a can of stop-leak to the cooling system. New aluminum castings sometimes "sweat" through miniscule pores in the casting for a short period of time.

If it has been a while since you first pre-lubed your engine, you may want to remove the distributor and spin the oil pump over again. Before you pull the distributor, mark its position in the engine and pay attention to where the rotor is positioned.

Exhaust System

If you're sticking with the factory exhaust manifolds, chances are that they'll bolt right in place without much fanfare. Headers, however, can be a different story. Headers are a great addition to your engine and can even add power, but you need to check with the manufacturer if they will interfere with brackets such as the power steering or air conditioning. Also, they can cause issues with clutch linkage or transmission linkage and chances are you should install the starter and its wiring prior to mounting the header. There are many header designs available from "shorty" models to different tube diameters from a variety of companies such as Hooker, JBA, Hedman, Edelbrock, and others.

Also, when installing headers, there is a very good chance that you need to have the engine lifted up just slightly to get the headers in position. This was the case with our Chevelle installation (and the Hooker instructions even warned of this). We were able to do this with the transmission connected to the engine, so you don't have to lift it too high, just a little over the engine mounts.

If you're going from manifolds to headers, remember that the exhaust system will require modification to connect and seal to the new headers. It is recommended to take your vehicle to a muffler shop, or plan on bolting some sort of makeshift exhaust system before starting and breaking-in the engine. With open headers, it will be so loud you won't be able to hear the mechanical side of the engine, not to mention you'll drive your neighbors nuts with the engine at 2,400 rpm for 20 minutes!

Headers can present a challenge. We had to lift our engine up slightly to get the new Hooker headers to slide in. Once we did that, they slid in easily. It's a tight fit, but the headers easily cleared the upper control arm, the frame, and fit as designed. You may need to remove the oil filter to ease the install too.

Header gaskets and bolts can be tough to align, but here's a little trick. Install the two outside bolts by a few threads. Next, take the gasket and cut a groove under the corresponding bolt holes (some gaskets come like this). The gasket will then slide right in place with the holes aligned for easy tightening.

CHAPTER 9

10 Install Radiator

Next up is the radiator and cooling system. If you're going to a bigger engine, or one with more power, now would be a good time to consider an updated radiator. Use care when installing the radiator as not to damage the fins. Also, if you're using an automatic transmission, connect the cooler lines at this time.

11 Install Hoses and Clamps

With your new engine, it's time to install new hoses and clamps. To aid in installation of the hoses, apply a small bead of grease to the inside of the hose. This will help the hose slide over the inlet and even add to the sealing of the connection.

12 Install Carburetor, Lines and Linkage

Remove the duct tape, install the new gasket, and position the carburetor. Connect the fuel line from the pump to the carb. If you changed carburetors, make sure to route the new line away from any moving parts (fan) and secure it away from edges and high heat sources. We used a braided line from Edelbrock that features a built-in filter and routes from the carb to the fuel pump. Also, connect the throttle linkage and return spring making sure it moves freely and returns to its closed position.

13 Install Fan and Shroud

Cooling your new engine is very important. Using the proper clutch fan and shroud is imperative to keeping the engine from overheating. If space is an issue, or if you are looking to upgrade the system, moving to an electric fan is a popular choice. Companies such as Be Cool offer direct-fit radiator fan kits for a variety of applications. This kit is supplied with dual fans and a fan controller. They're easy to wire and very effective in keeping your engine in its proper operating temperature range.

14 Check Electrical Connections

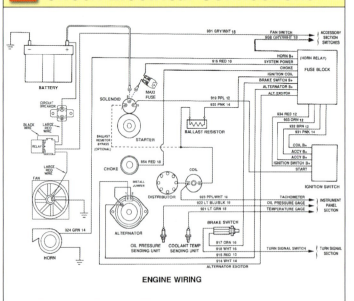

This wiring diagram shows many of the common electrical connections you need to make to the engine. This diagram from Painless Performance Products is a helpful tool in checking off your starter, ignition, distributor, and charging system.

INSTALLATION, BREAK-IN AND TESTING

Brackets, Pulleys and Belts

With the engine installed, one of the next challenges is to reinstall the brackets, accessories, and belts. If you took detailed photos and notes of the disassembly this should not be a problem. However, if you did an engine swap like our 6-cylinder to small-block change, the brackets and pulleys will be different.

Our plan is to find original brackets to use for our power steering, air conditioning, and the alternator. There are many alternatives out there that you can find at restoration suppliers like YearOne, by junkyard scrounging, and at swap meets to find the brackets you need. Other alternatives include a new serpentine system such as those offered by Vintage Air. These are complete, modern systems that include all of the main accessory components and that run off one belt. They are convenient, but pricey for many budgets.

When you're looking at pulleys and brackets it is important to maintain proper belt alignment among the accessories. Also, when mixing and matching parts, coming home with the proper-size belts may take a couple different trips to the parts store.

There are a variety of different brackets available for mounting the alternator or other accessories. In some applications, the alternator may require to be mounted on the opposite side to incorporate air conditioning or power steering.

As with brackets, there are also a variety of pulleys available. Pay attention to the V-groove depths, dimensions, and spacing. Ensure that the pulleys are properly aligned and that the belts do not contact any spark plug wires or hoses.

15 Double-Check Everything

Our engine is getting close to firing up for the first time. This is also a time to step back and review all of your steps and pay attention to the details. Are all of the hoses connected? Are the brackets installed and the belts tightened? Check the gauge connections and fuel lines again. In short, take your time to ensure the engine is ready to go.

TECH TIP: Before You Start the Engine

- Check the fuel lines and coolant hoses.
- Be sure all vacuum lines are connected properly.
- Check the wiring to the alternator, sensors, and other accessories.
- Confirm the throttle linkage operates smoothly.
- Be sure there is a ground strap from the engine to the chassis or battery.
- Be sure oil pressure gauge and temperature gauge are ready.
- Confirm there is water in the cooling system.
- If in the car, be sure the transmission is in park and the brake is applied.
- Be sure to have a fire extinguisher nearby (you never know).
- Use common sense and be safe.

REBUILDING THE SMALL-BLOCK CHEVROLET

CHAPTER 9

16 Check Fluids

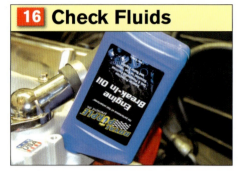

Confirm that your engine is topped with coolant mixture and you have more standing by. Generally, an engine will accept more coolant once the engine fires up and the fluid is rotated throughout. Also, check the fuel lines and oil level. We used Royal Purple's break-in oil, a non-synthetic oil that is formulated to assist in proper ring sealing and engine break-in. It also contains important additives and high levels of zinc and phosphorous to optimize longevity in flat-tappet engines.

17 Check Spark Plugs and Wires

Make sure all of the spark plug wires are connected to the plugs, and that they're positioned away from engine heat sources. Trace the wires to the distributor cap and check the position and firing sequence one more time (1-8-4-3-6-5-7-2).

18 Check Throttle Linkage

Make sure the throttle linkage and return spring are connected and move smoothly with no binding. At initial startup, you'll need to adjust the linkage to hold the RPM in the 2,300 range for over 20 minutes.

Dyno Testing

A dyno test session, whether on an engine dyno or a chassis dyno, is both an interesting and sobering experience. It's one thing to "guesstimate" how much power your shiny new engine will produce—an exercise that often borders on delirious optimism—but a dyno test can be like a bucket of ice-cold realism splashed in your face. A dyno is a giant polygraph so be prepared for the truth.

Finding a chassis dyno is a great idea once your engine is broke in and you have 500 miles or more racked up on it. A chassis dyno will give you the opportunity to really dial-in the performance of your new engine. Plus, the dyno staff should be able to help you decide what way you need to go in your tune-up. The beauty of the chassis dyno is that you are measuring output at the rear wheels while you're running through the exhaust and transmission. It is as real world as you can get!

An engine dyno is also an excellent tool in tuning your engine, but you don't get to run the power through your transmission or rear axle, or even your exhaust (well, with some work in the dyno cell you may be able to). The engine dyno gives you a chance to find small oil leaks or other minor problems that otherwise could be a big ordeal with the engine in the car. Also, if you want to test one intake against another, or see how different timing affects your engine's performance, this is the perfect opportunity.

If you get the chance to run your engine on a chassis dyno or an engine dyno, go for it!

An engine dyno break-in and test can be well worth the expense. For starters, if there is a problem or oil leak, you have the opportunity to fix the issue. Second, it gives you the ability to tune the engine. You'll be able to adjust the timing and jet combinations to obtain the best performance for your application. When you do install the engine in your car, it will be broken in and tuned up to be ready to roll and enjoy.

INSTALLATION, BREAK-IN AND TESTING

19 Pour Fuel Into Carburetor (if applicable)

If your vehicle has an electric fuel pump or electronic fuel injection, jump to Step 20. Before you start the engine, make sure there is fuel in the carburetor. Don't crank over the engine just to fill the carburetor, you could damage the camshaft before the carburetor is filled. A better alternative is to pour a small amount of clean gasoline directly into the carburetor. Using a "lipped" cup and/or a small funnel, carefully pour about 2 to 4 ounces of fuel into the primary bowl vent. This should be enough fuel to keep the engine running for several seconds—plenty of time for the fuel pump to take over and fill the carburetor.

20 Start Engine

Once the engine fires bring it up to 2,000 to 2,500 rpm immediately (if it didn't fire, see below). Be sure to confirm that there is ample oil pressure and be alert for fuel leaks. Adjust the idle stop and don't let the RPM drop during these first 20 to 30 minutes. This higher RPM is required to properly break-in the cam and lifters. While the engine is running, watch for leaks, smoke, and oil and temperature pressures. Having an extra set of hands and eyes is a good idea during the initial startup.

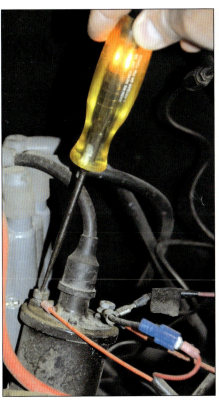

If your engine won't start, or spits and backfires, don't continue cranking. Find out what's wrong before you continue; when everything is right, most engines start after only 1 or 2 seconds of cranking. The first thing to check is the ignition system. If you installed a capacitive-discharge ignition control such as an MSD 6A or Crane HI6, follow their troubleshooting procedure to check for spark. If you used a stock-style distributor and ignition, check to make sure that there are 12 volts on the coil's positive terminal. You can then remove the coil wire at the distributor and hold it about 1/4 inch from a grounded object. Crank the engine; you should see an intense blue-orange spark jump from the wire. If there is no spark, recheck ignition timing then look into the fuel system.

When the engine has run about 20 to 30 minutes, back off the idle speed to about 500 to 700 rpm. Take another minute to check everything over one last time. Make sure there are no fuel, oil, or water leaks. Make sure no electrical wiring or vacuum hoses are near the hot exhaust system. Finally, shut the engine off and recheck the oil and water levels. When everything looks good, it's time to take your new engine out for a test drive. Don't plan on any all-out power blasts. For the first 200 to 300 miles, pick destinations that will keep you out of stop-and-go traffic. Don't "baby" the engine; drive normally, keeping peak engine speed below 4,000 rpm. After your initial break-in drive, drain the cooling system and add the correct mix of antifreeze. After about 500 miles, change the oil and the filter.

REBUILDING THE SMALL-BLOCK CHEVROLET

APPENDIX

Cylinder Numbers and Firing Order

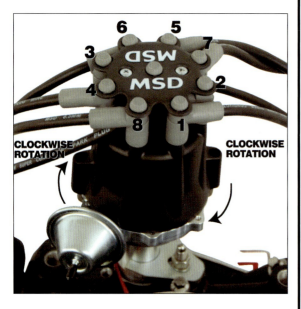

Firing Order:
1, 8, 4, 3, 6, 5, 7, 2

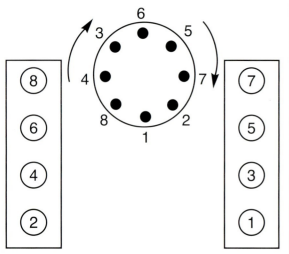

Illustrated here is the correct position for the spark plug wires on the distributor cap, as well as the correct firing sequence.

Torque Sequences

Head Torque Sequence

Intake Torque Sequence

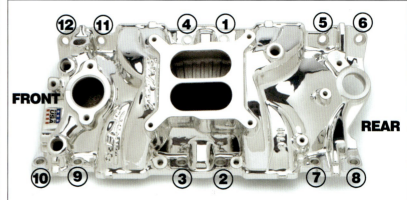

Mains Torque Sequence

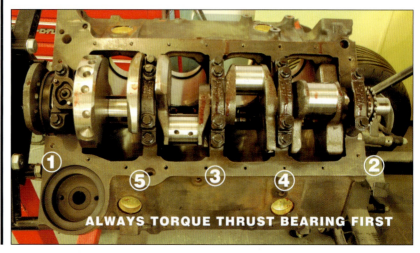

APPENDIX

Torque Specifications

Recommended Maximum Torque for General Automotive Applications (in ft-lbs)
See the table below for specific bolt torque recommendations

U.S. Standards for Bolt Dimensions				Grade: SAE 2 Tensile: 74,000		Grade: SAE 5 Tensile: 120,000		Grade: SAE 7 Tensile: 133,000		Grade: SAE 8 Tensile: 150,000		Special Alloys 180,000+	ARP** Tensile 170,000	ARP** Tensile 190,000
Bolt Diameter (in.)	Threads per inch	Decimal Equivalent	Bolt Head	Dry	Lubed	Dry	Lubed	Dry	Lubed	Dry	Lubed	Lubed with Washers	With ARP Lube	With ARP Lube
1/4 stud	20/28	.250	-	-	-	-	-	-	-	-	-	14	8	9
1/4	20	.250	7/16	5.5	4	8	6	10	8	10	8	12	9	10
1/4	28	.250	7/16	6	4.5	10	7	12	9	14	10	15	10	11
5/16 stud	18/24	.3125	-	-	-	-	-	-	-	-	-	30	18	19
5/16	18	.3125	1/2	11	8	17	13	21	16	25	18	26	19	21
5/16	24	.3125	1/2	12	9	19	14	24	18	25	20	26	20	22
3/8 stud	16/24	.375	-	-	-	-	-	-	-	-	-	60	30	40
3/8	16	.375	9/16	20	15	30	23	40	30	45	35	36	33	36
3/8	24	.375	9/16	23	17	35	25	45	30	50	35	38	35	38
7/16 stud	14/20	.4375	-	-	-	-	-	-	-	-	-	83	50	65
7/16	14	.4375	5/8	32	24	50	35	60	45	70	55	61	57	62
7/16	20	.4375	5/8	36	27	55	40	70	50	80	60	67	58	63
1/2 stud	13/20	.500	-	-	-	-	-	-	-	-	-	130	76	83
1/2	13	.500	3/4	50	35	75	55	95	70	110	80	105	84	92
1/2	20	.500	3/4	55	40	90	65	100	80	120	90	110	89	97
9/16 stud	12/18	.5625	-	-	-	-	-	-	-	-	-	181	n/a	115
9/16	12	.5625	7/8	70	55	110	80	135	100	150	110	155	116	127
9/16	18	.5625	7/8	80	60	120	90	150	110	170	130	175	121	132
5/8	11	.625	15/16	100	75	150	110	190	140	220	170	215	160	175
5/8	18	.625	15/16	110	85	180	130	210	160	240	180	250	172	188
3/4	10	.750	1-1/8	175	130	260	200	320	240	380	280	340	-	-
3/4	16	.750	1-1/8	200	150	300	220	360	280	420	320	380	-	-

Size	Bolt Head	Usage	Recommended Torque (ft-lbs)
1/4-20	7/16	Timing chain cover	7
		Oil pan to crankcase	6
		Oil filter bypass valve	7
		Oil pump cover	7
		Rockerarm cover	4
5/16-18	1/2	Camshaft sprocket	20
		Oil pan to crankcase	9
		Oil filter bypass valve	14
3/8-16	9/16	Clutch pressure plate	35
		Distributor clamp	20
		Exhaust manifold	20
		Exhaust manifold (inside bolts on V-8 engines	30
		Intake manifold	32
		Manifold water outlet	30
		Water pump	30
		Lower pulley	30
3/8-24	9/16	Connecting rod	45
7/16-14	5/8	Cylinder head	65
		Main bearing cap	75
		Main bearing cap (outer bolts, with 4-bolt caps)	65
		Oil pump	65
		Rockerarm stud	50
7/16-20	5/8	Flywheel	60
		Damper	60
1/2-14	3/4	Temperature send unit	20
1/2-20	3/4	Oil filter	25
		Oil pan drain plug	20
14 mm and 5/8		Sparkplug	25

Unless otherwise indicated, the torque specifications given on this page are for lubricated fasteners. While you can install fasteners dry, you will find that lubrication allows fasteners to screw in easier, prevents thread seizure, and gives more accurate torque readings. If you decide to use lubrication, use Vaseline or petrolatum. To compensate for lubrication, torque values are often reduced by about 10 to 25 percent. This reduction may not be required for the small (under 1/4 inch), high-quality fasteners. Refer to the Sidebar, "Bolt Torquing Techniques," on page 120 for more information before applying the torque specifications listed on this page or elsewhere in this book.

Tables Courtesy of Automotive Racing Products (ARP).

Piston Ring Gap Alignment

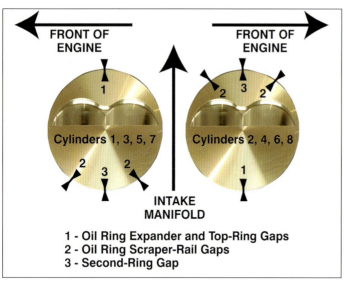

1 - Oil Ring Expander and Top-Ring Gaps
2 - Oil Ring Scraper-Rail Gaps
3 - Second-Ring Gap

End gap on oversize ring sets must be properly set. Doing so will imporve horsepower, reliability, and fuel economy. For more information, see pages 106–108.

Timing Belt/Chain Alignment Marks

Rotate the crank so that the keyway points to approximately 2 o'clock, and rotate the cam so that the dowel pins point to approximately 3 o'clock. For more information refer to step 37 on page 129 or the Sidebar on page 131.

General Specifications

Small-Block Chevrolet Basic Engine Displacements and Related Specs
(Dimensions in inches unless otherwise noted)

Engine	Year	Bore	Stroke	Main Journal Diameter	Rod Journal Diameter	Main Bearings	Cylinder Volume	Rod Length	Compression Height
262 ci	1975–76	3.671	3.100	2.450	2.100	2 Bolt	32.811	5.703	1.750
265 ci	1955–56	3.750	3.000	2.300	2.000	2 Bolt	33.134	5.703	1.800
267 ci	1979–81	3.500	3.484	2.450	2.100	2 Bolt	33.520	5.703	1.560
283 ci	1957–67	3.875	3.000	2.300	2.000	2 Bolt	35.398	5.703	1.800
302 ci	1967	4.000	3.000	2.300	2.000	2 Bolt	37.718	5.703	1.800
302 ci	1968–69	4.000	3.000	2.450	2.100	4 Bolt	37.718	5.703	1.800
305 ci	1976–94	3.735	3.484	2.450	2.100	2 Bolt	38.479	5.703	1.560
307 ci	1968–73	3.875	3.250	2.450	2.100	2 Bolt	38.347	5.703	1.675
327 ci	1962–67	4.000	3.250	2.300	2.000	2 Bolt	40.861	5.703	1.675
327 ci	1968–69	4.000	3.250	2.450	2.100	2 Bolt	40.861	5.703	1.675
350 ci	1967–94	4.000	3.484	2.450	2.100	2 & 4 Bolt	43.803	5.703	1.560
400 ci	1970–72	4.125	3.750	2.650	2.100	4 Bolt	50.139	5.565	1.560
400 ci	1973–80	4.125	3.750	2.650	2.100	2 Bolt	50.139	5.565	1.560

Work-A-Long Sheet   Also available at www.cartechbooks.com

DISASSEMBLY

Project Statistics
Your Name _____
Today's Date _____ Vehicle Engine Removed From _____
Engine Year _____ CI _____ Block Casting _____ ☐ 2 barrel   ☐ 4 barrel   ☐ Fuel Injection

Accessories Attached to Used Engine
☐ A/C Pump   ☐ AIR Pump   ☐ AIR Distributor Lines and Hoses   ☐ Water Pump
☐ Flywheel   ☐ Clutch   ☐ Flexplate   ☐ Transmission
☐ Starter   ☐ Fuel Pump   ☐ Exhaust Manifolds   ☐ All Pulleys; Except _____
☐ Alternator   ☐ Distributor   ☐ Coil   ☐ Carburetor
☐ Motor Mounts   ☐ Motor Mount Attaching Brackets   ☐ Spark Plug Heat Shields
☐ EGR Valve   ☐ Dipstick Tube   ☐ All Bolts; except _____
☐ _____   ☐ _____   ☐ _____   ☐ _____   ☐ _____

Operational Notes
Oil consumption _____   Compression check pressure variation _____ psi
Leak-down percent _____   Other observations _____

Disassembly Notations
Crank uses centerbolt   ☐ Yes   ☐ No
Heat riser restricted on   ☐ Left   ☐ Right   ☐ Both
Head gaskets   ☐ Steel shim ☐ Composition
Worn/damaged lifters   ☐ No   ☐ Yes; where _____

Vibration damper pulley screws   ☐ 3/8-NC   ☐ 3/8-NF
Location of timing-pointer attaching points:
Oil filter adapter type:
    ☐ Spin-on
    ☐ Long cartridge (late)
    ☐ Short cartridge (early)
Type of rear main seal:
    ☐ Rubber—two piece
    ☐ Rubber—one piece (late)
    ☐ Rope (early)

INSPECTION

Initial Parts Inspection Observations
Block OK   ☐ Yes   ☐ No; describe problem _____
Heads OK   ☐ Yes   ☐ No; describe problem _____
Crank Ok   ☐ Yes   ☐ No; describe problem _____
Bearings OK   ☐ Yes   ☐ No; describe problem _____
Pistons OK   ☐ Yes   ☐ No; describe problem _____
Cam/lifters OK   ☐ Yes   ☐ No; describe problem _____
Damper OK   ☐ Yes   ☐ No; describe problem _____
Intake manifold OK   ☐ Yes   ☐ No; describe problem _____
Exhaust manifold OK   ☐ Yes   ☐ No; describe problem _____
Oil pump OK   ☐ Yes   ☐ No; describe problem _____

APPENDIX

Oil pump/rear main cap mating surfaces damage/abnormalities ☐ No ☐ Yes
Identifying mark you placed on all parts: _____

AT THE MACHINE SHOP
Parts Delivered to the Machine Shop
☐ Block ☐ Main Caps ☐ Crankshaft ☐ Oil Pump ☐ Oil Pump Pickup
☐ Connecting Rods ☐ Pistons ☐ Piston Rings ☐ Camshaft ☐ Lifters
☐ Vibration Damper ☐ Main Bearings ☐ Rod Bearings ☐ Cam Bearings ☐ Rod Bolts
☐ Gasket Set ☐ Push Rods ☐ Rockerarms ☐ Head Bolts ☐ Main Bolts/Studs
☐ Miscellaneous Nuts/Bolts/Brackets for Cleaning
☐ Water Pump ☐ Timing Cover ☐ Oil Pan ☐ Flywheel/Flexplate
☐ Clutch ☐ Exhaust Manifolds ☐ Motor Mounts ☐ Motor Mount Attaching Brackets
☐ Assembled Heads ☐ Disassembled Heads with: ☐ Valves ☐ Springs ☐ Retainers ☐ Keepers
☐ Rocker Balls and Nuts ☐
☐ Intake Manifold ☐ With Heat Riser Shield ☐ Installed ☐ Not Installed
☐ _____ ☐ _____ ☐ _____ ☐ _____ ☐ _____
☐ _____ ☐ _____ ☐ _____ ☐ _____ ☐ _____
☐ _____ ☐ _____ ☐ _____ ☐ _____ ☐ _____
☐ Other Accessories _____

Special Instructions for Machine Shop
☐ Bore block ☐ Use torque plates ☐ Desired piston-to-wall clearance: 0._____-inch
☐ Grind crank ☐ Rod bearing clearance: 0._____-inch ☐ Main bearing clearance: 0._____-inch
☐ Deck to clean ☐ Surface heads ☐ Install cam bearings
☐ _____ ☐ _____ ☐ _____
☐ _____ ☐ _____ ☐ _____
Is pilot bushing to be installed in crankshaft (required for manual transmission)? ☐ Yes ☐ No
Are intake manifold heat shield holes to be tapped for 8-32 screws? ☐ Yes ☐ No

After You Pick Up Your Parts
☐ Yes ☐ No Threaded holes reconditioned/chased ☐ Yes ☐ No Drilled holes and edges chamfered
☐ Yes ☐ No head/block dowels properly installed ☐ Yes ☐ No Are cam bearings properly installed
☐ Yes ☐ No Galleries tapped for screw-in plugs ☐ Yes ☐ No Add 0.030-inch hole in gallery plug
☐ Yes ☐ No Add 0.030-inch hole in thrust face ☐ Yes ☐ No Core plugs properly installed
☐ Yes ☐ No Retaining straps on core plugs ☐ Yes ☐ No Crank keys properly installed
☐ Yes ☐ No Manifold heat-shield holes tapped for 8-32 screws

PRE-ASSEMBLY FITTING
Measured and Recorded During Pre-Assembly Fitting
☐ Yes ☐ No Do all valveguides have proper clearance? If no, which are correct _____
☐ Yes ☐ No Do all valveseats meet dimensional specs? If no, which are faulty _____
☐ Yes ☐ No Do all valveseats hold solvent? If no, which leak _____
☐ Yes ☐ No Have all valveguides been machined concentric for press-on seals?
Retainer to Valveguide clearance 0._____-inch; adequate on all valves? ☐ Yes ☐ No If no, which valves have insufficient clearance? _____
Recommended valvespring seat pressure _____ psi at _____-inches installed height.

Measured valvespring installed height:
1 _____ 3 _____ 5 _____ 7 _____
2 _____ 4 _____ 6 _____ 8 _____

APPENDIX

Spring shims used to obtain correct installed height:
1 _____ 3 _____ 5 _____ 7 _____
2 _____ 4 _____ 6 _____ 8 _____
Measured valvespring solid height _____ -inches
Calculated compressed spring clearance:
1 _____ 3 _____ 5 _____ 7 _____
2 _____ 4 _____ 6 _____ 8 _____

Connecting rod bore OK? ☐ Yes ☐ No; Which rods are defective _____
Crank straightness OK? ☐ Yes ☐ No Runout on center main of 0. _____ -inch
Main bearing clearance OK? ☐ Yes ☐ No Measured clearance 0. _____ -inch
Crank thrust OK? ☐ Yes ☐ No Measured clearance 0. _____ -inch
Main bearing clearance OK? ☐ Yes ☐ No Measured clearance 0. _____ -inch
Camshaft bearing fit OK? ☐ Yes ☐ No; Describe problem _____
Block required clearance grinding for upper sprocket? ☐ Yes ☐ No
Pin end clearance OK? ☐ Yes ☐ No Measured clearance 0. _____ -inch
Piston-to-wall clearance OK? ☐ Yes ☐ No Measured clearance 0. _____ -inch
Pistons with incorrect clearance _____

Measured ring end gap:
1 Top _____ 2nd _____ 3 Top _____ 2nd _____ 5 Top _____ 2nd _____ 7 Top _____ 2nd _____
2 Top _____ 2nd _____ 4 Top _____ 2nd _____ 6 Top _____ 2nd _____ 8 Top _____ 2nd _____

Rod bearing clearance OK? ☐ Yes ☐ No Measured clearance 0. _____ -inch
Rod side clearance OK? ☐ Yes ☐ No Measured clearance 0. _____ -inch
Piston-to-head clearance OK? ☐ Yes ☐ No Measured clearance 0. _____ -inch
Cylinders with incorrect clearance _____
Offset bushings/key used: ☐ +-2° ☐ +-4° ☐ +-6° ☐ +-8° ☐ +-10° ☐ +-12°
Rotating assembly clearance OK? ☐ Yes ☐ No; Cause of interference _____
Crank index OK? ☐ Yes ☐ No Maximum _____° out of index on journal no. _____
Cylinder-to-cylinder deck height accurate? ☐ Yes ☐ No Maximum 0. _____ -inch variation.
Rocker geometry OK? ☐ Yes ☐ No; Describe problem _____
Rocker-to-stud clearance OK? ☐ Yes ☐ No Maximum 0. _____ -inch (Intake); 0. _____ -inch (Exhaust);
Piston-to-valve clearance OK? ☐ Yes ☐ No Maximum 0. _____ -inch (Intake); 0. _____ -inch (Exhaust);
Oil pump drive clearance OK? ☐ Yes ☐ No Measured clearance 0. _____ -inch
Intake manifold end-rail clearance OK? ☐ Yes ☐ No Measured clearance 0. _____ -inch
Manifold surface parallel with head? ☐ Yes ☐ No; Describe problem _____
Pulleys/accessories aligned? ☐ Yes ☐ No; Describe problem _____

SOURCE GUIDE

A&A Machine Shop
6006 North State Road
Davison, MI 48423
810-653-1891

ACCEL/Mr. Gasket
10601 Memphis Avenue
Cleveland, OH 44144
216-688-8300
mrgasket.com

Arias Industries
13420 S. Normandie Avenue
Gardena, CA 90249
310-532-9737
ariaspistons.com

Air Flow Research
10490 Ilex Avenue
Pacoima, CA 91331
818-890-0616
airflowresearch.com

Auto Meter
413 West Elm Street
Sycamore, IL 60178
815-895-8141
autometer.com

Automotive Racing Products (ARP)
1863 Eastman Avenue
Ventura, CA 93003
805-339-2200
arp-bolts.com

Barry Grant Inc.
1450 McDonald Road
Dahlonega, GA 30533-9773
706-864-2206
barrygrant.com

Crane Cams
530 Fentress Boulevard
Daytona Beach, FL 32114
386-252-1151
cranecams.com

COMP Cams
3406 Democrat Road
Memphis, TN 38118-1541
800-999-0853
compcams.com

Edelbrock
2700 California Street
Torrance, CA 90503
310-781-2222
edelbrock.com

Eastwood
236 Showmaker Road
Pottstown, PA 19464
610-323-2200
eastwoodcompany.com

GM Performance Parts
800-GM-USE-US
goodwrench.com

Goodson Tools and Supplies
156 Galewski Drive
Winona, MN 55987
800-533-8010
goodson.com

Hedman Heddars/Trans-Dapt
16410 Mannin Way
Cerritos, CA 90703
562-921-0404
hedman.com

High Desert Machine
North 17th Street
Las Cruces, NM 88005
866-448-HEMI
highdesertmachine.com

Holley Performance Products
1801 Russellville Road
Bowling Green, KY 42102-7360
270-745-9544
holley.com

Hooker Headers
1801 Russellville Road
Bowling Green, KY 42102-7360
270-782-2900
holley.com

Hot Rod Connection
8407 Dyer Street
El Paso, TX 79904
915-755-7637
billygrahamracing.com

Isky Racing Cams
16020 S. Broadway
Gardena, CA 90248
323-770-0930
iskycams.com

JBA Headers
7149 Mission George Road, Suite D
San Diego, CA 92120
619-229-7797
jbaheaders.com

JE Pistons
15312 Connector Lane
Huntington Beach, CA 92649
714-898-9763
jepistons.com

Mallory Ignition
550 Mallory Way
Carson City, NV 89701
mrgasket.com

Milodon
20716 Plummer Street
Chatsworth, CA 91311
818-407-5436
milodon.com

MSD Ignition
1490 Henry Brennan Drive
El Paso, TX 79936
915-857-5200
msdignition.com

Moroso
80 Carter Drive
Guilford, CT 06437
203-453-6571
moroso.com

Pit-Pal Products
2009 Horizon Court
Zion, IL 60099
888-PIT-PALS
pitpal.com

Powerhouse Products Inc.
3402 Democrat Road
Memphis, TN 38118
800-872-7223
powerhouseproducts.com

Powermaster Motorsports
1833 Downs Drive
West Chicago, IL 60185
630-957-4019
powermastermotorsports.com

Ross Racing Pistons
625 South Douglas Street
El Segundo, CA 90245
310-536-0100
rosspistons.com

SCAT Enterprises
1400 Kingsdale Avenue
Redondo Beach, CA 90278
310-370-5501
scatenterprises.com

SCE Gaskets
1122 West Avenue, L-12
Lancaster, CA 93534
800-427-5380
scegaskets.com

Scoggin-Dickey Parts Center
5901 Spur 327
Lubbock, TX 79424
800-456-0211
sdpc2000.com

Snap-on
877-762-7664
snapon.com

Total Seal
22642 N. 15th Avenue
Phoenix, AZ 85027
800-874-2753
totalseal.com

Trick Flow
565 Kennedy Road
Akron, OH 44035
330-630-0270
trickflow.com

Venolia Pistons and Rods
2160 Cherry Industrial Circle
Long Beach, CA 90805
323-636-9329
venolia.com

World Products
51 Trade Zone Court
Ronkonkoma, NY 11779
631-981-1918
worldcastings.com

Year One
P.O. Box 521
Braselton, GA 30517
800-932-7663
yearone.com